Social Policy: A Critical Introduction

Social Policy: A Critical Introduction

Issues of Race, Gender and Class

Fiona Williams

Polity Press

Copyright © Fiona Williams 1989

First published 1989 by Polity Press in association with Blackwell Publishers.
Reprinted 1989, 1990, 1991, 1992, 1993, 1994

Editorial office:
Polity Press
65 Bridge Street, Cambridge CB2 1UR, UK

Marketing and production:
Blackwell Publishers
108 Cowley Road, Oxford, OX4 1JF, UK

238 Main Street
Cambridge, MA 02142, USA

Cataloguing in Publication Data is available from the British Library

A CIP catalogue record for this book is available from the British Library.

Library of Congress Cataloging in Publication Data

Williams, Fiona.
  Social Policy.
  Bibliography: p.
  Includes index.
  1. Great Britain—Social Policy.   2. Welfare state—
History.   3. Racism—Great Britain.   4. Sexism—Great
Britain.   I. Title
HN390.W48   1989   361.6′1′0941   88–28499
ISBN 0–7456–0149–9
ISBN 0—7456–0150–2 (pbk)

Typeset in 10 on 12 pt Times by Witwell Ltd, Southport.
Printed in Great Britain by T. J. Press, Padstow.

Contents

Acknowledgements

I have been very aware of my limitations as a white person of understanding fully the impact of racism. At the same time, as a socialist and feminist with a longstanding commitment to anti-imperialism and anti-racism, I feel a responsibility to take seriously the struggles and writings of those who do experience racism, acknowledge their criticisms, and apply these to my own spheres of knowledge and practice.

I would like to acknowledge those who contributed in different ways to my writing this book. First of all, my late father, Leonard Williams, who taught me some very early lessons in anti-imperialism in Cairo in the early 1950s and to Arif Hussain, whose long friendship in many ways crystallized this understanding. Next are those who offered support, interest and encouragement through the book's long gestation: Miriam David, Yasmin David, Julia Szalai and, especially, my children, Rowan and Joe Deacon. In addition, I have gained stimulation and support from the meetings and work of the Editorial Collective of Critical Social Policy. I am particularly grateful also to Sidney Jacobs, Norman Ginsburg, Rowena Vickridge and to John Thompson and the anonymous reader of Polity Press, not only for their encouragement but for their comments on parts of the drafts. Finally, I must record my thanks to Lyvinia Elleschild who read the proofs and to Bob Deacon, who chivvied and cared, and shared his thoughts, and read almost all the words of several drafts.

Fiona Williams

Note on Terminology

'race', Black

I have followed the recent convention of putting race in quotation marks to distinguish it from any biological connotation the word otherwise has. However, it is not ideal as it is sometimes interpreted as a euphemism for 'Black people'. I have used it here for want of a less loaded abstract noun. I have used the capital B for Black similarly to distinguish it from mere description. However, usage of the word 'Black' in the following text carries two difficulties. The first is the danger of homogenizing and minimizing the important diversity of the histories, cultures and experiences of Black people of different ethnic and geographic origins – Asian, African, Middle Eastern, Caribbean, Central American, Latin American, North American and Oceanic. The second is to ignore the widespread racism directed at those other than Black people – in particular in Britain, Jewish, Irish, Chinese, Turkish people and gypsies. Whilst there are historical references to anti-semitism and anti-Irish racism, the contemporary references mainly concern racism directed at Black people of Afro-Caribbean and Asian origins, accepting that amongst Black people of different ethnic origins racism can be experienced differently.

'women and Black people'

I have used this phrase when I have wanted to convey both the separate *and* combined effects of racism and sexism. Black women experience a sexism augmented and reconstituted by racism, whilst white 'Anglo-Saxon' women do not often experience direct racism, nor Black men direct sexism. The phrase is a shorthand for 'white and Black women, and Black women and men'.

gender and 'race'

Similarly, this phrase denotes these dimensions as both separate and in the case of Black women, combined. References therefore to the oppressions of gender, 'race' and class are in general references to women, Black and white, Black men and women, and working-class men and women, Black and white.

Introduction: 'Race', Gender and Class – Towards an Integrated Approach in Social Policy

This book is about both the discipline of social policy and the provision of state welfare in Britian. It argues that 'race', gender and class, as interrelated and specific issues, are central to an understanding of the development of the welfare state and it presents a framework for the study of welfare drawn from three perspectives: from the political economy of welfare, from feminism, taking into full account the critique of white feminism by Black feminists, and from work on 'race' and class and racism and imperialism.

The Marginalization of Gender and 'Race' in the Discipline of Social Policy

In general 'race' and gender are issues that have been neglected or marginalized in the discipline of social policy, particularly in terms of a failure to, first, acknowledge the experiences and struggles of women and of Black people over welfare provision; secondly, to account for racism and sexism in the provision of state welfare; thirdly, to give recognition to work which *does* attempt to analyse the relationship between the welfare state and the oppressions of women and of Black people (and, historically, other racialized groups like the Irish and Jews); and fourthly, to work out a progressive welfare strategy which incorporates the needs and demands which emerge from such strategies and analyses.

Evidence for the neglect and marginalization of these issues can be drawn, at a superficial level, from a glance at contemporary social policy textbooks. The development of a feminist critique of the welfare state emerged from the struggles and campaigns in the late 1960s and the 1970s over women's rights in relation to social security, housing, health care, child care, education, training and work opportunities. Between the publication in 1977 of Elizabeth Wilson's *Women and the Welfare State* and Jen Dale and Peggy Foster's *Feminists and State Welfare* and Gillian Pascall's *Social Policy: A Feminist Analysis* in 1986, a wealth of material from different feminist perspectives emerged about the relationship between the state and the family, and about the financial, emotional and physical relationships within and outside the family. Much of this work offered new dimensions to key questions in social policy analysis: issues of caring, dependency, needs, of the relationship between work and income, of the relationships between the providers and users of welfare provision, as well as theoretical questions about the relationship between patriarchy, capitalism and the state. Yet by the mid-1980s two of the most widely read textbooks on social policy (see Mishra, 1984; George and Wilding, 1985) made no more than passing reference to the theoretical or empirical observations advanced by the feminist critiques of the welfare state or the impact of different strategies and policies upon women. While one or two texts in social policy *do* exist which acknowledge the feminist critique or look at the effect policies upon women (e.g., Ginsburg, 1979; Clarke et al., 1987), the general pattern has been to have a token acknowledgement in terms of a single (often excellent) chapter or single issue (often 'community care') which appears to have no great impact on the rest of the text (Bean and MacPherson, 1983; Glennerster, 1983; Hill and Bramley, 1986).

The neglect of issues of 'race' and racism and 'race' and gender is far more marked in social policy and has been the result of a different process. Very few recent social policy textbooks deal with Black experiences of welfare or general policies in relation to Black people. Mishra (1981, 1984), Klein and O'Higgins (1985), Hill and Bramley (1986), Jones et al. (1978), Loney et al. (1983) make little or no reference to racism or race-related policies. Nor do those texts which seek to assess theoretical perspectives in social policy give us any clue as to how these perspectives approach 'race' and racism (e.g., Taylor-Gooby and Dale, 1981; George and Wilding, 1985; Taylor-Gooby, 1985). Nor, too, do those who offer us strategies for welfare consider the application or implications of strategies against racism (Bosanquet, 1983; Deacon, 1983; Mishra, 1984; Walker, 1984). (It should also be added that until very recently little of the feminist literature on the welfare state considered the experiences of Black women or the relationship between 'race' and gender.) Where 'race' is brought in, it is often, like gender, as a discrete issue, a dimension of inequality, an 'ethnic' or 'minority group' or 'special needs' issue (Bean and MacPherson, 1983; Glennerster, 1983) or it is subsumed under a general problem such as 'the inner city' or 'poverty'. From the 1960s the study of 'race-relations' and the promotion of race-relations policies based on the ideas of 'integration' and later 'multiculturalism' was carried on separately from the study of social policy. However, these models still tend to dominate much writing on social policy and social work even though there have been considerable developments in work on 'race' and racism and in spite of the fact that the models themselves have faced extensive critiques (Sivanandan, 1976, 1978, 1979; Hall et al., 1978; Bourne, 1980; CCCS, 1982; Gilroy, 1982; Mama, 1984). In addition, there are an increasing number of accounts of struggles against Black oppression in welfare, especially from Black feminists (Carby, 1982; Ohri et al., 1982; Black Health Workers and Patients Group, 1983; Mama, 1984; Bryan et al., 1985; Bhavnani, 1986), but few of these have been drawn into the social policy literature. Some particular areas of study have been more open to the development and application of 'race', gender and class questions – educational studies (Brah and Minhas, 1985; Brah and Deem, 1986; Sarup, 1986), youth studies (Cross, 1981, 1982; Solomos, 1985), cultural studies (CCCS, 1982). However there are emerging in social policy and social work an increasing number of articles and books which critically explore 'race' and welfare themes: Doyal et al. (1981), Gordon (1983, 1985, 1986), Cohen (1985), Jacobs (1985) Stubbs (1985), Ahmed et al. (1986), Ben-Tovim et al. (1986), Ely and Denney (1987). One of the aims of this book is to explore not just how but why gender and 'race' issues have been marginalized, and the challenge that existing work on these issues poses for welfare thinking and strategies.

Work, Family and Nation: the Organizing Principles of Welfare Development

To speak of the 'marginalization' of gender and 'race' in social policy is to tell only half the story. It is also the case that historically and today many welfare policies have been quite explicit about the role of women or of Black people and their families, for example, in the denial of social security benefits to dependent wives, or to immigrants or non-nationals. One of the arguments advanced in this book is that the themes of *Family* and *Nation* have been central organizing principles in the development of the welfare state. That is to say, welfare policies have both appealed to and reinforced (and occasionally challenged) particular ideas of what constitutes family life, and what constitutes national unity and 'British culture', although the notions and reality of Family and Nation have themselves changed over time. Much critical analysis of welfare begins, quite appropriately, with an analysis of the relation of welfare policies to *Work*, that is to the economic and social organization of production – the needs of capitalism (for a literate, healthy and obedient workforce) on the one hand, and the struggles of the working class to improve their working and living conditions on the other (Gough, 1979). However, problems arise for an acknowledgement of 'race' and gender when the analysis ends there. By situating an analysis of the welfare state not only in terms of the organizing principle of *Work* but in terms also of the adjacent and interconnected themes of *Family* and *Nation* we can be led towards a deeper understanding of the differential impact of welfare policies, to a more complex picture of the gains won and the losses suffered by the working class as a result of the way in which the welfare state in Britain has developed. These themes, Work, Family, Nation, which shape welfare policies, reflect the divisions of class, gender and 'race', respectively. In this picture the welfare state has to be understood as developing within a capitalism which absorbed and recreated the social relations of imperialism and the social relations of patriarchy, which themselves have changed over time and according to the nature, strength and composition of class struggle. In short, an analysis is presented here of the welfare state within a patriarchial and racially structured capitalism.

It is often the case when introducing new or previously neglected elements into an analysis (in this case gender, but more particularly 'race') that the emphasis which is necessary to make a case for their acknowledgement appears to 'privilege' these elements over and above existing ones (in this case class). In the account that follows in this book I have given more emphasis to 'race' and gender and the elaboration of the themes of Family and Nation in order to shift thinking in those directions. This should not be read as an implicit ranking of these two issues above class, but as an attempt to remedy their marginalization. A related distortion is one which has already been referred to in the 'Note on Terminology' above but it requires emphasis here. To insist upon an emphasis of the '*Black* experience of welfare' in order to counter its previous neglect risks losing sight of the importantly diverse cultures, histories, experiences of colonialism and of racism that people of Asian and Afro-Caribbean origins have. Where possible I have attempted to acknowledge, albeit briefly, such diversity.

Other Forms of Oppression

In asserting that class, gender and 'race' are the most significant divisions in our society from the point of view of understanding the welfare state, the question may be asked: what of other forms of oppression and the struggles that flow from them upon which welfare practice and policy have important bearing? What of disability, age, sexual orientation, intellectual impairment? Unfortunately this book does not do justice to the attempts by people within these groups to analyse their oppressions and assert their demands for change (e.g. Finkelstein, 1980; Phillipson, 1982; Oliver, 1985).

Nor does it cover Britain's imperialism in Ireland and the experiences of Irish immigrants. To create the theoretical umbrella capable of acknowledging the role of welfare in relation to different kinds of oppression is a task that has yet to be done, though there are important developments in writing and in practice which examine the interrelationships between different forms of oppression – see, for example, Naomi Connelly's *Care in the Multiracial Community* (1988), which examines the 'race' aspects in relation to the arrangements for community care of older people, mentally ill, people with learning difficulties and severely physically disabled people.

I hope that the following analysis, which links 'race' and gender to each other and to class, but at the same time stresses the specificity of the effects of welfare policies upon women or Black people, can be a useful guide to the analysis of other forms of oppression. Some of the issues raised by 'race' and gender may inform or be informed by these different forms of oppression: issues of power, the social construction of dependency, the relationship (in the case of gender, disability, age and intellectual impairment) between biology and society, the marginalization of those struggles from the traditional organizations of the working class, the importance of autonomous organization – all these are relevant to different forms of oppression. In contrast, it also becomes obvious that each oppression has to be considered as specific: they are not parallel forms. Gender, for example, is a biological construct, whereas 'race' is a social construct; disability denotes physical impairment but also reflects as much the disabling norms of able-bodied society. In addition, physical impairment is not a condition to be celebrated in the way that 'women's culture' or 'Black pride' sometimes are, although the celebration of a culture of resistance and the value of disabled people is important.

The Welfare State Under Attack: the Need for an Integrated Strategy

Students, teachers and practitioners of welfare may find themselves at present in a dilemma, faced with two counterveiling pressures: on the one hand, a movement, of which they may well be part, for equal opportunities for oppressed groups, for anti-racist and anti-sexist strategies, for a critical re-evaluation from the interests of women and Black people and other oppressed groups, of the policies and practices of social services and housing departments, hospitals, clinics and surgeries, DHSS offices, schools and not least the content and accessibility of their own courses in higher education. On the other hand, the social and economic policies of the past decade have led to a situation where the poor are getting poorer, where their access to decently paid employment and public housing is dwindling along with the value of state benefits and pensions and where education, youth training and the social security system are being streamlined to fit the development of a low-wage economy. In this situation some may ask whether it is appropriate to reassert the Marxist and feminist critiques of welfare and to add to these an anti-racist critique, when it appears we should be defending, not criticizing what still exists in universal state provision. Similarly, those working in schools or social services departments may be told that the pursuit of anti-racist and anti-sexist strategies are diversions from the main task of resisting the rationalization of resources. Can we still defend and criticize at the same time? I think we have to, but more than that, we have to work towards a welfare strategy which combines class, race and gender interests within democratic user-led services. It is women and Black people who are dispro-portionately represented amongst the poor, the low paid and the unemployed. Furthermore, appeals to and policies to reinforce the sanctity and values of family life, along with appeals to nationalism and 'British cultural traditions' and policies which reinforce the marginalization of other 'cultures' and the civil rights accorded to their members, are essential ramparts in the restructuring of the welfare state, and in the pursuit of economic policies capable of maintaining the profitability of capital at the particular expense of sections of the working class. Whilst it is the specific-ities of 'race' and gender which result in women and Black people being a significant section of the poor, the unemployed and the low paid, this situation is also the result of social and economic policies which undermine the interests of the working class. 'Race' and gender have their specific dynamics but they are at the same time interconnected to class. Similarly the demands for a system of welfare which benefits the working class must encompass demands which serve the interests of women and Black people too. This is why it is not enough merely to defend, or propose a strategy based upon the post-war welfare state with its predominantly white, male forms of full employment, universalism and egalitarianism. It has to be acknowledged that no simple common denominator of a 'race', class and gender strategy exists. Nevertheless, if a system of welfare is to be fought for which represents an alternative to that being pursued by the New Right, it must be based on new concepts of employment, universalism and egalitarianism which embody class, 'race' and gender interests. A programme of realizable demands which can be struggled for and which could include, along with is more general demands, policies for women and Black people – for example, universal nursery provision, positive action and equal opportunities programmes for women, Black people and other oppressed groups, disaggregation of the social security system (i.e. doing away with the assumption that a woman is a man's dependant), discon-nection of social security, housing, health and education systems from immigration controls, no restriction to eligibility to welfare provision or benefit by nationality or length of residence, and, importantly, a shorter and more flexible working week fitted around the needs of home-life; such a programme can emerge from an analysis that recognizes the welfare state as operating within the constraints of a capitalism which is both patriarchal and imperialist.

Re-evaluating Curriculum Content as Part of Anti-racist and Anti-sexist Strategies in Higher Education

This book represents an attempt to contribute to one part of an equal opportunities programme within higher education: that is, to provide a re-evaluation of the theoretical content of social policy and sociology of welfare courses, and to present the possibility of an integrated approach to 'race', class and gender issues. This should not displace or replace the specialist studies of 'race' and gender issues but should exist alongside them. An understanding of the world from the point of view of women and Black people is important not only in an attempt to provide meaningful teaching to the women students and Black students we would wish to encourage into higher education, but also it begins to provide a framework for the pursuit of anti-racist and anti-sexist strategies within the colleges, polytechnics, universities and future workplaces of all students, Black and white, women and men.

Structure of the Book

Part I deals with the discipline of social policy. Chapter 1 looks at the origins and development of the discipline and suggests that the empirical and atheoretical characteristics of the discipline, along with prevailing political thinking about the family and imperialism, prevented it from developing any critical evaluation of the unmet welfare needs of women and Black people. By the 1970s the Fabian-dominated tradition of the discipline began to be challenged by the re-emergence of different perspectives of welfare thinking from the political left and right, and this generated the theoretical basis of the discipline. Chapter 2 elaborates this theoretical basis – the classification and evaluation of different perspectives or theories of welfare whilst noting the exclusion of feminist or 'race' theories from most existing classifications. (Readers who are familiar with this should move straight to the critiques in Part II).

Part II examines and evaluates the different strands of feminist critiques of welfare and what might be called 'anti-racist' critiques of welfare and discusses their implications for welfare theory, policy and strategy. Chapter 3 looks at six different approaches to feminism – libertarian feminism, liberal feminism, welfare feminism, radical feminism, socialist feminism and Black feminism – whilst chapter 4 looks at six different approaches to the study of, and policies related to 'race' and racism – integration and assimilation, cultural pluralism, the underclass theory of John Rex, the relative autonomy of racism, the autonomy of racism and the political economy of migrant labour. In Chapter 5 we then return to the existing welfare perspectives outlined in Chapter 2 – anti-collectivism, non-socialist welfare collectivism, Fabian socialism, radical social administration and the political economy of welfare – and re-examine them in terms of their conceptualizations of the relationships of welfare policies with women and the family and 'race', and racism.

Part III draws on the evaluation we have made of existing welfare theory and the feminist and anti-racist critiques of welfare, and presents a framework for the analysis of gender, 'race' and class in the welfare state. This is a historical and materialist framework whose focus is broad enough to include both production *and* reproduction, that is both the relations of paid employment *and* of unpaid work in the family, and whose context is wide enough to include an understanding of the international aspects of different forms of imperialism and their impact upon the lives of Black and ethnic minority welfare workers and users. Chapter 6 looks at the development of significant policies from the nineteenth century up to the impact of New Right welfare policies upon women and Black people. Chapter 7 provides an analytical framework for understanding the welfare state as part of a racially structured and patriarchal capitalism in terms of the role of Black male workers and women workers, Black and white, in maintaining lower social expenditure; the reproduction of sexual and racial divisions of labour in welfare provision; the maintenance of the non-working white population, and the limitation of the Black non-working population; varieties of social control applied to women and to Black men and women including Black cultural pathology, ideas of dangerousness, containment and incorporation and internal controls; and, finally, the implications for welfare strategy of the struggles against women's oppression and Black oppression.

Part I   The Discipline of Social Policy

1 The Origins and Development of the Discipline of Social Policy and the Construction of Ideas around Family and Nation

Introduction

This chapter paves the way for the main themes of this book. These themes may be summarized as follows:

1   The neglect of the issues of gender and 'race' in the discipline of social policy.
2   The consistent, but differing, use of ideologies of the family, nation and 'race' in the development of British state welfare provision.
3   The consequent failure to recognize or meet many of the specific needs of women and Black people (and other racialized groups), as well as, in many cases, the consequent reproduction by state welfare of aspects of their exploitation and oppression.
4   The marginalization in practice and theory of challenges to this failure.
5   The need to attempt to rectify this by understanding these processes, by examining the theoretical and practical challenges to social policy posed by issues of gender and 'race', and by attempting to centralize the separate and convergent aspects of gender, 'race' and class in the study and practice of social policy. In other words, to create a framework for the study of the welfare state which is broad enough and internationalist enough to acknowledge the social relations of capitalism, of patriarchy, of racial domination and of imperialism.

As such we are concerned with both social policy as a *discipline* as well as social policy as the development and operation of *state welfare policies and practices*. Clearly these two aspects are interlinked, the first being an attempt to understand the second.

This chapter starts with an overview of the discipline, and begins to indicate some of the ways in which the construction of both the discipline and the welfare state itself inhibited the recognition of the welfare needs of women and Black people. Those aspects of the way the discipline has treated gender and 'race' issues which are asserted in this chapter, are substantiated in the following chapters. We start by looking at the origins of the discipline, at the nature of the 'mainstream' of the discipline which developed in the two decades after the Second World War, and at the challenges to this posed in the 1970s and 1980s.

Origins of Social Policy as a Discipline

The establishment of the discipline of social policy (or 'social administration' as it was usually known until relatively recently) emerged from the politics of collectivism and the practice of state intervention to deal with social problems in the beginnings of the twentieth century. Although there had been significant state intervention in the nineteenth century by way of, for example, the Poor Law, the Factory Acts, public health measures and state education provision, large-scale acceptance of the arguments for the principle of collectivism did not emerge until the turn of the century. The Liberals, socialists and the Fabian Society all supported collectivism in different ways, but it was in the ideas and practices of Beatrice and Sidney Webb of the Fabian Society that the 'empirical strengths and theoretical deficiencies' (Pinker, 1971, p. 94) of the discipline of social administration took its root. Fabianism was characterized by its proposals for practical policies aimed at social problems. It developed the method of empirical social investigation into, for example, the failure of the free market to mitigate poverty, which formed the basis of pamphlets and reports which were used to lobby and influence government officials and politicians. Their objectives were to move gradually to socialism through the state's reforms which would bring about good health and freedom from destitution for the working class through a system of state administered, professionally provided welfare and state regulation of the economy. In so far as the discipline of social administration established itself in the traditions of Fabianism it rejected other major political traditions of the time. The first was an anti-collectivist, free market individualism represented by the social philosopher Herbert Spencer; the second was Marx's critique of capitalism which argued for the international working class to organize to overthrow capitalism and bring about socialism for themselves; and thirdly, an earlier tradition of Utopian socialism, which flourished from the 1820s to the 1840s and emphasized the need to build alternative cooperative communities in which egalitarian relationships between all people, all 'races' and men and women could develop (Taylor, 1983). These other traditions remained relatively submerged features of the discipline until the emergence of a more articulated anti-collectivism, and Marxist and feminist approaches in the 1970s.

There were two further characteristics of early Fabianism which also influenced both the discipline and its policies for welfare reforms. These were its ideas about the family and motherhood and about nation and 'race'. In terms of the former this was an assertion of the family as constituted by the breadwinner father and dependent wife and children as the basic unit of society and of welfare provision. In this sense, the financial dependence of women on men and their primary responsibilities to society as mothers and wives, were taken for granted. In terms of ideas on nation and 'race', Fabianism, like many of the contemporary political philosophies, was influenced by the theories of 'survival of the fittest' of Darwin and by support for Britain's imperialist role. The writings and speeches of these early Fabians are marked by a racial bigotry and superiority (see Chapter 5), by a belief in a hierarchy of 'races' and by a nationalist programme of social imperialism. Social imperialism linked the necessity of welfare reforms to the maintenance of imperial strength: the promotion of the imperial 'race' required a fit and healthy workforce, a fit and healthy army and the cooperation of fit and healthy mothers. The ideas of the eugenics movement, which also influenced the Fabians, linked the two sets of ideas about the family and the 'race' through a belief in encouraging the procreation of the fitter, more intelligent of the classes and 'races' and discouraging the unfit and unintelligent. The 'endowment of motherhood', from which the family allowance system emerged, was central to these ideas.

Fabian ideas are generally seen as *distinct* from the competing anti-collectivism and Liberal ideas by the emphasis upon a major and direct role for the state in regulating the economy and providing for welfare reforms and redistribution of wealth (see, for example, George and Wilding, 1985). What is often overlooked is the extent to which it *shared* with these groups, as well as with sections of the growing labour movement, assumptions about the role of women, of racial superiority and the attempt to replace class solidarity with nationalist pride, which in turn found their expression in the developing welfare state.

The Development of the Discipline

Many of these characteristics and objectives of early Fabianism were carried into the post-war discipline of social administration which was dominated until the 1970s by the Fabian-influenced mainstream. There did exist, nevertheless, undercurrents of different perspectives of social policy: from the left there was Saville's Marxist analysis of the history of the welfare state (1957), Dorothy Wedderburn's 'Facts and Theories of the

Welfare State' (1965) and Coates and Silburn's *Poverty, the Forgotten Englishman* (1970). All attempted to place the welfare state in the context of the conflicting interests of capital and the working class. From the right the 'anti-collectivist' Institute of Economic Affairs produced a steady stream of pamphlets critical of what they saw as the welfare state's undermining of initiative and self-reliance. Within mainstream social administration the former ideas tended to be ignored whilst the latter were used as a foil to present the case for state intervention and universalism in welfare provision (see, for example, Titmuss's *Choice and 'The Welfare State'*. 1967).

Mainstream social administration was largely empirical and pragmatic, concerned with collecting facts and evidence, about, for example, the extent of poverty, in order to influence governments to improve their welfare provision. Its subject area was the statutory social services, and its teachers often practitioners and government advisers on policy-making. Both Richard Titmuss (first professor of social administration at the London School of Economics) and David Donnison became chairmen of the now extinct Supplementary Benefits Commission. The authority that this approach held over studies of the welfare state was both paralleled and fuelled in post-war Britain by a faith in economic growth and a policy followed, with different emphases, by both Conservative and Labour governments, of expansion of the welfare services (the so-called post-war 'consensus'). Its political and economic context was thus one of economic growth and increased public spending as well as one in which the labour movement was led by largely reformist ideas of piecemeal and gradual change. Common to all of these – social administration as a discipline, welfare provision, the 'consensus' and large sections of the labour movement – were unquestioned assumptions about the family and nationalist chauvinism. Indeed, central to the new Welfare State of 1945 were the themes of Family and Nation. Within the discipline of social administration these assumptions can be identified in both its explicit familism (see below) and nationalism as well as implicit within its main characteristics: its empiricism, idealism, its state and government orientation and its belief in the welfare state as integrative, universalist and redistributive. (These aspects are discussed more fully in later chapters.)

As with the earlier Fabians, policies aimed at women were in terms of an emphasis on the needs of women as mothers and dependent wives, rather than as individuals or wage-earners. The maintenance of the family was seen as integral to society's stability. This was part of a dominant ideology of 'familism', that is to say, a set of ideas which characterized the 'normal' or 'ideal' family form as one where the man was the main breadwinner and his wife's main contribution to the family was through her role as mother, carer and housewife, rather than as wage-earner, and who was therefore, along with her children, financially dependent upon her husband. Those households not conforming more or less to this model were thus seen as deviant or potentially problematic. Social administration's references to the 'voluntary' sector took for granted women's unpaid work within and outside the home. Its arguments for state intervention gave no room for the analysis of the relations of dependency or power between men and women, and could not encompass the negative experiences women had of the paternalism and sexism of the welfare state. In addition, its assumptions of female dependency and responsibility for care blinkered it to the fact that the welfare state was built upon the unpaid and the low paid work of women.

The nationalist and racialist superiority of the earlier Fabians re-emerged in social administration as a form of moral evangelicalism, a pride in Britain and the British welfare state. As the power and profits of imperialism declined only its civilizing mission remained. And it was this to which, in 1943, Titmuss referred when he wrote in *Problems of Population*, 'Western civilisation slowly evolved a higher way of life and it was our duty to help and guide the teeming millions of India and Africa to a more abundant life' (p. 9).

Many of the proposals concerning motherhood and family life in the 1942 Beveridge Report were couched in terms of maintaining the British race and British values. The national unity derived from Empire would be replaced by a unity derived from Welfare. The post-war situation was one where Black men and women from the Commonwealth were brought into the country to solve the labour shortage, but whose access to the welfare services, particularly housing and education, was neither acknowledged nor planned for and often denied. This went largely unquestioned by the labour movement and by academics in social administration. The subsequent hostility of a white working class whose historical concessions to racialist and racist ideology combined with a fear that post-war welfare capitalism was shortchanging them in relation to housing, in particular, produced appalling racism (as was evidenced by the uprisings in Notting Hill in 1958). The reaction of social administration to one of the most significant failures of the welfare state to provide for those in need, and one of the most startling examples, to use its own terms, of a lack of altruism, was fourfold: to ignore it, few social policy texts made reference to this denial of access; to categorize it as 'race relations', a separate problem, whose solution was that of changing the prejudices of whites (Race Relations Acts) or the cultures of Blacks (assimilation, integration, dispersal, and so on); to produce empirical evidence to show how Black people did not use many services after all; to subsume it under a general social problem – poverty or urban decline, or deprivation, or as a dimension of disadvantage.

These reactions of social administration can be partly explained in terms of the general characteristics of the mainstream of the discipline to which we now turn. At the heart of mainstream social administration was empiricism: the collection of facts and evidence about social problems, charting the dimensions of poverty, of homelessness, of the shortcomings of welfare administration, of improved forms of redistribution. The aim of these painstaking and thorough documentations was to persuade governments to improve their welfare provision, to tug at social conscience, to, as the Webbs had put it, 'convince the 2,000 who mattered'. Empirical documentation became the tool of persuasion. This emphasis on facts, reality and practicality presented itself as a counter to dogma, utopia and ideology. At the same time this led to an emphasis on prescription and remedy for social ills at the expense of a wider diagnosis based on evaluation and explanation. Its pride in its avoidance of so-called dogma or ideology from the left or right, inclined it to side-step theory, alternative explanations and the tools of self-criticism. Its empiricism and pragmatism meant that what it took for granted – economic growth, the family, the capacity of the welfare state to solve social problems, the supremacy of 'British' welfare, imperialism, the recruitment of cheap labour from the Commonwealth – was as significant as that which it questioned; and what it ignored – international economic forces, racism, the sexual division of labour – was as significant as that which it studied.

This empiricism was linked to its idealism, that is to say, the assumption that changes can be effected by ideas, or by the presentation of evidence, or by rational debate. This meant that in so far as racism was acknowledged in the mid-1960s, then associated policy recommendations were for anti-discriminatory legislation (the Race Relations Acts of 1965 and 1968). This identified racism as individual prejudice, and evidence was gathered to show the irrationality of such attitudes (Rose and Deakin, 1969). But this study of 'race relations' remained quite separate from social administration.

A further characteristic of the mainstream was its focus upon the state. It was governments who were to be lobbied, the state which could bring about reforms and their professional, trained experts who could carry out the policies. Not only did this exclude any appreciation that the working class, the patients, clients, or claimants might have any say in welfare provision, or impact in changing it, it also led to social administration's tendency to view social probems from 'the perspective of the state' (Taylor-Gooby and Dale, 1981). In other words, by not questioning the limitations of the state's capacity to solve problems, the approach unconsciously defined problems in the state's own terms, and thereby upheld the status quo. Successive governments had only seen Black immigrants as cheap labour. The state had overlooked their needs and social adminstration followed suit.

Associated with this was the faith placed upon the welfare professional or expert which excluded a subjective assessment of the welfare state on behalf of those who used the system and especially those who experienced it as bureaucratic, authoritarian, sexist and racist. This absence was reinforced by a belief in the power of the welfare state to promote integration and social harmony. Titmuss believed a free, universally available Nation Health Service would create national unity and harmony, and many Fabians believed the welfare state was a 'half-way house to socialism'. Within this framework it was not easy to raise questions about the ways the welfare state reinforced the oppressions of women and Black people.

The arguments of the mainstream for redistribution between rich and poor, for universal as against selective welfare provision, for the state and not the market, failed to acknowledge the need for redistribution within families as well as between them, to recognize the specific as well as the general needs of women and Black people. If these needs were identified they became dissolved in social problems of family stability or 'unsupported' mothers, or poverty, 'disadvantage' or urban decay, or in the case of 'race', ghettoized into 'race relations' studies.

Challenges to the Mainstream

Challenges to mainstream social adminstration came from within the discipline through the development of different perspectives of the welfare state, as well as outside the discipline through the economic crisis and the breaking of the post-war consensus of economic growth, full male employment and a secure welfare state. In particular, the beginnings of welfare cutbacks from the early 1970s seemed to begin to challenge the post-war project of the welfare state.

First, within the discipline there was the development of a 'political economy of welfare' (Gough, 1979) which was a refined and influential application of Marxist theory to welfare capitalism. Part of Gough's analysis of the welfare state is based on O'Connor's explanation for the crisis of welfare capitalism in *The Fiscal Crisis of the State* (1973). In this O'Connor identifies a basic contradiction in the development of welfare capitalism, that is, a tendency for state expenditures to increase more rapidly than the means of financing them (p. 9). According to O'Connor, intervention of the increasingly centralized state to grant social and economic reforms works partly to aid the accumulation of capital (the profitability of industry, for example) and partly to salve the demands of the organized working class for better welfare services. However, this process generates its own conflict which is exacerbated by economic decline: as the working class demand improvements (in health provision, for example), the state has to demand that capital (from the profits of industry) or labour (from greater taxation of the working class) pays for this. Unless it is able or prepared for a confrontation with capital, one way out is for the government to cut back on social expenditure on welfare, as the Labour government did in 1975/6 and 1977/8, and the Conservative governments have in subsequent years (see chapter 6). Welfare cuts represent, then, an attempt to solve the fiscal crisis, to reduce taxation and provide more resources for private investment.

A second set of ideas which contributed to the sense of ebbing of the welfare state's ideals stemmed from social critiques of it by feminists and socialists. The feminist critique exposed the way that the main institutions of welfare – health, social security, housing, education and the personal social services – all in different ways either failed to give women the benefits they needed, or reinforced material and ideological aspects of their oppression, both as consumers of welfare or workers in the welfare services. Alongside this, critiques emerged from socialists which attempted to link the contradictory experiences of those who worked in the welfare services to those of their consumers. In particular the London–Edinburgh Weekend Return Group in *In and Against the State* summed up the contradiction of welfare in the following way: 'We seem to need things from the state, such as child care, houses, medical treatment. But what we are given is often shoddy or penny-pinching, and besides it comes to us in a way that seems to limit our freedom, and reduce control we have over our lives' (LEWRG, 1979, p. 8). They pointed also to the contradiction in the important struggle to defend the welfare state against cutbacks, that is, the necessity to go beyond a defence of the welfare state: 'to limit our actions to demands for "more of the same" is to fail to take the opportunity to challenge capitalism fundamentally by rejecting its agenda, its definitions, its social relations' (p. 83). These 'social relations' are those of individualism, competition, bureaucratic formalism, sexism and racism, and the organization of struggles against these should themselves, the authors argued, attempt to incorporate or 'pre-figure' anti-capitalist relations of cooperation, anti-sexism and anti-racism.

Other writers expanded these specific criticisms of the welfare state as remote, authoritarian and bureaucratic into a critique of post-war social democracy. Stuart Hall (1980b, 1984), for example, sees these contradictions of the welfare state reflected in the operation of post-war social democracy which the welfare cutbacks of the 1974–9 Labour government particularly exposed. Whilst social democratic governments win elections on the claim that they are the party of working-class interests they have at the same time to 'manage' capitalism. They have done this by disciplining their workforce, by appealing to ideas of the nation, family or of 'law and order' over and above the ideas of 'class' and 'struggle'. Their socialism, Hall argues, is statism, where people experience the state and all its institutions not as their own, but as distant and bureaucratic. As such, the Labour government of 1974–9 in particular disarmed its own working class and left the way wide open for the New Right, who were able to exploit such themes of nation, family and the need for law and order, and the negative experiences of the state into a more thorough-going philosophy of anti-collectivism and anti-statism. Hall's work also identifies how the continued but shifting appeal to 'national unity' has given rise to the rationalization of various forms of state racism, particularly in relation to the policing of Black youth and to immigration controls (CCCS, 1982; Hall et al., 1978).

A further significant challenge to the apparent permanency of the post-war welfare state came through the philosphies and practices of the New Right Conservative administration which appear in some ways to invert the philosophies of the consensus of the post-war welfare settlement that went before it. New Right philosphy switched the role of the welfare state from the Fabian interpretation of *solution* to our ills to the monetarist one of *cause* of our ills. It presented state intervention and the welfare state as a *hindrance* to economic growth, first because the burden of taxation and interference with market forces acts as a disincentive to investment; secondly, because the provision of welfare encourages scroungers, saps individualism and initiative, and generally acts as a disincentive to work; thirdly, because the state is seen as inefficient, wasteful and bureaucratic, whereas the private market is a superior mode of organization offering freedom of choice. Inequalities are seen as natural, God-given or culturally determined.

The impact of these new and different critiques upon the mainstream tradition of social administration was a fragmentation and a regrouping into three different strands. First a non-socialist approach, arguing for a 'mixed economy of welfare', that is to say that welfare provision need not necessarily just be state-provided, but could come from the voluntary and the private sectors too, (Pinker, 1979; Hadley and Hatch, 1981; Owen, 1981). Secondly, a more wary and self-critical Fabianism has emerged (Glennerster, 1983; Deakin, 1987); and thirdly, a radical strand of social administration which combines the traditional concerns of Fabianism – poverty, inequality – with a structural analysis of social problems and a radical programme of redistribution through social planning (Townsend, 1983; Walker, 1984).

As far as the discipline of social policy is concerned, the articulation, and in some cases the practice, of new and different approaches to the welfare state has done two things. First it paved the way for attempts to develop a theoretical basis for the discipline and move it beyond its empirical orientation (George and Wilding, 1976, revised in 1985; Mishra, 1977, revised in 1981; Pinker, 1979; Room, 1979; Taylor-Gooby and Dale, 1981). The strengths and limitations of these attempts are discussed in the following chapter, but it is significant that very few of these took on board the feminist critique, and that the implications of this critique remained at best marginalized in most subsequent social policy texts. It is also interesting that from the mid-1970s theoretical approaches to 'race' and racism and critiques of race-relations policy were emerging but found no place in social policy texts. This is perhaps even more suprising since many of the political debates about the New Right (see Hall, 1980, 1984) began to acknowledge the centrality of the traditional themes of the family and nation to the management of the crisis by the New Right.

The second effect of the challenges to the mainstream's concept of the welfare state was a debate about whether the welfare state was in crisis, whether it had lost its legitimacy not simply amongst writers of social policy but amongst the public at large (Corrigan, 1979; Leonard, 1979; Golding, 1983). This debate has focused upon how far the electoral successes of the New Right and their commitment to privatization and welfare expenditure cuts mean an end to the welfare state and public support for it. What is also at issue in this debate is how far present changes taking place in the welfare policies – which are discussed in the final section of this book – represent continuities or discontinuities with past practices and philosophies of welfare. Without going into the twists and turns of this debate (see discussion in Mishra, 1984, 1986b; Offe, 1984; Therborn, 1984; Taylor-Gooby, 1985), the following exploration of the welfare state in terms of gender and 'race' lends support to Peter Taylor-Gooby's observation that 'the changes that are taking place have deep roots leading back into the original structure of the welfare state and the continuing pattern of public support for it' (1985, p. 2). In other words, as far as women and Black people are concerned, the policies emanating from the welfare state 'in crisis' represent not so much a break with past practice as an intensification in a much harsher way, as well as being justified in a much more explicit manner, of elements of a familism, a nationalism and a variety of racism inherent in the development of the welfare state. From our point of view we need to understand the reasons for the continued marginalization of the issues of gender and 'race' in the discipline, as well as the reasons for the consistently limited achievements of the welfare state in these areas.

2 Perspectives of Welfare: the Existing, but Inadequate Theoretical Basis of Social Policy

Introduction

This chapter is about the different perspectives of welfare, that is to say, the different theoretical approaches to the understanding of the relationship between welfare and society, and different views on the best means of maximizing welfare in society. What we are concerned with is the way these different perspectives have been classified and differentiated. In addition, we begin to indicate how the conventional classifications have marginalized issues and perspectives derived from feminism and work on 'race' and racism.

In the previous chapter it was noted that the Fabian-dominated mainstream in the discipline of social policy began to be challenged in the 1970s by different and more critical perspectives of the welfare state: from the left was a Marxist 'political economy of welfare perspective'; from the right, a new and more assertive form of anti-collectivism from the New Right in the Conservative Party; from the women's movement, a feminist critique of welfare. In the wings, not particularly recognized by the discipline was emerging a powerful critique of race-relations policies and of the relationship of the state to Black people. At the same time, the Fabian mainstream appeared to fragment into three stands: those arguing for a pragmatic mix of private, voluntary and state welfare provision – the welfare pluralists; those Fabians who continued in the mainstream and insisted on the primacy of documenting social problems, elaborating policy solutions and demonstrating the inequalities of the market; and more radical Fabians influenced by the methods of Fabianism as well as the critique of Marxism.

The emergence of a plurality of perspectives, and the recognition of them provided the discipline of social policy with a new theoretical terrain: the classification and analysis of the philosophies, objectives and theories of these different perspectives of welfare. (It was not *entirely* new – as I shall describe later on, both Richard Titmuss (1974) and Dorothy Wedderburn (1965) had attempted classifications of different welfare perspectives – nor is the development entirely welcomed: Howard Glennerster (1988), from the old mainstream Fabian position, comments about this development, 'If we had worried less about critical theory and more about cleaning people's rubbish we would have served humanity better'.) Nevertheless, this development was seen by most as an important step forward in the discipline. Ramesh Mishra (1986a), for example, argues that these classifications and analyses are 'at the core of social administration as a theoretical discipline' (1986a, p. 33). If this is the case, that these classifications represent the core of the theoretical basis of the discipline, then we are forced to ask two questions: why is it, despite the fact indicated in chapter 1 that familist and nationalist ideologies have been central to much welfare development and thinking, that these aspects find little mention in most conventional classifications and analyses; and secondly, that with one or two exceptions, the feminist critique of welfare, or an 'anti-racist critique' of the state and race-relations policies, similarly find no acknowledgement? It could be argued on the second question that the discipline of social policy, like most of us, is a creature of its time and that *eventually* these perspectives will get recognition. However, as I shall argue in chapters 3 and 4 which elaborate the feminist critique of welfare and the empirical and theoretical basis for an anti-racist critique of welfare, the answers to these two questions lie in an examination of the implicit consensus about what constitute the important policy concerns in social policy, and secondly, in questioning whether the theoretical terrain of existing welfare analysis is broad enough to encompass issues of gender and 'race'.

This chapter covers the ground of the conventional classifications and analyses of welfare perspectives (i.e. those that make no reference to feminism or to critical 'race' theory), bearing in mind the qualifications just made above. First, we look at the broad areas of similarity in the ways social policy writers have classified different welfare perspectives. We then look at the two ways in which these writers have sought to describe and analyse the perspectives. Some writers have examined the philosophies or *values* which different perspectives have and the implication of these for their goals or objectives for welfare provision, other writers have included an analysis and evaluation of how the different perspectives *explain* the existence of social problems, or the nature of social change. These are often referred to as *normative* and *explanatory* approaches, respectively. Sticking to the conventional classification of welfare perspectives, we examine and evaluate them using both these methods. Finally we return to the question of the missing perspectives of feminism and anti-racism, and the unanswered questions of how the perspectives we have examined approach questions of gender and 'race'. These three areas are taken up in detail in the following three chapters.

Different Perspectives of Welfare and their Classifications

In table 2.1 seven different perspectives of welfare are, very briefly, summarized. The characteristics of the first five will be expanded further later in this chapter and the last two, feminism and anti-racism, examined in separate following chapters. For the moment, we very briefly outline these perspectives. The first, *anti-collectivism*, comprises the now various strands of economic liberalism which emphasize distribution through the free market and minimize the state role in providing welfare – nineteenth-century *laissez-faire*, neo-liberalism and the policies of the New Right. The second, third and fourth perspectives represent the divergent strands of social reformism all with varying commitments towards and reasons for collectivism, that is, state-provided welfare. Those who believe in state intervention to provide welfare but who would not see themselves as socialists, more as pragmatists, I have labelled *non-socialist welfare collectivists*, whose beliefs stretch from the Liberal Party of the early twentieth century, through Beveridge and Keynes to social policy writers like Robert Pinker, welfare pluralists and politicians like David Owen of the Social Democratic Party.

The *Fabian socialists* were discussed in chapter 1 and similarly their tradition covers three important periods: the early Fabians, like the Webbs, the post-war welfare writers, like Anthony Crosland and Richard Titmuss, and present-day social policy writers such as David Donnison and Howard Glennerster. The *radical social administration* stream is new: it combines the empiricism of Fabianism with the structuralism of Marxism and argues for redistribution through social planning; Peter Townsend and Alan Walker represent this perspective. The *political economy of welfare* represents the application of Marxist economic and political theory to the twentieth-century development of welfare capitalism. This is mainly a critique of capitalism, which is seen as ultimately antagonistic to the welfare needs of the working class, but nevertheless forced by working-class struggle, or for the sake of political stability, or because it also suits its own needs, to concede welfare reforms. Ian Gough, Norman Ginsburg and Claus Offe represent different strands within this perspective. The *feminist critique* contrasts the welfare state as a potential provider of some of the material necessities to improve women's lives, such as nurseries or access to safe contraception, with the

Table 2.1 Different perspectives of welfare: a simple account

Type	Attitude to the welfare state	Political tradition (associated writer/ policy-maker)
Anti-collectivism	State welfare limits individual freedom; initiative and choice, and leads to excessive demands. Provision to come from private/ voluntary sector as well as through family and self-help	Right-wing, freedom of the market, economic liberalism, New Right (Hayek, Friedman, Joseph, Boyson)
Social reformism (three types)		
Non-socialist welfare collectivism	State welfare provision necessary for national efficiency and alleviation of worst deprivation, but can also come from private/voluntary sectors ('mixed economy of welfare' or 'welfare pluralism')	Political liberalism and social democracy (Beveridge, Keynes, Hadley and Hatch, Pinker, Owen)
Fabian socialism	The welfare state is central to the transformation of society through redistribution of wealth and the creation of a more equal, just and harmonious society to counter the inequalities of the private market	Social democracy, Fabian socialism (Tawney, Titmuss, Crosland)
Radical social administration	Welfare state to be central to a socially planned society which consists of radical redistribution of wealth and resources and the pursuit of equality	Fabian socialism, democratic socialism, Marxism (Townsend, Walker)
Political economy of welfare	Welfare state as outcome of fundamental conflict between capitalism and working class, but unable to meet need under capitalism	Marxism (Gough, Ginsburg, Offe)

Table 2.1   *cont.*

Type	Attitude to the welfare state	Political tradition (associated writer/ policy-maker)
Feminist critique	State welfare provision important for amelioration of women's lives but also reinforces female dependency and the sexual division of labour	Liberal/socialist/radical feminism, Marxism (Land, McIntosh, Pascall, Wilson)
'Anti-racist critique'	State policy reflects shifting relations between imperialism, capitalism and patriarchy. Welfare state is part of institutionalized racism of society, by denial of access, second-class provision, reproduction of racial divisions and maintenance of immigration controls	Black radicalism/ socialism/Marxism/ Black feminism (Gilroy, Lawrence, Solomos, Hall, Carby, Sivanandan, Rex, Ben-Tovim and Gabriel, Miles and Phizacklea)

ways in which aspects of welfare provision reinforce women's financial dependency and their responsibilites for caring for the young, the sick and the old, and their limited access to low paid work. This perspective too has historical variations and is informed by different feminist theories: liberal feminism, radical feminism, socialist feminism and Black feminism; this is discussed in chapter 3. The last perspective also flows partly from Black feminism, as well as from theoretical analyses of the relationship of the state to Black people, and critiques of race-relations policies (Sivanandan, 1976; Hall et al., 1978; CCCS, 1982) from the few analyses that do look at racism and the welfare state (Rex, 1973; Ben-Tovim et al., 1986) and from the political economy of migrant labour (Sivanandan, 1976, 1979; Miles and Phizacklea, 1984). I have labelled this an *'anti-racist critique'* though this is an unsatisfactory description on two counts: first because 'anti-racist' does not connote fully enough the internationalist and anti-imperialist dimensions of this critique; secondly, because it hardly exists as a coherent perspective *within* social policy (although the aim of chapter 4 is to rectify this). Nevertheless, this perspective, which is elaborated in chapter 4, identifies the welfare state as part of the institutionalized racism in society, by denying Black people's access to benefits and provision, by reproducing racial divisions of labour within the welfare state and by using welfare agencies to police Black people and immigrants.

Table 2.2 Different classifications of welfare perspectives

Author(s)	I Anti-collectivism	II Non-socialist welfare collectivism	III Social reformism / Fabian socialism	IV Radical social administration	V Political economy
Wedderburn (1965)	Anti-collectivism	Citizenship	Integrationism	Functionalism	*
Titmuss (1974)	Residual welfare	Industrial achievement performance (handmaiden)	Institutional redistributive*		
George and Wilding (1976, 1985)	Anti-collectivism	Reluctant collectivism	Fabian socialism	*	Marxism
Mishra (1977, 1981)[a]		Citizenship Functionalism	Welfare as social reform Convergence theory		Marxism
Mishra (1977, 1981)[b]	Residual		Institutional		Normative*
Pinker (1979)	Classical economic theory	Neo-mercantile* collectivism			Marxism
Room (1979)	Market liberalism	Political liberalism	Social democracy*		Neo-Marxism

*Denotes the standpoint of the author(s).
Mishra uses two types of classification: [a] refers more to theoretical influence; [b] refers to view of the role of the welfare state.

Most existing classifications of welfare perspectives follow broadly the same pattern, except of course that they do not include feminism or anti-racism. (Two recent exceptions to this are Clarke *et al.* (1987) and Sullivan (1987), which include feminism but have litte to say on racism or anti-racism). These conventional classifications are illustrated in table 2.2.

It is possible to see three broadly similar areas represented by a continuum which moves, politically speaking, from the right through to the left: anti-collectivism – social reformism – political economy of welfare. Both the earlier classifications of Wedderburn and Titmuss excluded a Marxist perspective. Titmuss's classification is threefold: residual welfare, which sees state provision of welfare as a last resort to those few whose needs cannot be met through the market; industrial achievement performance (or 'handmaiden') model which sees the welfare state as subordinate to, yet important for, the development of the economy; and the institutional redistributive model, to which Titmuss was committed, and which is depicted as playing a major reforming role in providing for need outside the market and creating through redistribution, a more egalitarian society (Titmuss, 1974). Generally, at least two areas are represented within the middle-group – social reformism. What appears to be the logic of this continuum is the extent of support each perspective exhibits for a collective commitment, via the state, for welfare provision: minimum at one end (the anti-collectivists), working up to maximum at the other end (the political economy of welfare). Alternatively, it could be said that the anti-collectivist end represents a market-based society and the continuum works along to a needs-based society at the other end. Either way, these give us some clue as to why it is difficult to include perspectives such as the feminist critique and the anti-racist critique on this continuum because neither critique is *centrally* concerned with promoting a particular role for the state in the provision of welfare, what they are concerned with is forms of oppression and inegalitarianism between men and women and whites and Blacks and the fact that the state may reinforce these every bit as much as the market. Two further points are made in table 2.2: first, that in some cases the writers refer to a theoretical classification (e.g. 'functionalism') rather than a *welfare* perspective. The reason for this will be clearer when we deal with 'explanatory' accounts below. Secondly, most writers argue for one particular perspective, thus Mishra (1977) argues for a position combining the empiricism and humanitarianism of Fabianism, particularly of Titmuss, with the theoretical clarity of Marxism. Though Wedderburn does not mention Marxism, in effect she analyses from that standpoint. Pinker and Room, on the other hand, come from the mainstream tradition, recognize they have to confront Marxism and anti-collectivism, but dismiss them and argue for social administration to be brought back to its empirical and social democratic roots.

Normative and Explanatory Accounts

We now turn in greater detail to the question of how to distinguish between different perspectives. The first method, used for example by Titmuss in 1974 and by George and Wilding in their first edition (1976), is *normative*, that is, it aims to show the values or political philosophy of a particular perspective (e.g. liberty or equality) and to show how this relates to that perspective's goals for social welfare. So, for example, anti-collectivism believes in the freedom of the individual which is limited by state intervention; by contrast, Fabian socialism believes in equality which can be enhanced by state intervention. A typical normative-based classification would distinguish its perspectives by asking of them the following questions.

• What are their political traditions and values?
• What role for the state do they envisage in the provision of welfare?
• What is their principle of distribution of welfare (that is, to everybody, or selected few and so on)?
• What is their view of the preferred relationship between economic policy and social policy?

Table 2.3 sets out these questions in relation to the five perspectives in conventional classifications. Note that most normative accounts have not asked how these values, such as freedom of the individual, apply to women, or indeed what role is played by the family, and women within it, in the provision of welfare. Neither have they asked how these values apply to non-nationals or what are the boundaries (e.g. national) of welfare obligation or what is their attitude towards racism. The contents of table 2.3 will be elaborated shortly, when the perspectives are discussed in turn.

A number of shortcomings arise from using this normative method of analysis on its own. One has already been mentioned and is highlighted by Lee and Raban (1983) – that the presentation of different perspectives along a continuum or axis of anti-state values at one end and pro-state values at the other, leaves no room for perspectives that are centrally concerned with different conditions, or whose political traditions cut across some of these classifications. An example here is feminism. A second limitation is that which applies to any attempt to classify perspectives in a descriptive manner, which is that it exaggerates the characteristics of each perspective, and underestimates the degree of blurring between the perspectives, or contradictory elements within any one perspective.

A final substantive criticism is raised by Taylor-Gooby and Dale (1981), who argue that a normative presentation of these perspectives fails to do two things. First, it fails to recognize some of the most important distinctions between the perspectives. These are not only in the values and

Table 2.3 A typical normative account of different welfare perspectives

	Values	Role of the state in the provision of welfare	Principle of distribution of state welfare provision	Relationship between economic policy and social policy
Anti-collectivism	Liberty of the individual; freedom of the market; individual choice	Minimal	Extremely selective, otherwise through choice in the private market	Freedom of the market dominates
Social reformism Non-socialist welfare collectivism	Individual liberty within an efficient, compassionate, capitalism; pragmatism	Medium, combined with private and voluntary provision: pragmatic mix	Some universalism, some selectivity	Social policy compensates for and supports economic policy
Fabian socialism	Equality, collectivism, social harmony	Large	Universal needs-based	Social policy influences economic policy to become more socially responsible
Radical social administration	Equality, humanitarianism, collectivism	Large, decentralized, local control	Universal needs-based	Unification of social and economic policy through social planning to redress inequality
Political economy of welfare	Values determined by nature of economic production	Large . . . to dissolved, decentralized	Universal needs-based	Irreconcilable conflict between economic and social policy under capitalism. Under socialism, economy to serve human needs

goals they have for welfare, but in the sorts of *explanations* they have of social problems and social change. As it stands in table 2.3, the political economy perspective merely seems a more extreme version of Fabian socialism or radical social administration. In fact the real difference between the political economy perspective and the other two is, as we shall see, in the way it explains how social change happens. The second failure is that the normative account provides us with no basis to *evaluate* the theoretical and strategic adequacies of the different perspectives. Certainly some *appear* 'nicer' than others, but what tools do we have to evaluate that appearance?

Various writers do provide evaluations of the types of explanations used by different perspectives: Taylor-Gooby and Dale (1981), Gough (1978), Mishra (1981) and, to a lesser extent, Wedderburn (1965). Here we follow loosely the explanatory classification of Taylor-Gooby and Dale, being the most thorough. These two writers identify four main types of explanation used by social welfare writers and policy-makers. These are individualism, idealism and two types of structuralism: functionalism and materialism.

Individualism locates the causes of social problems in individual failure or misbehaviour and identifies social change as being affected by individuals trying to maximize their personal self-interest. An explanation which indentifies people's lack of control over their eating habits as the cause of ill-health, or their poor budgeting habits as the cause of their poverty, is an individualist explanation. As a method of explanation it is inadequate because of its 'denial of any role to social structures and institutions in shaping people's ideas and actions' (Taylor-Gooby and Dale, 1981, pp. 116–17). In this example of ill-health, no adequate consideration is given to differential access to food, the pricing and availability of food, or environmental factors such as transport, work, housing, incomes, stress, pollution and so on.

Idealism identifies change coming about through the agency of changed ideas. The Fabian socialist belief, noted in chapter 1, that it was possible to bring about change through rational discourse, through moral persuasion or by fostering collective values, is idealist. Another commonly held idealist view is that it is possible to educate people to think and act differently, for example, to stop discriminating against women or Black people. The problem with this view of change is that it fails to recognize the bearing that society itself has on the creation and sustenance of ideas. Ideas do not float through the air for us to catch and discard as we may, they are rooted in our day-to-day life, in the material conditions of our existence. Thus, in the example of education, it is not enough to tell people gender discrimination is wrong when the material conditions of women's lives (work, childcare, housing and so on) continue to make them financially dependent on men and responsible for servicing their needs. Both individualism and idealism, then, in different ways, underestimate the objective social conditions which shape individuals' behaviour, or which shape ideas and ideologies.

By contrast, *functionalism* acknowledges and gives primacy to the structure of society shaping people's behaviour, or the changes in welfare development. Thus the welfare state would be identified by functionalists as functional to society as a whole, ensuring people were housed, fit, skilled and so on (Parsons, 1951); others have identified the welfare state as a necessary corollary to industrial development (Wilensky, 1975) – sometimes also called convergence theory or technological determinism. The strength of these theories is that they see society as a totality, but the weakness is that they leave human action totally out of account. By concentrating on the welfare state as functional to the integration of society, they fail to account for areas of conflicting interests between the welfare state and those who use it, or the fact that certain welfare policies may be beneficial, or functional, to some, but not to others. In addition, it cannot explain, as Gough (1978) points out, the divergences in the development of social welfare in industrialized societies, only the general trends.

Materialism, the Marxist method of explanation, identifies the structures of capitalism as the forces which shape the social relations of everyday life, but explains that, at the same time, these social relations are based on a conflict of interests: the interests of capitalism to get profit out of their workers, and the interests of workers to maximize the social and economic conditions of their lives. This antagonism leads to class conflict, class conflict leads to struggle and struggle leads to change. In this explanation both the structure of society – the objective conditions, *and* the role of human actions are acknowledged. In addition, as Gough points out, it offers a historical method that unites the subjective (human action) element of social change with an account of the objective conditions in which that action takes place. In this way materialism accommodates structure *and* the individual *and* conflict *and* change. In fact, it should also be said that not all Marxist explanations necessarily account for both subjective and objective in this way. Some Marxist analysis tends to be functionalist; for example, Bowles and Gintis (1976) give an account of the United State's education system as one which grades and selects and skills according to the requirements of industry, and little mention is made, for example, of the forms of resistance by pupils and teachers in this process, and whether they have any impact on change.

In the end then both Gough and Taylor-Gooby and Dale agree that one of the criteria for evaluating the adequacy of any theory is that it must take account of the extent to which our lives are constrained by social forces but it has to account as well for the extent to which we act for ourselves. We are not puppets, totally moulded and our actions determined: 'Any theoretical approach must be capable of doing justice to both areas: the objective and the subjective . . . on the one hand the objective development of the welfare state as a social form . . . on the other hand, the story of how citizens as free subjects have collectively willed such development' (Taylor-Gooby and Dale, 1981, p. 126). Individualism recognizes the human actor but not the structure; idealism proposes change through the collective adoption of superior values – for example, fraternity, equality – but offers no analysis of the roots of these values. Functionalism neglects human action, but materialism with its account of the structural forces of capitalism *and* of class struggle offers the possiblity of a more fruitful method. Furthermore, materialism succeeds where idealism fails: not only does it acknowledge both human action and social structure but within this it is able to offer an account of ideology which roots ideas in the material social relations of production. For example individual self-interest or ideas of property stem from the forms of activity in which people are engaged under capitalism. Oppositional ideas of equality similarly are rooted in the struggles people engage in against exploitation and oppression.

Taylor-Gooby and Dale suggest that it is this distinction between, in particular, the individualism of anti-collectivism, the idealism of social reformism and the materialism of political economy of welfare which is missing in the 'countinuum' classifications of social policy writers. Instead, the crucial distinctions should be made between the different types of explanations: table 2.4 summarizes the explanatory methods of the five perspectives. These as well as their values and objectives for welfare will now be discussed and evaluated.

Anti-collectivism

There are three historical variations of anti-collectivism: first nineteenth-century classical liberalism of Adam Smith, which promoted the idea of only minimal state intervention on the basis that the market economy was the key to social order and through which individual's needs and desires could best be secured. The associated practice of *laissez-faire* policies in the nineteenth century believed in charity work to promote self-help and a highly deterrent, punitive and minimal form of welfare provided through the workhouse under the Poor Law. Second are the modern philosophers of liberalism, the *neo-liberals* Hayek and Friedman; and thirdly, the policies of the New Right which combine the economic liberalism of Hayek and Friedman with the social authoritarian approach of neo-conservatives like Roger Scruton and John Casey (whose ideas are discussed in greater detail in chapter 5). Straddling the second and third group are writers like Keith Joseph, Enoch Powell and Rhodes Boyson who have expounded critiques of the welfare state.

Common to all is a fundamental belief in the *freedom of the individual*.

Table 2.4   An explanatory account of different welfare perspectives

	Social problems explained in terms of	Changes effected by	Method
Anti-collectivism	Individual failure or inadequacy	Individual action	Individualist
Social reformism			
Non-socialist welfare collectivism	Individual failure plus dysfunction-ing of economy	Pressure group action; fostering collective commit-ment to national interest	Idealist
Fabian socialism	Dysfunctions of capitalism, malad-ministration of welfare state	Fostering collectivist and moral values of equality, fraternity, altruism	Idealist
Radical social administration	Structure, class relations and mal-distribution within capitalism	Transformation of state by fostering socialist values to press for radical state action	Idealist/ structuralist
Political economy of welfare	Conflicting interests between working class needs and capital's needs	Class struggles to change economic production result-ing from conflict between capital and labour	Materialist/ structuralist

Friedman emphasizes freedom to act in the market economy, whilst Hayek's stress is on freedom from coercion as the basis of economic freedom. Rhodes Boyson expresses it in terms of freedom to choose between good and evil which is the basis of morality, but also it is a freedom which applies to the economy: the freedom to take risks and be held responsible for your actions (Boyson, 1971).

It follows from this that if this individualism, this ability to stand on one's own two feet, is properly fostered, then state welfare is undesirable and becomes unnecessary for the vast majority of the population. Liberal economists writing in the 1950s and 1960s saw the development of state welfare as a passing phase whose real objective was to make people do without it.

Since then a critique of post-war welfare has emerged from anti-collectivists, particularly via the Institute of Economic Affairs, which the New Right has elaborated in a number of ways. The main points of this critique are that the welfare state inhibits individual freedom, it is inefficient and wasteful and is morally disruptive. First of all, individual freedom is limited through the imposed burden of taxation necessary to fund state welfare, by planning and legal controls which inhibit private enterprise – rent control, for example, which inhibits private landlordism – and by the monopoly that state welfare has over welfare provision. State welfare, it is argued, is paternalistic and authoritarian in dictating how needs should be met. These arguments have been taken up by the New Right and built into a radical critique of professionalism and bureaucracy in the welfare state which points to the lack of choice and control welfare consumers have in health, education and the personal social services in particular. This lack of choice is reinforced by there being no readily available alternative to state provision.

These 'monopoly' characteristics also mean, according to anti-collectivists, that state welfare services are wasteful and inefficient since they are faced with no competition and are not controlled by any cost-effective principles. This wastefulness is fuelled by the belief that the existence of state welfare has led to a spiralling of demands and expectations: the more people get the more they expect. This aspect was condemned by Enoch Powell as the dangerous process whereby a want or need becomes a right. It is argued that many of the benefits of state provision, like child benefit or NHS treatment, go to those who do not need them or could afford to buy their own. In addition, state welfare bureaucracies have created self-interested groups of professionals and administrators who demand that the growth of the welfare state be maintained. Finally, the welfare state is seen as morally disruptive by sapping people's initiative and self-reliance and inducing them into states of dependency upon provision. Social security, it is argued, removes people's incentive and responsibility to find work.

What then, apart from minimal state provision for those really in need, do anti-collectivists propose to remedy all this? One solution being followed in Britain is the re-privatization policies of the New Right (which are discussed in chapter 6). These take three forms: the encouragement to the private sector to provide alternative privately based welfare, the contracting-out to the private sector of parts of the state welfare services, and the application of private market principles within state welfare provision. The assumption here is that the logic of the market will provide a more accountable, efficient service, responsible to its consumers whose freedom, choice and control lies in their purse, now heavier with lower taxation. Another important part of anti-collectivist objectives for welfare is to encourage the family rather that the state to exercise greater responsibility for the care of its young and old dependants. This aspect is discussed in chapter 5.

Finally, it is clear in this perspective of welfare that not only are the needs of the economy seen as central and social needs subsumed under them, but that the principles of economic life are to be reflected in social life: initiative, responsibility, discipline, authority and ultimately, through these, freedom. It is also clear that the type of explanation for social change underlying this perspective is an *individualist* one. Individual action and initiative are seen as the prime motors of change to be guarded and preserved. The influence of the objective world is not accounted for: thus, the processes which render some people less able to choose or buy their housing, health or education are considered unimportant. The social causes of problems are minimized as are the social costs of industrial change and economic policy. Poverty is to be overcome by self-help and self-reliance. In the early 1970s the notion of 'culture' rather than 'individual' emerged from Keith Joseph as an explanation for poverty. His argument was that families in poverty transmitted a 'culture of deprivation' to their children who then continued this when they grew up. This 'culture' consists of lack of achievement at school, problematic relationships and casual, unskilled work, or unemployment. Such an explanation again fails to account for the effect of social circumstance, and seeks to explain a social phenomenon through the supposed characteristics of the family or 'culture' to which they belong. Anti-collectivism as a theory of welfare is totally inadequate. The effects of its contemporary application in Britain are detailed in chapter 6.

The three different perspectives under the general category of social reformism all believe in some form of collective state provision for welfare. We will now look at each in turn: non-socialist welfare collectivism, Fabian socialism and radical social administration.

Non-socialist Welfare Collectivism

This perspective has similarities with that identified by Titmuss (1974) as the 'handmaiden model' and by George and Wilding (1976) as 'reluctant collectivism'. Contemporary adherents are generally referred to as 'welfare pluralists'. Historically this perspective has moved from the Liberal reformers of the Lloyd George government at the beginning of this century to Keynes and Beveridge in the 1930s and 1940s, through to Social Democratic Party politician David Owen and Conservative Party 'wets' like Ian Gilmour, and supporters of a 'mixed economy of welfare'. In terms of their political values they share with anti-collectivists a belief in the maintenance of capitalism and free enterprise along with individual liberty. At the same time these values are tempered by a pragmatism. They see the warts on capitalism's face, Disease, Want, Squalor, Ignorance and Idleness (i.e. unemployment), as Beveridge termed them in the Beveridge Report of 1942, and they believe that with judicious state intervention these warts can be removed to reveal capitalism with a caring and compassionate face. State intervention in this way is also seen as promoting political stability and maintaining capitalism more effectively. Beveridge and Keynes were architects of large-scale state intervention and regulation of the economy in the post-war welfare state, but they did not come from the tradition of socialist collectivism. They ensured the maintenance of capitalism and encouraged private enterprise and self-help; for example whilst Beveridge guaranteed a national minimum in his national insurance system, he still saw an important role for the private insurance companies, and also reinforced the principles of self-help and thrift by the system where workers compulsorily contributed to their own benefits. This was an extension of Lloyd George's programme of national insurance established as part of the Liberal government's reforms of 1906–11. Both these sets of reforms also exemplify the non-socialist welfare collectivists' emphasis on combining collectivism with capitalism for national efficiency and unity. In practice this approach combines universalism, that is, that state welfare is available to all, but only at a minimal level (as, for example, state pensions), with selectivity, that is, the provision of certain services to targeted individuals or groups.

Contemporary social administration writers of this persuasion, the welfare pluralists, emphasize a 'mixed economy' of welfare, in which provision is a pragmatic balance emanating not simply from the state but from the informal sector (the 'community' or family), the voluntary sector and the private market. Decentralization and participation also feature strongly in this perspective, and are linked to the argument to increase the role of the voluntary and informal sectors (Hadley and Hatch, 1981). Like the anti-collectivists, they criticize the bureaucratic inefficient aspects of state welfare but do not associate that with the need for the privatization of welfare. Their solution is to decentralize not simply central government, but local government, to much smaller localized units or patches, in which people feel more able to participate. The role of the state would be reduced in terms of *providing* welfare, its resources would go instead to *supporting* voluntary organizations from local self-help groups, community groups, national pressure groups, as well as the organization of informal care within communities, neighbourhoods or families. Hadley and Hatch do see some forms of centralized state provision as necessary – for example, in social security provision, and they do not rule out private provision so long as it is properly regulated and monitored.

However, not all those who share this middle-ground perspective agree with Hadley and Hatch. Robert Pinker (1979) argues for a non-socialist commitment to welfare more in the Beveridge tradition, where welfare enhances people's commitment to family and nation. At the same time he has opposed the neighbourhood system. In expressing his dissent to the Barclay report on social workers which advocated this, he suggested that such a system would reinforce the stigmatization that already exists in small communities, as well as be open to the abuse of confidentiality (Barclay, 1982).

Pinker's point, that local communities themselves often reinforce 'stigma', leads us to a more fundamental problem common to the various strands within this perspective, which is the tendency to see social problems and the solutions to them as quite independent of the social and economic structure, particularly as independent of the conflicting interest of the social and economic structure. The assumption that local decentralized structures will more easily promote participation and representation takes little account of the extent to which conflicts of interest and ensuing relations of power at the societal level are reproduced at the local level, particularly in terms of class, 'race' and gender. How far does the 'community' represent the interests of all? Secondly, the solution of the problem of bureaucracy and hierarchy of the state sector is to turn to the non-state sector. This fails to analyse *why* those problems exist in the first place and also the extent to which the non-state sectors suffer from similar problems, or could generate similar sorts of inequalities as the state sector. For example, the development of informal community care rests on the assumption that women are available and ready to care (see Finch and Groves, 1983 and chapters 3 and 5 below); the voluntary sector is characterized by bureaucracy, unaccountability, patchiness, lack of coordination (see Beresford and Croft, 1984; Johnson, 1987). Furthermore, there may be conflicting goals between sectors: while the voluntary and the informal sectors may represent the values of altruism, the private sector exists to make profit; where the two sectors co-exist there are bound to be conflicts of interests and the operation of the private market has the capacity both to undermine and take over the voluntary sector (see Beresford and Croft, 1984, p. 25). Whilst welfare pluralists see the role of the state to regulate such a tendency, this could give rise to a situation where the state became *more* bureaucratic, not less. This piecemeal and pragmatic approach of this perspective has been criticized for being opportunistic. Thus Beresford and Croft argue that contemporary welfare pluralists have stepped into the gap vacated by the Fabians and come up with proposals which by their emphasis on the voluntary, private and informal sector, appeal to the cost-cutting New Right whilst their emphasis on decentralization and participation appeals to the radical left.

Finally this perspective is idealist in that change is seen as the outcome of changing ideas and attitudes. Beveridge insisted that the argument for the welfare state was fundamentally a *moral* argument. This idealism combined with a minimal reference to structural issues can be seen in the following statement about a poverty strategy from David Owen of the Social Democratic Party:

The only way of achieving a more equitable distribution of income in a democracy is to secure *a greater awareness by the mass of the population* of the facts about poverty and by greater diffusion of wealth ... Nationalization is neither a necessary nor a sufficient condition for social change of this kind: reliance must be placed *on changing people's attitudes*, on promoting industrial democracy, and on industrial co-operatives, wider share ownership and, above all, wider home ownership. (Owen, 1981, p. 247; quoted in Clarke et al, 1987; my emphasis)

Fabian Socialism

The dominant values of Fabianism are equality, freedom and fellowship (George and Wilding, 1985, p. 70). Fabians are deeply committed to equality for the sake of social harmony, social efficiency, natural justice and the realization of collective potential. Alongside this they are humanitarians, they give priority to the alleviation of misery, and put a premium on cooperation and on democracy. Their argument against capitalism is a moral one: it is unethical, unjust and undemocratic, but it can be transformed, not least by government action. Central to this transformation is the welfare state, which with its commitment to the promotion of equality of opportunity, social harmony and redistribution of wealth, promotes material changes and wins people over to altruism and egalitarianism. Anthony Crosland writing in the 1950s saw the welfare state as a major stepping-stone to socialism (Crosland, 1956). T. H. Marshall's account of the development of the welfare state contained in *Citizenship and Social Class*, first published in 1949, has been influential in Fabian socialism, particularly in its concept of the welfare state as a progressive force. Marshall sees the welfare state as part of the gradual development of citizenship rights. These are made up of three elements: civil rights – liberty and equality before the law, developed largely in the eighteenth century; political rights – the right to vote and seek office, developed in the nineteenth century; and social rights, a right to a minimum of economic and social security developed through the welfare state in the twentieth century.

So, for Fabian socialists, capitalism is not an ugly face, but a tiger to be tamed and transformed. They oppose the means test, and support basic universal services provided by the state but with a top-up of selectivity (positive discrimination) for areas or groups with greater needs. Titmuss felt many aspects of the National Health Service exemplified the Fabian ideals in terms of its accessibility to all. In *The Gift Relationship* (1970) he suggests that the way the National Health Service is able to rely on a *volunteer* blood donor system indicates how altruism can be fostered, unlike the United States, where donors are paid and blood is bought by hospitals, with the consequence of an inefficient, unsafe and profit-dominated system. Thus, he and other Fabian socialists argue strongly for the state as the source of welfare provision, as against the private sector, which they see as catering for the rich rather than the poor, undermining state provision, encouraging selfish attitudes and basically undemocratic. (Titmuss's short essay, *Choice and 'The Welfare State'*, written in 1967, is still a good summary of arguments against the idea that the private sector offers choice.) The welfare state – the social market – with its socialistic collectivist principles, is thus seen as running alongside the economic market, and hopefully influencing it towards a more socially responsible economic policy. (See also the description of 'mainstream social administration' in chapter 1 above.)

Contemporary social policy writers working in the Fabian tradition are more critical of the bureaucratic, centralizing tendencies of state provision – for example, Deakin (1987) stresses the need for democracy and accountability in the welfare services: smaller rather than larger units of government and a move towards the decentralization of local government services and new forms of representation based on local neighbourhood forums (1987, p. 188). These objectives are linked to a strategy of equality through 'direct and sustained use of the powers of the central state' (p. 184) to redistribute resources and promote the interests of the disadvantaged. Glennerster (1983) also argues for accountability as the best way to engender support for the welfare state: 'Making services open and accountable to local people is in the end the best way to preserve them' (p. 8). He argues for a larger concept of 'citizenship that derives from a sense of shared obligations and common rights to be full members of society in terms of work living standards and the capacity to share our common living and working environment' (p. 223).

Although Deakin and Glennerster are more critical of the nature of state welfare, they share a number of characteristics with the post-war Fabians, outlined in chapter 1 and above. First, an overestimation of the capacity of the state to act independently of, or even contrary to, the interests of the economic system. Secondly, their stress on changing people's values in order to change society for the better exemplifies their idealism, which fails to identify the material circumstances and conditions which might inhibit such a change. For Tawney and Titmuss it was necessary only to counter the acquisitive values of capitalism with the socialist values of freedom and equality. The first condition for change to a better society was for Tawney 'intellectual conversion'. Titmuss emphasized the values necessary to foster integration and to discourage alienation. Deakin shares this idealist position; if there is a crisis, he suggests, it is a 'crisis of values':

The project is not merely concerned with the ending of the grosser forms of inequality, which [Tawney] discusses as a relatively straight-forward technical operation . . . It is also concerned with the creation and maintenance of a common culture, in which mutual aid and fellowship ... replace the 'tadpole' values of competitive capitalism which seeks to retain the loyalty of its citizens by offering them a one-in-a-thousand chance of turning into a prosperous frog. (1987, p. 184)

In this perspective then, social change is generated by the state's actions which effects and is effected by changes in commonly held ideas and values from the competitiveness of capitalism to the altruism of socialism. These changes in ideas are brought about by reason and by example of altruism in practice – most demonstrably by the welfare state itself.

Radical Social Administration

Some social reformist welfare writers of the 1980s offer a more structural approach to social problems than the Fabian socialist writers described above. Townsend, for example, classifies his theory of poverty as a 'radical social administrative approach' ... going 'beyond Fabian gradualism because the analysis implies the need for dramatic change or transformation of social structure and of corresponding social and economic institutions, though not necessarily implying revolution in the sense of political seizure and abandonment of the democratic process ... identifying large-scale poverty and calling for large-scale redistributive policies' (1983, p. 62). Other social policy writers, like Ramesh Mishra and Alan Walker, argue for the necessity to combine the moral humanitarian commitment and pragmatic empiricism of Fabianism with more structural-based explanations derived from Marxism of inequality and social problems which stem from unequal distribution of wealth and opportunities. They still share with the Fabian socialists a number of values: equality, humanity and cooperation, the goals of redistribution, a high priority on the assertion of *values* and morals to counter capitalism, and an emphasis on the welfare state as an important vehicle of change, and a belief in change through parliamentary democracy. As Townsend puts it:

Welfare as the attempt to meet need (which involves extensive empirical knowledge and therefore communication); welfare as the assertion of social or collective over individual interests; welfare as compensation for the social costs or 'diswelfares' of economic, technological and social change; welfare as the pursuit of social equality and welfare as the reorganization of private relationships. (1983, p. 62)

Where this group differ from other social reformists is on their insistence upon the predominace of social policy over economic policy, social policy as creative and preventative rather than reacting to and compensating for economic policy. Walker's (1984) main theme is that social and economic policy need to be unified through a democratic decentralized process of social planning according to need. Secondly, whereas many Fabians saw the persistence of poverty and inequality resulting from technical or administrative faults within the welfare system, Townsend (1979) clearly locates poverty as rooted in the structure – the 'class relations' – of society. This group is also critical of the role of the central state, bureaucracies, and professionals in the provision of welfare, stressing instead decentralized provision and citizen-power over welfare allocation. Both Walker and Townsend employ a *structuralist* analysis of social problems. But at the same time they lean back to the idealism of the Fabian socialists to explain change. Two of Townsend's more recent works on poverty (1979, 1984) both show this idealist tendency. In the latter Townsend argues for a radical strategy of structural change to abolish poverty, and almost echoing Tawney he says, 'The creation of a mass dependent underclass is by no means inevitable. *It must be fought intellectually, socially and morally*' (1984, pp. 31–2, my emphasis). Gough (1981) offers a critique of Townsend's 1979 poverty survey, suggesting that although it pushes at the 'outer limits of Fabianism', it still stays very firmly within that tradition. Whilst Townsend's notion of relative deprivation (the idea that the measurement of poverty is not through an absolute standard but in terms of the relative conditions of those around you) recognizes the role of social forces, it does not have a material analysis of the way capitalism's economic and social organization shape people's needs, and the way it consistently creates new consumption needs which remain unsatisfied for many. Secondly, in elaborating the radical strategy of distributional justice for all, Townsend neither recognizes 'the strong interlinkages ... between the state and the capitalist economy', nor does he identify any 'class or other social group ... to press for the radical changes he espouses' (Gough, 1981, p. 325). In other words, Townsend elaborates his explanation of poverty in terms of the class relations in society, but he does not identify the role of those classes themselves, historically or in the future, in effecting change.

Walker, too, tends to idealism in his analysis of a strategy for socialist welfare. Whilst this would be based on an integrated, structural social and economic policy, and would only be possible when some of the basic structures of society are altered, nevertheless he says this does not necessarily mean the abolition of the market 'but rather the assertion of socialist *values* over capitalist *values*' (Walker, 1984, p. 210, my emphasis). He also quotes Tawney's famous conviction that socialism will happen not through the creation of mystical historical necessity but the energy of *human minds and wills*. In this way both Walker and Townsend's idealism as well as the idealism of the previous two perspectives distinguish them from the materialist method of Marxism and its insistence that ideas and values are only changed through changed material circumstances. This is represented in the next perspective: the political economy of welfare.

Before turning to that perspective, it should be pointed out that a more sophisticated attempt has been made, too recently for this book to do it justice, by Phil Lee and Colin Raban (1988), to assert the importance of a perspective which is based on a fusion of Marxism and Fabianism. This represents, as they call it, 'a third way' – a combination of a critical Fabianism with a realistic Marxism. They suggest that the Marxist attack on Fabian writers in social policy has been too heavy-handed, neither recognizing the critical variants within the Fabian tradition (G. D. H. Cole, Tawney), nor acknowledging the importance of Fabianism's pragmatism, that is, its commitment to presenting realistic and realizable welfare policies from which the working class could benefit. Marxism's importance is in its ability to analyse the 'contextual constraints' of capitalism which prevent the meeting of welfare needs within capitalism, but it has been less forthcoming on strategies for the pursuit of welfare needs in the here and now. The 'third way' can provide us, they argue, with an alternative and politically feasible welfare strategy to achieve a socialist welfare system, based on 'a fusion of alternative social planning and local socialist welfare strategies' (p. 222).

The Political Economy of Welfare

We now encounter one of the difficulties of classifying the perspectives just according to their norms and values: whilst the other perspectives have clear values, ideals and goals which they wish to promote, it is not so easy to find a value-tag for the Marxist political economy perspective. This is not to say that many Marxists are not inspired to work towards a better world (or that no debate exists about the nature of a Marxist morality – see, for example, Geras (1983). What *is* different is that Marxists do not offer values as such, rather they understand values, or ideologies, whether they be equality or individualism, as emerging from the reflecting the material conditions and social relations in society. The economic organization of capitalism depends on and fosters an individualist ideology – the selling of one's labour in the market place. Thus one of the values that permeates people's lives is individualism. This means that if values are to be changed, this is possible, not through moral argument, but when the economic organization of society is changed. At the same time, collectivist values may spring from and be fostered by class struggle which can occur as a result of the fundamental conflict of interests between the capitalist class and the working class in capitalist society. It is these material struggles rather than simply the conflict of ideas they generate, that provide the key to overthrowing capitalism.

The political economy approach sees the development of welfare under capitalism as the result of this same conflict between the classes: the working class struggling for changes in their interests, for greater security or more rights, and the capitalist class attempting to maintain political stability, but also ensuring policies for the maintenance of capitalism. Gough summarizes the main goals of welfare under capitalism under three headings (these are derived from O'Connor's *The Fiscal Crisis of the State* (1973), described in chapter 1, which sets them out as the function of the modern capitalist state).

1 *Accumulation*: maintaining conditions favourable for the accumulation of capital (e.g. council house building programmes often have stimulated the private building sector).
2 *Reproduction*: the most important goal, ensuring a healthy, educated and housed workforce, but at the same time disciplining and controlling through that provision (education teaches discipline as well as skills, social security benefits reinforce sexual divisions and labour discipline as well as offering benefits).
3 *Legitimation/repression*: maintaining political stability, social harmony and social control. The growth of the welfare state in post-war Britian is identified as an important way governments have maintained credibility. Another aspect of this is social control, particularly of 'threatening' groups in society: youth, Black immigrants, the 'undeserving' poor.

Gough stresses two points: that these very functions may conflict with each other – for example, extensive social control programmes, like the Youth Training Scheme, may well take money that could otherwise be ploughed into the private sector, at the same time it could encourage accumulation by providing the private sector with a cheap workforce, but this in turn could threaten the government's credibility. The second point is that welfare should not be seen simply as a function of the state to maintain capitalism but as the outcome of class struggles to improve social and economic conditions for the working class. In this way Gough avoids the functionalism of some earlier Marxist accounts which stressed welfare as a tool of the ruling class, and teachers, social workers and so on, merely the 'agents of social control'. Gough therefore tries to give a materialist account of both human action *and* social structure. Ginsburg (1979) also stresses this duality of the welfare state but adds an extra twist by showing, with reference to the development of housing and social security provision, that whilst welfare may be the outcome of struggle and benefit the working class, the *forms* that this welfare takes reinforce the values of capitalism and tie the working class more securely to it: thus, whilst social security benefits the working class by insuring them – albeit minimally – against the ravages of capitalism, unemployment, ill-health, loss of breadwinner, at the same time it is administered and rationed so as to reinforce the work ethic, the dependencies of women, youth, disabled people and elderly people.

How far these reforms affect the move towards socialism depends on the view taken of the state and its relationship to capitalism, and here Marxists differ: the more *autonomous* the state from the capitalist class the more effective reforms can be in effecting a gradual and peaceful move to socialism. 'Autonomy' means the extent to which the state is able to act independently of the interests of the capitalist class. The less autonomous the state then the more necessary that the road to socialism will involve greater conflict between groups representing the interests of one or other class. For example, Ginsburg's interpretation above show the state's actions as *ultimately* more bound to capital's interests (and therefore less autonomous) than in Gough's interpretation.

The political economy approach is largely an analytical critique of welfare under capitalism. Unlike the other approaches it is more abstract and theoretical rather than prescriptive which has led to the charge of its not 'dirtying its hands' with practical solutions (Donnison, 1975; Pinker, 1979). Some writers have looked at Russia, or Eastern Europe for practical evidence of the implications for future social policy flowing from the political economy critique (Pinker, 1979; Mishra, 1981), but this is a rather misplaced venture as many Marxists would argue that these 'state-controlled' socialist countries have represented a distorted legacy of Marxism (for a discussion of this see Deacon, 1983, p. 46). In fact, Deacon has suggested that the task of creating visions of socialist welfare from struggles over welfare issues is an important one. In this way he suggests that the socialist social relations of welfare would eventually be according to need, and distributed through decentralized, community-controlled forms of provision, with the distinctions between user and provider and work and home being broken down (Deacon, 1983, chapter 1). His discussion does not centre on the amount of welfare provision society can afford but on the *forms* that welfare might take; it is not about the politics of *access to* welfare, but the politics of *creative control* over welfare. These forms of socialist social relations of welfare cannot be seen as separate from the realization of social relations of reciprocal cooperation at work, but part of them. Deacon insists, however, that such change is dependent upon a materialist strategy of identifying those forces in society whose struggles attempt to demand these changed social relations. Another attempt to tie Marxism to the practices and concepts of present welfare struggle has been Doyal and Gough's search for a 'theory of human needs'. In their view a future socialist welfare society has to be able to create the conditions where 'the *maximization* of creative choice about ways of satisfying health and autonomy needs' is possible (1984, p. 24). Tables 2.3 and 2.4 summarize this discussion on perspectives.

Conclusion: Missing Perspectives and Unanswered Questions

The above account of perspectives of welfare to be found in conventional classifications has distinguished the perspectives in terms of their welfare norms and goals and their values; it has also indicated how we might also evaluate the perspectives in terms of their methods of analysis in explaining the relationship between welfare and society. In particular it has been argued that theoretical adequacy entails being able to account for change in terms of both human action and the impact of social structure. According to these criteria, only the historical materialist method of the political economy of welfare came close to such adequacy.

However, as has already been mentioned, this classification has not included feminist or anti-racist critiques as (i) perspectives in their own right; (ii) perspectives giving rise to new norms or concerns which are central to welfare policy, such as the relationship between the welfare state and the family, or the welfare state and immigration control; or (iii) perspectives which demand explanations by welfare theory for the ways in which social policy reflects or challenges the patriarchial and racially structured society in which it operates.

The discipline of social policy in the mid-1970s cast off its empiricist past and embarked on establishing its theoretical base. Yet it stands in danger of overlooking the importance to this of an established feminist critique and a newly emerging 'anti-racist' critique. We need now to be able to do two things. We need to understand these two critiques and the challenges they pose to existing welfare theory, both in terms of prescriptions and policies for welfare, and in terms of explanations of welfare. Since these critiques are themselves made up of different perspectives, we shall also apply to them some of the criteria of theoretical adequacy drawn from this chapter, that is, whether their explanations are individualist, idealist, functionalist, materialist. Then we need to look again at the perspectives of anti-collectivism, social reformism and political economy of welfare to see how they measure up to some of the new requirements relating to gender and 'race' in terms of welfare prescription and explanation. The next two chapters explore the missing perspectives and the unanswered questions of existing welfare analysis.

PART II   New Critical Approaches to Welfare

3 Feminist Critiques of the Welfare State

Introduction

The re-emergence of the women's movement in the late 1960s has regenerated amongst other things the development of feminist theory and feminist critiques of the welfare state. Significant tests now exist which examine and develop these critiques: Wilson (1977, 1980a), Bryan et al. (1985), Ungerson (1985), Dale and Foster (1986), Pascall (1986), as well as numerous analyses of the individual welfare services – health, housing, education, social security and the personal social services. However, as is clear from the previous chapter, the integration of this into the theoretical accounts of social policy has been less noticeable. In general, in so far as any feminist critique has been accepted within social policy, it has been as a dimension of inequality, or a further form of discrimination, or a minority-group issue, often represented by a single chapter within a textbook. Whilst this development goes some way towards acknowledging the specificity of welfare issues for women, it ignores another, more far-reaching aspect, that issues of sexual divisions and the family are both specific and *central* to the study of the welfare state. The aim of this chapter is to evaluate the different theoretical and strategic positions within feminism which inform the feminist critiques, looking at libertarian feminism, liberal feminism, welfare feminism, radical feminism, socialist feminism and Black feminism. It will become clear that some of the welfare issues and theoretical questions raised by the feminist critique pose significant challenges to existing approaches to welfare within the dsicipline of social policy, described in the previous chapter.

The contribution of feminist critiques of the welfare state has been to focus more intensely and critically upon the areas know as 'reproduction' or 'social reproduction'. These terms cover not only the process of bearing children, but also the physical, emotional, ideological and material processes involved in caring for and sustaining others – not just children. The conditions in which this social reproduction takes place, and the consequences and expectations flowing from it are crucial for women's lives and central to welfare policies. The question feminist analysis has asked is: *Why do women play such a major role in social reproduction? What does this experience, and the way the state intervenes, mean for women? Should it be changed and, if so, how?* In other words, rather than simply accepting that women provide unpaid caring and nurturing, or that they form an army of cheap labour in paid employment, because it is natural, or because it suits the accumulation and labour force needs of capitalism, feminist analysis asks: why women? The emphasis is, therefore, upon the dynamics of social reproduction, upon women's attempts and struggles to change them, and upon the implications of these for strategies to change the welfare state.

It is common to identify three dominant approaches within contemporary feminism in the late twentieth century: liberal feminism, radical feminism and socialist (or Marxist) feminism. However, in the classification which follows, three further approaches have been identified. The first is an important critique of these approaches emerging recently from Black and Third World feminists. The second is welfare feminism, which has historically rather than contemporarily, a particular significance for welfare policy. And the third is the recent development of a right-wing feminism – libertarian feminism.

In evaluating these different approaches to feminism and their implications for welfare theory we shall focus on how they explain women's oppression and, in particular, the account each gives for the role of women's biology in these explanations; whether they emphasize the public sphere of 'work' and politics or the private sphere of home and caring, or both; and whether they emphasize the generality of women's oppression or the differentiated needs and experiences of different groups of women. In addition, we shall use the criteria elaborated in the last chapter to assess how far these approaches are individualist, idealist and materialist. In terms of welfare policy we shall examine what these different approaches have to say about the relationship between the welfare state, the family, women and the sexual division of labour; about the basis of women's eligibility to welfare provision (as mothers, workers, in their own right, etc.); and about how welfare provision should be organized (for example, on non-sexist, non-racist, non-hierarchical lines). Table 3.1 on pages 82–5 represents a summary of the application of these issues to the different feminist approaches.

Feminist Approaches to Welfare

The categorization of feminist theories or approaches which follows will be open to argument, especially because very few of the strategies described are the monopoly of one single feminist approach. At the same time, feminists (and non-feminists) who work side by side in many welfare campaigns and projects do not share the same explanation of why women are oppressed. It is these differences which this section aims to explore. The choice of particular approaches and the different emphases placed on them is influenced by their relevance to social policy and welfare strategy. In addition, more space is devoted to radical feminism, socialist feminism and Black feminism because these are, in my view, the most significant approaches in feminism in Britain today for the theory and practice of welfare policy.

Libertarian Feminism

Account should be taken of this emerging feminist offshoot of neo-liberalism, particularly in view of the political successes of the New Right and women within this political group. Somewhat misleadingly they call themselves libertarian feminists. The emphasis of this group is on individual liberty achieved through the freedom of the market, rather than, say, through laws for equality and social justice. Their slogan is *For Life, Liberty and Property.* For them, it is partly state intervention which prevents women achieving liberty – first, protective employment legislation which has led employers not to hire women employees, and secondly, benefits like child benefit, or rights to custody, which reinforce a particular domestic role for women. Institutional discrimination can be removed only by fostering greater competition where firms would be forced to hire according to abilities. There is, of course, a certain truth in the first two assertions but the final reliance on the freedom of the market is a strategy from which highly paid professional women or women with capital might benefit, but not necessarily the majority of women with children whose income would not allow them to buy the domestic help necessary to permit them to enter the labour market in equal competition with men. Indeed without the state's intervention to provide help for childcare the assumption must be that other women (or perhaps men) are available to do this work. This class-blind individualism is reflected in the assertion of one libertarian feminist: 'A women's place is where she chooses to be' (quoted by Campbell, 1986).

In this way, some libertarian feminists retain the individualism of neo-liberalism but reject the biological determinism implicit in the writings of neo-liberal philosophers like Friedman, Hayek or Mount who see women's ability to bear children and 'natural instincts' determining their role as mothers and homemakers (see chapter 5). However, others like Mary Kenny (1986) seek to combine a belief in liberty for women through the freedom of the market, with an insistence on preserving and protecting the natural domain of women – motherhood and the family. For them, the 'Life' part of their slogan is an unswerving opposition to abortion, a position not necessarily shared by their more achievement-oriented sisters.

The libertarian feminists, then, are made up of some women who deny the significance of women's biology, and some who see it as a fundamental role in women's lives. What they share is a belief in individualism and neo-liberalism. As such they have little to say about the organization of welfare since for them state intervention one way or another is not conducive to the improvement of women's lives, either because in 'protecting' them it restricts them as individuals, or by intervening in women's lives it regulates and confines the natural state of motherhood. However, as Georgina Waylen points out, these beliefs are the antithesis of feminism: 'a consideration of women as individuals would entail a radical restructuring of the family and the protected domain which would destroy the foundations of neo-liberalism' (1986, p.99). Although their slogan acknowledges the private sphere of reproduction in 'Life' and the public sphere in 'Property', the notion of individual freedom in 'Liberty' is insufficient and unable to link these two spheres because it does not acknowledge the impact of structural forces – the family, the labour market, class and other divisions – on women's lives. Neither is any link made between the contradictory stances of an acknowledgement of biology on the one hand and a rejection of it on the other, both evident in this strand of feminist thought. (See summary in table 3.1. pp. 82–5.)

Liberal Feminism

The development of liberal thought in the eighteenth century emerged from the opposition of the rising bourgeoisie to feudalism. Under feudalism birth determined social status. Liberalism insisted that social status should be determined by individual ability and skill, and this could be measured by the achievement of the individual competing with others in the market place. Mary Wollstonecraft's book *A Vindication of the Rights of Women,* written in 1798, applied this argument to women: that since women have reasoning powers equal to men, they should be granted equal rights with men. The belief that society's treatment of women violates their rights to liberty, equality and justice, and in addition creates a waste of women's skills and abilities is the basis of liberal feminism, and informs the campaigns which most characterize it: for the right to vote, to equal education and equal employment. In contemporary society the work of the Equal Opportunities Commission (EOC) and the campaign for equal pay in Britain are clear descendants of Wollstonecraft's ideas. Liberal feminism has in many ways been much stronger in the United States with the development in the 1960s of the National Organisation of Women (NOW) and its campaign for the Equal Rights Amendment to the Constitution – 'Equality of rights under the law shall not be denied or abridged by the United States or any State on account of sex' – passed in 1972. (Although since the 1980s there has been a significant anti-feminist backlash, see David, 1983.)

For contemporary feminists the main focus is on gender inequalities caused by sex discrimination, which is seen as being caused by irrational prejudice, stereotyping and outdated ideas. So one plank of liberal feminist strategy in welfare consists of reforming laws which are sex-biased, and challenging the sexism of those who administer, or provide welfare services. The removal of discrimination in social security legislation in 1984 in the form of the household duties test imposed on married women (checking whether she is still able to do 'normal' household duties) before she receives a non-contributory invalidity pension, is one example of this sort of progressive law reform. Use of the law to change people's attitudes and outmoded behaviour is also seen as important; for example, the Sex Discrimination Act of 1976 makes it illegal to discriminate against an individual girl or woman on the grounds of sex. In addition, the processes of socialization and education are considered key areas where stereotyping takes place, therefore a further strategy is challenging the sexism of teachers in school, and providing alternative sex-roles and models. The EOC has been concerned to eradicate discrimination against girls in schools by providing information, anti-sexist teaching material and by encouraging girls to go into male dominated areas like science and engineering. Rational argument, education of the public about the irrationality of discrimination and prejudice mark this theory as fundamentally *idealist*.

A second plank of action for liberal feminism has been pressurizing for reforms to make it possible for women to take advantage of opportunities and rights. Whilst liberal feminists acknowledge that child-bearing is often given as a reason for their limited access to opportunities and rights, their argument is that this need not necessarily be so because rights to contraception and abortion, maternity leave, state provision of day-care facilities for dependants, create the conditions in which women can be free to compete and use their skills and abilities. Thus, this approach is characterized by a belief in the state as a vehicle for reforms, and a minimizing of any role biology may play in women's lives.

In general, this theory seeks to deny the relevance of any differences between men and women, and in so far as women are the ones who bear children, then laws, provisions and changed attitudes and behaviour can counter this. There is, however, one form of action followed by liberal feminists which is not quite consistent with this. Within the strategy of equal opportunities for women in welfare work is the goal of getting women into positions of power in the welfare professions – as headmistresses, doctors, consultants, directors of social services. In part, this is argued for in terms of providing useful role-models for children to aspire towards, as in the case of headmistresses of large comprehensive schools. On the other hand it is often also argued that women in positions of authority would humanize and tenderize these often bureaucratic and remote forms of welfare. The inconsistency of this idea is in its acknowledgement of the idea that men and women *are* different, in this case, possessing different management characteristics. Less inconsistent is an associated strategy for women working in the state welfare services to put feminism into practice in working with female users of the provision, and to support each other in doing so: thus teachers devise anti-sexist schemes, social workers and health visitors attempt to devise practices which do not cast their female clients as responsible for maintaining the well-being of their families. A third strategy in the representation of women in welfare work has been the pressurizing of local authorities to institute 'equal opportunities policies' and this is often done in conjunction with employment policies with regard to 'race', disability and sexual orientation. In relation to women the strength of these policies varies from a formal paper commitment to equal opportunities, to programmes of monitoring, non-discriminatory application and promotion procedures, training and retraining and provision for employees with parental responsibilities.

All these various strategies described here, however, are not the monopoly of liberal feminists and with perhaps the exception of women seeking positions of authority and power, most of these forms of action would be supported by radical and socialist feminists. Indeed, one of liberal feminism's strongest points is its commitment to action now for social justice. At the same time, radical and socialist feminists would have different reasons for supporting these strategies.

I have already indicated that liberal feminism is idealist, and that it does not consider biological differences between men and women as a significant obstacle in the quest for equality. The main direction of strategy associated with liberal feminism is for action in the *public* sphere, although contemporary liberal feminism has also drawn on work done on the socialization of girls within the private sphere, that is, the home. The rationale for anti-sexism in schools is often framed in terms of social learning theories. These examine the ways girls and boys learn their 'appropriate' gender roles and destinies initially from observing the behaviour of their parents, and then from the reinforcement and reward their own 'appropriate' behaviour receives from parents, other adults, peers and teachers, through, for example, the encouragement of different emotional responses (allowing girls but not boys to cry), the use of toys or images in books. The implication of social-learning theories is that self-conscious attempts at role-reversal between mothers and fathers, encouragement of less gender-specific behaviour and self-awareness by teachers of differential treatment towards boys and girls, can broaden the identities of girls and boys and make them more able to exercise real, and not gender-determined, choices about their schooling, their work and the way they care for *their* own children. Such theories have provided the basis for feminists of all perspectives to do important studies, especially in education. However, the questions left unanswered by social learning theories are whether such role-reversal is fully possible if it threatens men's power in the context of the family, and whether society provides the material conditions (for example in the conditions and hours of paid work) to make role-reversal feasible. These are questions taken up by radical and socialist feminism respectively.

Nevertheless, it is for its view of the public sphere that liberal feminist theory and practice has been most criticized, particularly for underestimating the structural forces limiting women's equality and for reducing the causes of inequalities to discriminatory ideas and attitudes. Paid work, with its own divisions and hierarchies, is taken for granted. It is for this reason that liberal feminism is often chastised by radical feminists for encouraging women to see liberty in terms of entering the male-defined world of work and absorbing male, competitive values. Radical feminists see discrimination as a manifestation of attempts by men, singly and as a group, to hold on to their power. They would suggest, for example, that the sexual division of labour and sexist practice within health care is not simple discrimination, but stems from an historical struggle between men and women for control over health care provision. Socialist feminist and Black feminists criticize liberal feminism for offering strategies that have more relevance to the interests of white middle-class women. In terms of promoting the educational achievement of girls at school or equal opportunities in the professions, factors other than sexism, such as class or 'race' have a significant influence over the career opportunities offered to young women.

Radical feminists would suggest that whilst such campaigns are absolutely necessary to improve women's lives in the here and now, and important in that they provide a collective basis and experience on which to struggle for greater change, they are not sufficient in themselves. Reforms and laws alone cannot undermine the institutionalization of women's oppression within the very structures of the labour market, the family, education system and welfare state. The demand of liberal feminism is for justice and for equal *rights*, but as Rosalind Petchesky has pointed out in her discussion on *Reproductive Freedom: Beyond 'A Woman's Right to Choose'* (1980), the concept of rights is tricky, because it is 'a concept inherently static and abstracted from social conditions. Rights are by definition claims that are staked within a given order of things and relationships. They are demands for access for oneself, or for "no admittance" for others, but they do not challenge the social structure itself, the social relations of production and reproduction' (p. 670).

A further criticism of the liberal feminists' reformism is of their view of the state. In pressing for reforms and changes in the law to attain equality, the state is represented as a proper and neutral arbiter, open to reasoned argument and pressure. Radical feminists would insist that the state was run by men and protected men's interests and power; socialist feminists would argue that there is no guarantee that the state can bend to women's interests, particularly if these interests conflict with the interests of the more powerful representatives of capitalism, and/or patriarchy. For example, gains were made in employment and social security legislation in the 1970s and 1980s towards equality for women: the 1970 Equal Pay Act, the 1975 Sex Discrimination Act, the equalization of the arrangements for contributions and benefits in the National Insurance system in 1977, the rights of married women to Family Income Supplement and to be a 'nominated breadwinner' for social security in 1983. At the same time other changes outside and within the law countered the impact of these policies: women's access to segregated, low paid and part-time jobs rather than full-time jobs has increased since the late 1970s so women are less eligibile for either equal pay or National Insurance benefits. Furthermore, the value of insurance and supplementary benefits has decreased in the same period. Also cuts in public expenditure and closing down of nursery facilities have reduced women's employment opportunities. So what the state gives away with one hand it can take back with the other. Furthermore, as I shall discuss later, Black feminists have identified many of the state's actions and policies as racist in content and impact. Both radical and socialist feminists would, in addition, point to the fact that although women, for almost 200 years, have been proving the irrationality of women's inequalities in the face of liberal ideas of equality, liberty and justice, very little had been achieved by the law or state reforms alone. When legislation is introduced, like the 1975 Sex Discrimination Act, it may only improve the lot of individual women, or small groups, or it may be notoriously easy to avoid, like the 1970 Equal Pay Act, or it may be countervailed by structural forces like unemployment. It may, like giving women the vote, have little impact on the representation of women in politics, because it leaves unaffected the sexual division of labour in the home. On the other hand, it may, and does, raise women's hopes and give them the confidence to organize the necessary collective struggles of groups of women to fight for these rights. So whilst liberal feminism pushes for important changes in legislation, it does not challenge the distinction between the public world of work and politics and the private world of home and family. The significance of such reforms should not be underestimated but at the same time the liberal feminist strategy fails to acknowledge the structural conditions which impede the success of such reforms, as well as the differential impact these reforms have for women of different class, ethnic origin, age, disability and sexual orientation. Claims about women's biology determining their inequality have no place in liberal feminism, which rejects any influence of biology in favour of a view that women are conditioned and socialized into the roles they play. By the same token, equality is sought by changes in laws, practices and ideas about women's potential. In this way liberal feminism is *idealist* in method, and it does not envisage any fundamental changes in the relationship between the family, women and the welfare state beyond the provision within the existing framework of non-sexist and non-discriminatory welfare to women in their own right. (See summary in Table 3.1, pp. 82–5.)

Welfare Feminism

We turn now to a third variant of feminism where the struggles for reforms for women are aimed not towards their access to opportunities in the public sphere, but at their needs as mothers and wives within the private sphere. One good example of this is the campaigns by women in the inter-war years for improvements from the state for mothers and their children. It represents, in this way, something of a shadow to liberal feminism's reformism, a shadow which has its historical antecedents. Ursula Vogel (1986) describes two variants of thought on the women question in the eighteenth century, both emerging from liberalism. One was the rationalist argument represented by Mary Wollstonecraft, already outlined above; the other was a romantic or aesthetic conception of women's liberation represented by the German writer Friedrich Schlegel. Here, it was not an emphasis on the universal human nature of men and women, but the special, and superior nature of women, particularly, 'a woman's capacity to harmonize experience and knowledge from an inner centre of intuitive understanding and reflective feeling' (Vogel, 1986, p. 38). Although Schlegel was a man, and writing in the romantic tradition, nevertheless this direction of thought, towards a positive reappraisal of women as products of their nature and circumstance, finds reflection at different historical times in different feminist strategies. The campaign by feminists for the vote shifted its focus after the First World War to campaign for state welfare improvements in maternal and child health services and for maternity benefits. This shift was paralleled by a shift in politics generally. The defeat of the 1926 General Strike marked a decline in the influence of more radical and revolutionary socialism to which some of the earlier feminists, like Sylvia Pankhurst, aligned themselves. Labour Party politics became more dominated by a gradualist, constitutional and paternalistic approach to change. The goals of feminism tended to be restricted to welfare reforms for wives and mothers, and, to a lesser extent, for equal pay. In contrast to earlier feminism and much contemporary feminism, the state was seen very much as a potential benefactor, and far less as the regulator of women's lives. Activists like Stella Browne campaigned for contraceptive rights for women and others like Elizabeth Abbott maintained a critical view of policies which reinforced women's domestic role, and others like Ada Nield Chew continued the fight for rights of working-class women at work. Nevertheless, this 'welfare feminism' as Olive Banks calls it (Banks, 1981), was a dominant theme in feminist campaigns between the wars and up to the 1945 welfare reforms. The involvement earlier of organizations like the Women's Co-operative Guild, which had the support of large numbers of working-class women, was particularly significant. The main advantage of campaigns based on women's interests as wives and mothers was that they were often able to represent the needs of working-class women, there and then, and seek material improvements in their conditions. The preoccupation before, during and after the First World War with motherhood or more specifically the maintenance of the 'Imperial Race', meant that some concessions could be won from local authorities and the state, for example, the successful campaign led by Margaret Llewellyn Davies, secretary of the Guild, for maternity benefit to be included in the 1911 National Insurance Act (and its payment to be made to the woman and not the man) (see Davies, 1915/78; Davin, 1978).

The immediate concerns of many women in the 1920s were their children's and their own ill-health, and the inadequacy of the family wage combined with the unreliability of the male wage-earner to distribute his income within the family. A particularly moving account of this can be found in Margery Spring Rice's book *Working Class Wives*, a collection of interviews with women published in 1939. Thus campaigns for infant health centres, (Maternity and Child Welfare Act 1918), for ante-natal clinics, for birth control, for family allowances paid to women and for maternity benefits found massive support. At the same time the winning of these reforms has also attributed to the fact that they also gathered support from other groups with different interests: from social imperialists keen on maintaining the numbers and fitness of the British race, from employers who saw family allowances as a way of resisting wage claims, and from the state, keen to reinforce the familist ideology of a woman's responsibility to care for her family. It is particularly in relation to these points that this sort of strategy has been most criticized, especially in basing its demands on women's role in the family, for it reinforces the very conditions that give rise to women's financial dependence in the first place, and although it protects women, it perpetuates the idea that women are *victims* of male power and social injustice. It takes the family and its privatization as given, women's biology as their destiny, and its rests on the belief of an essential difference between men and women.

Eleanor Rathbone, champion of family allowances, believed that women were 'the natural custodians of childhood', though she added 'that at least is part of the traditional role assigned to us by men and one that we have never repudiated' (quoted in Lewis, 1984, p. 105, where a good discussion of these issues can be found). Contemporary adherents of this position have often started with these points as a justification of this particular path to women's liberation. The late Mia Kellmer-Pringle, Director of the National Children's Bureau, argued very strongly that the way forward for women was a reassertion of the value and role of caring and motherhood. She saw the promotion of equal rights and benefits as simply expecting women

to become more like men in their aspirations, values, behaviour and attitudes ... But surely this is not enough and it does not touch the basic question. This is that equality does not necessarily mean 'sameness'. The central issue is how the role and relationship of both sexes will have to change if women are to be enabled to take their place is society in their own way and in accordance with their values. (Kellmer-Pringle, 1980, p. 4)

These values, according to Kellmer-Pringle, spring from the fact that only women can conceive and bear children, which endows them with 'a greater capacity for nurturing and caring which has been further enhanced by the division of labour between the sexes' (p. 5). The difficulty with Kellmer-Pringle's argument is, like the earlier welfare feminists, that she returns us to a view of women's lives *determined*, albeit positively, by their biology, and it therefore retains a clear distinction between the public and the private spheres of work and family. To some extent, especially with the earlier welfare feminists, there was a recognition of the particular needs of working-class women and of the poverty inflicted upon them from the combination of their exclusion from paid labour, from the insufficiency of the 'family wage' and from the patriarchal attitudes of their husbands. Relief from this situation was sought via state welfare reforms, but without any fundamental challenge to the existing relationship between the state and the family, nor the paternalistic organization of welfare provision. Sheila Rowbotham comments thus upon the hey-day of welfare feminism:

The assumption in the 1938 report [Spring Rice, 1939] is that the conditions of motherhood can be improved by asking more from the capitalist state – more clinics, better maternity provision, an extension of welfare. The power relations behind the machinery of welfare are obscured. Nor do they see the poverty, suffering and hardship of the pregnant working class woman and the oppressive form which child-rearing in capitalism assumes, as the result of the sexual division of labour in the family and the organization of capitalist production as a whole. In presenting their 'reasonable' demands and in reacting against the dismissal by the feminist movement earlier of motherhood, these liberal and labour women never fundamentally questioned the society they sought to reform (1974, p. 148)

In keeping with liberal feminism, welfare feminism is idealist, but in contrast it does not eschew biology but regards motherhood and marriage as women's destiny, and the basis upon which improvements be sought. Whilst this may meet the material needs of women of different classes, at the same time it has also served to create the conditions for a propagation of a respectable white familism. (See summary in table 3.1, pp. 82–5.)

Radical Feminism

Radical feminists see women oppressed, as a group or class, by men as a group or class. In relation to welfare policies, these are characterized as the exercise of male power over women through the state. Evidence of this power can be observed from the extent of male domination in all areas of the state (as well as the major institutions of capitalism), – in the civil service, government and upper echelons of the institutions of health, social security, social services and housing, and of the judiciary. Men's power or control over women is institutionalized as patriarchy, which has been defined in different ways. An earlier radical feminist writer, Kate Millet, described it as a general relationship of 'dominance and subordinance' enduring through history: 'sturdier than any form of segregation, and more vigorous then class-stratification, more uniform, certainly more enduring' (1970, p. 24–5). However, it is mainly in two specific ways that patriarchy has been defined by radical feminists: male power and control over women's sexuality and male power and control over women's biology, namely, their reproductive capacity. Shulamith Firestone's *The Dialectic of Sex*, written in 1970, was an exposition of this second idea of patriarchy, which she saw as *the* fundamental class oppression giving rise to other forms of oppression. Its abolition could only be possible by relieving women of their biological reproductive role. (For an enlightening view of the possibilities of this, see Marge Piercy's novel *Women on the Edge of Time*, 1979). This particular interpretation of patriarchy has had a revival recently in analyses of the developments in reproductive technologies which writers like Gene Corea (1985) see as male attempts to control women's reproductive powers or to turn them into breeding machines.

The other definition sees patriarchy as rooted in male aggression, or men's *physical* power over women, in particular over her sexuality. Susan Brownmiller (1975) argues that because a man can force a women to have sexual intercourse against her will, the possibility of this violence serves as 'the perpetuation of male domination over women by force' (1975, p. 209). This analysis has been influential in issues and campaigns over male violence (Reclaim the Night Marches), war (Greenham Common), pornography and incest. Some of these analyses see pornography, male violence and aggression and rape as interlinked forms of male terrorism upon women. The popular graffiti 'pornography the theory, rape the practice' and Andrea Dworkin's book *Pornography* (1981) support this theme. The idea of war and militarism as expressions of male desire for aggression has also been influential in feminist anti-nuclear campaigns and writing.

These concepts of patriarchy give rise to a number of difficulties. They are summed up by Sheila Rowbotham (1981): 'The word patriarchy implies a universal and historical form of oppression which returns us to biology.' Many writers who are *anti-feminist* or who take the family and the sexual division of labour within it for granted also offer explanations of women's alleged inferiority by resorting to a *biological-determinist* argument that women are 'naturally' more suited to childcare and housework because they have babies, or that their hormonal or chromosomal make-up makes them less aggressive and less able to compete with men in the world of work. Many feminists have attempted to clarify the distinction between the basic biological *sex difference* (women have babies) between men and women, and their *gender roles* (men are aggressive, women submissive), and identify the latter as *socially constructed* differences between men and women, that is to say, differences which emerge as a result of men and women reacting and adjusting to the different social conditions, arrangements and expectations they meet. The above radical feminist definitions of patriarchy blur this distinction by explaining patriarchy in terms of biological characteristics. In a sense, we are returned back to square one. In a discussion of radical feminist explanations of sex and violence, Lynne Segal comments:

One way or another, and despite insistent assertions to the contrary, we are forced to leave behind the complex historical formation of men's social power – and how this social power confers a symbolic power to the penis as the defining characteristic of the male – to return to a naked sexual capacity which can be, and therefore is, used to control women. In the description of the relentless power of the steely prick, the biological, so forcefully ejected from the front door, swaggers in, cocksure, through the back. (Segal, 1987, p. 101)

However, Christine Delphy (1984) is a radical feminist who offers a materialist, rather than a biological, definition of patriarchy: using Marxist terminology she cites the family as a 'patriarchal mode of production' (rather than reproduction) where a man pays a women (or does not as the case may be) for the domestic and other services she provides him with through her labour. The point of Delphy's argument is to argue that women are a class and their class-enemy are men. She has been criticized (see Walby, 1986, pp. 37–42) for concentrating on the family and not explaining the relationship between patriarchy at home and patriarchy at work. Some of the criticisms levelled above at the previous radical feminists also apply to Delphy. These raise questions over the ahistorical and universal nature of the concept of patriarchy, that is to say, patriarchy is presented as an unchanging and universally applicable set of relations. Even if it becomes accepted that forms of patriarchy do change over time and across cultures, there still remains the difficult assertion of a 'false universalism', as Hester Eisenstein calls it (1984). This is the idea that women constitute a *class*. What this ignores is the differences of interest between women created by divisions of class and 'race' and culture, to name but a few. Many working-class women, for example, would not identify a universal bond tying them to Margaret Thatcher, nor she to them. Also, in practice, the assumption of universalism has sometimes led white women to underplay the influences of class and 'race' divisions on their own actions, and the racist and imperialist assumptions of their own traditions of thinking. For instance, in the mid 1970s in response to male violence and pornography, parts of the women's movement organized 'Reclaim the Night' marches through British cities, and some called for better policing to make the streets safe for women. This ignored the struggles of Black women (and men) against the increase of policing in their communities. In addition, whilst radical feminist writers do acknowledge (in a way that many other feminist do not) the situation of women from different cultures, especially the Third World, there have been two tendencies criticized by Black feminists (see later in this chapter). One is to see Third World women as simply the passive victims of more extreme practices of patriarchy – arranged marriage or bride-price, for example – in a way that comes dangerously close to notions of Western cultural superiority (see for example, Daly, 1978). The other is to explain imperialism – especially the imperialist use of reproductive technologies on Third World women – national chauvinism, women's global poverty, as consequences of male power and male culture to which women by virtue of their special nature, are *intrinsically* opposed.

A further difficulty associated with the biological-determinist aspect of patriarchy is this: what is the strategy for women's liberation? If patriarchy lies within men's nature, their violence, their aggression, how then, apart from patricide, can we, in the long term, rid society of patriarchy? One solution for many radical feminists is political separatism, that is campaigning, organizing, working separately from men. A further step for some is personal separatism, living and having relationships with women only, not only out of personal choice, but out of political choice. Relationships with men, it is argued, take up emotional time and energy, and often ultimately serve only to bolster a man's power, when this time and energy could be better spent upon the needs of women.

Out of these strategies of personal and political separatism there has emerged, first, a slightly different direction for radical feminism which has had influence upon a number of significant campaigns over welfare issues.

Radical feminism to some extent in the 1980s has moved away from the theorizing of earlier writers like Millet and Firestone, and away from the image of women as victims of men's power. Writers like Susan Griffin and Adrienne Rich write instead in terms which celebrate women's special values: their sharing, caring, tenderness and closeness to nature, and counter them to male values of competition, self-centredness, aggression and violence. In an irresistible and poetic appeal to women's special spirituality Griffin says:

We know ourselves to be made from this earth. We know this earth is made from our bodies. For we see ourselves. And we are nature. We are nature seeking nature. We are nature with a concept of nature. Nature weeping. Nature speaking of nature to nature. (Griffin, 1980, p.107)

The recreation, protection and provision of a 'women's culture' for the nourishment of women only, then, has become the mainstream of today's radical feminism and writing. Of course, this brings us back to the criticism that if we are to suggest that women *by their nature* possess special values, then we are talking the language of biological essentialism, or biological determinism, language which traps women back into their biology. It means it rejects those other feminist arguments which say that just as all women do not possess the characteristics ascribed to them by anti-feminists – passivity, illogicality, physical weakness – neither do they all possess the values of sharing, caring and so on. In addition, as a strategy, it is idealist in the extreme for it rests on the hope of change through the encouragement of female, or woman-centred values counter to society's dominate male ones. It has also been criticized for its retreatism and defeatism, and its inversion of the 'personal is political' to the 'political is personal' (Eisenstein, 1984; Segal, 1987). On the one hand radical feminism has forcefully questioned the tendency of much Marxist writing to explain women's oppression in terms of the needs and operation of capitalism (a tendency discussed more fully in the next section). This 'economic reductionism' is perceived by some radical feminists to be typical of androcentric (male-centred) thinking: objective, scientific and abstract, rather than subjective, intuitive and person-related. On the other hand, in distancing itself from economic reductionism, radical feminism has fallen foul of biological reductionism.

Nevertheless, the insights of radical feminist writing and campaigns should be recognized. The guiding principle of much feminism in the second half of the twentieth century, that the 'personal is political', has been at the root of much radical feminism. The idea that the relations of power between men and women deserve political and theoretical assessment, sets feminism apart from the major traditions of Western political thinking – liberalism and Marxism. (It can be argued that anarchism makes links between public and personal politics and that utopian socialism acknowledged gender relations.) Possibly because of their independence from the major traditions of political thought, radical feminists have more often than not been the first to bring out and generalize hitherto hidden areas of women's existence whether these be sexuality, rape, violence or, more recently, reproductive technologies, though not all feminists accept their analyses. Since, for radical feminists, the root of oppression lies in the control men exercise over women's biology and their sexuality, the 'personal is political' has been expressed in campaigns aimed at women gaining control over their bodies. This has influenced a whole number of issues: violence, rape, tranquillizing drugs, contraception, abortion, sexuality. What has further characterized such campaigns is not simply the attempt of women to challenge male power on these issues, but, along with notions of a women's special culture, to provide alternative, women-only forms of care and assistance based on feminist principles of shared knowledge and control and an opposition to hierarchies. As such they have in some ways represented important alternatives to the mainstream forms of state welfare provision, as well as meeting the specific needs of many women. In terms of challenging male violence in the home, radical feminists, along with other feminists, played an important part in setting up women's refuges, and in challenging the sexism of the medical profession by setting up well-woman clinics and health centres, where women can be treated by a woman doctor and where the emphasis is on women acquiring information and knowledge about their own bodies. Rather than relying on medical expertise, women have organized self-help groups for conditions where they have met indifference from the medical profession, such as pre-menstrual tension, or menopause-related conditions. In these ways the distinctions between the provider, often a professional, and the user of the service have been broken down. Women-only counselling services for victims of male violence, such as rape crisis centres, have also been important in exposing and challenging patriarchal assumptions within the courts and the police about female sexuality. Radical feminists have also been well represented amongst those women campaigning for the right of women to a self-defined sexuality and have applied this to campaigns over the rights of lesbians to have custody of their children after divorce. As such these campaigns have highlighted the marginalization of the needs of those women who do not fit the conventional nuclear family form.

On the one hand, while radical feminism roots women's oppression in the wider social structure, that is in 'patriarchy', it can be criticized for its ahistorical assumptions of a 'false universalism' of patriarchy, its lack of recognition of divisions of class and 'race' between women, its resort to biological differences to explain both women's subordination and their superiority, and the idealism of its view of change through the cultivation of women's culture. (See table 3.1, pp. 82–5, bearing in mind many radical feminists would reject such a methodological evaluation as 'man-made'.) On the other hand, their insistence on politicizing issues normally considered matters of private choice or personal destiny, their insistence (with other feminists) upon different values and methods of organization, has marked the women's movement of the second half of the twentieth century as significantly different from earlier forms of feminism, and has provided the catalyst for crucial questions to be raised over the material and ideological relationship between the private area of reproduction and the public area of production, a task which also belongs to the next group, socialist feminism.

Socialist Feminism

The label of 'socialist feminism' has covered quite a wide range of political actions and interpretations of feminism in Britain over the past 20 years. In general, though, this contemporary feminist theory, or set of ideas, is influenced by both socialist ideas, particularly Marxism, but also anarchism, utopian socialism and Maoism and also the feminist ideas already discussed. As we have seen, radical feminism offers crucial insights into relations between men and women, but it is seen by socialist feminists as unable to offer an adequate analysis or strategy to change the social and economic organization of society (as suggested above). By contrast, this is what Marxism does offer with its historical and materialist analysis of the relationship of class to the mode of production, capitalism and the role of class struggle in changing society. However, socialist feminists have also been critical of classical Marxism for ignoring the significance of the specific oppression of women, and of the practices of socialist groups and organizations representing the working class, especially the trade unions, for seeing the struggles by women against aspects of oppression as irrelevant or 'dividing the working class'. In the late nineteenth and early twentieth century this issue was known as the 'Woman Question' and was an important debate in revolutionary socialist organizations. Clara Zetkin in Germany, Sylvia Pankhurst in Britain and Alexandra Kollontai in Russia all argued for the need to make women and women's demands central in the socialist movement. The rise of Stalinism in Russia, reformism in Britain and fascism in Germany meant that in different ways, many of the fundamental questions about women's role in Society raised were dropped until the second wave of feminism in the 1960s. The concern of contemporary socialist feminists then, has been, at a theoretical level, to present a materialist analysis of women's oppression under capitalism which does not reduce all forms of women's oppression to the requirements of capitalism but does attempt to take account of the concept of patriarchy, and at a practical level, to demonstrate the importance, indeed the centrality of women's issues and struggles to the struggle for socialism: there can be no socialism without women's liberation, and no women's liberation without socialism.

The forms this practice now takes are fairly diverse and have been subject to much contentious debate within socialist feminism (see the debate in *Feminist Review*, no. 23, 1986a). In relation to welfare strategies, many socialist feminists continue to put their energies into either local or national autonomous women's groups and organizations fighting for better health, housing, social security, care for children and the elderly, education and employment services. These include national organizations like ROW (Rights of Women), National Childcare Campaign, as well as local well-woman groups, reproductive rights groups and employment projects. This has not just been in terms of *more* provision, but provision which is neither sexist nor racist, nor reinforces the dependencies of old age or disability, nor discrimination against lesbians or homosexuals. In addition the struggle has been to bring to these services some of the principles of feminist organization: the breaking-down of hierarchies or authority based on differences between the providers (the experts) and users of the service, and the recognition of the unpaid welfare work of caring carried out by most women. What further characterizes socialist feminist activity is the attempt to work inside the local state, inside the trade unions and inside the Labour Party and to get these organizations to recognize women's welfare concerns as central political issues.

Since the 1980s many of the New Left Labour councils in the major cities in Britain set up Equal Opportunities Units, monitoring and improving the opportunities of oppressed groups in their localities. Two other local authority developments have shifted a significant amount of women's energies to the inside rather than the outside of the local state: the first was the setting up of Women's Committees to campaign on local issues affecting women (childcare provision, transport, freedom from violence, employment, racism) and secondly the provision of subsidies to help local women's organizations run projects or campaigns. Two counter-developments, however, are set to limit severely the impact of such moves. First was the abolition of the Greater London Council and the metropolitan county councils in 1986, and second, the return in 1987 of a Conservative government aiming to restrict further the financial and other powers of local authorities. In the short term, however, some socialist feminists have viewed putting their energies into municipal socialism as important and a chance to put their visions into practice, to practise 'prefigurative politics'. For Lynne Segal, for example: 'such feminist involvement has brought the question of social need into economic planning: "domestic life" and "the quality of human relationships" are emerging from the silent secrecy of "the private" to enter the public world of town hall committees and challenge their bureaucratic language' (Segal, 1987, p. 224). In the long term, however, while the effect of such developments is to give important legitimacy to feminist politics, this legitimacy will only be maintained if the grass-roots women's organizations are able to determine local authority policies, and secondly if they are able to maintain links with other organizations of working-class groups and mobilize support for their demands. Without that we might see the incorporation of an able few to manage the increasingly disillusioned many.

A further shift of socialist feminist activity into mainstream politics is the presence of women in the Labour Party campaigning for feminist demands to become part of Labour Party policy, and, if elected, to be put into practice through a Ministry for Women. In 1981 Anna Coote wrote a critique of the Alternative Economic Strategy, a left reform strategy of the Labour Party, saying the crucial starting-point was not how to regenerate paid jobs on the old model of skilled full-time work for white men, but how to care for and support our children, how to reallocate labour and wealth within the family and then, how to structure paid employment to fit these needs. Hilary Wainwright (1987) argues that the politics and policies of organized feminism, along with other social movements (the peace movement, Black organizations) offer the opportunity for a radical alternative to both the New Right and reformist social democracy, based inside and outside the Labour Party.

Socialist feminists' work within the trade unions, especially within the public sector (NALGO, NUPE, NUT, etc.) has followed a similar pattern: getting the unions to take seriously issues like maternity and paternity leave, equal opportunities, positive action, sexual harassment, childcare, as well as guaranteeing female representation within national and local committees. A broader challenge to the labour movement to change its male-dominated spots is represented by Bea Campbell's powerful critique of what she calls the 'men's movement' in *Wigan Pier Revisited* (1984). This highlights the continuous collective struggles by working-class women over apparently small but crucial issues – provision of playspace, council house repairs, pedestrian safety. She concludes that if the labour movement is to be able to take these issues seriously it must put the 'reform of men' high on its agenda.

However, not all socialist feminists have welcomed these shifts. In an attempt to recall feminism back to its socialist and class-based roots, Angela Weir and Elizabeth Wilson (1984) are critical of this 'lifestyle feminism', that is, attempts by feminists to change the distribution of money and paid and unpaid labour between men and women within the home, discussed further below. They are also critical of constitutional feminism in the Labour Party, of feminism which puts redistribution from men to women in the home before redistribution from rich to poor within society, and of feminism which is too readily dismissive of the trade union movement. The central problems facing women today, according to Weir and Wilson, are caused by the crisis of capitalism: 'Women are becoming the new urban poor. The loss of full-time employment, cuts in social services and public housing and the decline in real value of state benefits are restricting the opportunities of many young women in a way not seen since the 1930s' (1984, p. 102). The best hope for an improvement in women's position, therefore, lies in a class- based attack on capitalism and to demand 'the expansion of the economy and the creation of secure, full-time jobs for women. To ensure this ... [we need] anti-discrimination and positive action programmes and expansion of socialised services, particularly collective childcare and caring services for the sick and elderly' (p. 103).

In terms of the theoretical development of socialist feminism there are some areas of general agreement: the importance of understanding differences between men and women's behaviour as socially constructed difference, and of recognizing the 'personal' as 'political', and of recognizing the *differential* as well as shared experiences of oppression of women of different class, race, age, disability, sexual orientation and religion. There is a difference of opinion on the relationship between and the relative importances of capitalism (class exploitation) to patriarchy (male oppression) in creating women's oppression, and on the extent to which the demands for women's liberation can be met without a massive reorganization of the economic and social structure of society, or without the mobilization of both women and the working class. These differences will now be scanned in turn.

First of all, the idea that women's oppression has its roots in the material and social arrangements of society, particularly in the material and social organization of reproduction, rather than in biological reproduction itself, has emerged from debate around Engels's work. Classical Marxist analysis of women's oppression is represented by his *The Origin of the Family, Private Property and the State* (1976, first published in 1884). Very simply, Engels's theory was that women's oppression emerged with the first development of private property (see Sayers, 1982, pp. 181–201, for a fuller account). In the very earliest communities the traditional division of labour was such that the part of men's work was tending animals. Within this work lay the possibility of the creation of surplus wealth through maintaining the herd and its young. However, women through their biology, retained the line of descent, because with free sexual relations, only a woman knew whose children were hers. For men to ensure that, as their wealth increased, the property was passed on to *their own* undisputed children, they instituted restrictive practices on women's sexual behaviour and fidelity. This was the basis, then, of women's oppression by men.

Engels's theory has been subjected to a number of important criticisms, but what is important about it is that he offers an account rooted in the material conditions of the development of private property and their *interaction with women's biology*. It is a historical-materialist account which in acknowledging biology is able to present a challenge to those theories which rest their claims on biological determinism. However, the theory is inadequate. First, it is not clear *why* men, in the first place, would want to ensure the inheritance of their wealth. Secondly, Engels uncritically attributed the early forms of sexual division of labour (men – hunting; women – food preparation) to a physiological difference between men and women, that is, differences in physical strength. Apart from the fact that the division of labour could have been based on other attributes, and the over-generalization of the claim that men are stronger than women, such apparent differences in physical strength between men and women have not prevented women in may agricultural societies from doing the heaviest physical labour. Thirdly, Engels suggested that one positive aspect of the introduction of machinery through industrialization was that it made irrelevant the argument of physical strength as a criterion of who enters paid work, and therefore potentially enables women to be accepted into paid work as equal to men. In retrospect, we know that other developments have meant that women continue to be in lower paid, less secure jobs and that lesser physical strength is still used as a argument against equality. Fourthly, whilst Engels shows the relevance of women's oppression to the maintenance and inheritance of private wealth, he does not make clear why the mass of the working class who have no wealth should adhere to such a bourgeois ideology. Finally, Engels's prescription that women's emancipation would be attendant upon their mass entry into paid work and the socialization of domestic work has been contradicted by the examples of such provision in so-called socialist societies in Eastern Europe, where the traditional sexual division of labour has remained relatively unaffected (Molyneux, 1981, 1984; Williams, 1986).

Subsequent Marxist theory has been criticized by socialist feminists for being gender-blind, in that it provides little by way of examination of the sexual division of labour in the home, and oppressive relations between men and women, and sees the family and relations within it only in terms of their relationship to capital. So, for example, the unpaid work of women in the home is identified as serving capital's interests by reproducing and maintaining the workforce. Such an analysis is an example of economic reductionism (and, incidentally, of functionalism) where gender differences are reduced to the needs of capital. In this instance socialist feminism has posed the question: to what extent does this unpaid labour also maintain the authority of men over women? In other words, many socialist feminists point out that is the intersection of capitalism with patriarchy which in our society gives rise to women's oppression. Capitalism is a system which survives by exploitation, that is, making a profit from the labour of men and women; patriarchy is a form of oppression – a system whereby men maintain their control and authority over women's lives. One example of this kind of explanation can be found in the following analysis of the family wage system, this is, the system which assumes that the man in the family earns sufficient to cover the needs of his wife and family and enable his wife to commit herself to domestic work. It forms the basis upon which much social policy has been built, either directly, in social security and national insurance policy, or indirectly, in social work, education, housing and health policies. It also has formed the basis, historically, of trade union wage bargaining practices. Not only does it perpetuate a myth that men earn enough to support their wives and families, it also reinforces the assumption that women are and should be financially dependent on a man, that the woman's wage is less important and that she is prepared to work for less money. In addition, it assumes there exists a harmonious and equitable redistribution of the male wage packet within the household. Many of these assumptions have been challenged by feminist writers (Land, 1978; Pahl, 1980) and by the demands by socialist feminists for 'disaggregation' in the social security system whereby married or cohabiting women have independent rights to social security on the same conditions as other people (see McIntosh, 1981). One socialist feminist explanation has suggested that the inception of the family wage system was a coincidence of the interests of capital and patriarchy. The factory system separated work from home; initially men, women and children all worked in factories for wages. This disrupted existing patriarchal relations within the household where husband had been head, but it also threatened the health of mothers and children. This was a problem not only for capital, in its need to guarantee a continuing supply of labour, but also, of course, for those families themselves. The protection and exclusion of women from certain work, their allocation to 'home' work, to less paid and less 'skilled' work combined with the practice of male collective bargaining for a 'family wage' ensured that the balance of power was retained by men in the household, and that a more satisfactory maintenance of their labour power (cared for and serviced by women in the home) existed for capital (See Barrett and McIntosh, 1982a).

This analysis identifies capitalism and patriarchy as two systems combining at a particular historical moment: capitalism reshaping an already existing patriarchy to suit its own needs. But it still begs the question of what is the root of patriarchy? Socialist feminists differ in terms of the definition as well as the significance and autonomy they attribute to patriarchy in relation to capitalism. Heidi Hartmann (1979) sees them as two interlocking systems, as suggested by the above analysis of the family wage. She proposes that there is a materialist basis to patriarchy, and generally this is the control men exercise over women's labour, but that this is historically changing. Hartmann's analysis has been criticized for emphasizing the accommodation and mutuality of capitalism and patriarchy, and thereby ignoring the amount of tension and conflict that can exist between the two systems. For example, while state policies have often reinforced women's economic dependence and domestic role in the home, capital has at times required the cheap labour of women outside the home. Also Hartmann emphasizes the distinction of the two systems and underplays the interweaving of the social relationships of one system with another. Thus, capitalist social relationships, say of exploitation at work, may also be patriarchal in form – men in positions of authority or power.

In relation to the study of the welfare state, socialist feminists have, in general, developed work in one of two directions. Taking the example of the role of the state in welfare provision, some writers have sought to emphasize the state acting first and foremost in the interest of capitalism. Mary McIntosh (1978), for example, describes the welfare state as directly maintaining a particular family form (though this may vary) which is benefical for capitalism, and indirectly upholding women's oppression, because it is this particular family form which oppresses women, particularly in its reinforcement of women's financial dependency within the family. Elizabeth Wilson, too, in her analysis of the welfare state as 'the state organization of domestic life' (1977, p. 9) locates the state as managing the overall reproduction of labour for the benefit of capitalist production, and being beset with contradictions in its attempts. Gillian Pascall (1986), however, seeks to give equal weight to the idea of the state's actions as patriarchal. She describes the welfare state as developing in order to articulate production needs, but doing so in a patriarchal way. Hilary Rose, following Hartmann's dual system analysis of patriarchy and capitalism operating as two separate but connected systems, analyses the development of the welfare state thus:

It is in this context that we can see the historic achievement of the welfare state – an accommodation between capital and a male-dominated labour movement – reached its maturity in the post-war years in North-Western Europe. ... this particular achievement which offered substantial gains for the working class, did so none the less at the price of the continued subordination and dependency of women. (1986, p. 81)

Sylvia Walby (1986) has attempted a theoretical refinement of Hartmann's ideas, taking account of the criticisms we outlined. She identifies patriarchy as a relatively autonomous set of relations operating differently on different sites – domestic work in the household, paid work, the state, male violence and sexuality. At the same time patriarchy constantly changes as it intersects with capitalism and racism in different ways, at different times. She, therefore, sees the state as capable of independently representing patriarchal interests over and above other interests. One example she gives is the lack of response of the state to male violence against women, despite the notion that the law exists to protect everybody equally from illegal violence. She explains her position like this:

The state should be considered equally as an arena for political struggle and an actor intervening in particular situations. Its actions should be seen as the result of struggles between different interests. It should not be seen as the interest of the dominant class or class fraction. In a theory like this, it is possible to conceive of the state as both patriarchal and capitalist. (Walby, 1986, pp. 58–9)

What Walby does is try so hard to avoid the economism (the stressing of capitalism as the power by which the state is influenced) of writers like McIntosh and Wilson, that she almost returns us to a liberal pluralist or liberal feminist conception of the neutral state balancing different interests.

What most of these socialist feminist analyses have in common at a theoretical level is an attempt on the one hand to acknowledge the significance of institutionalized power relationships between men and women which produce gender inequalities, and, on the other, an acknowledgement that capitalism gives rise to *differential* experiences of oppression by women of different classes. This is important for an understanding of welfare policy, not only in recognizing the different experiences different women have, but also in resolving a particular paradox: that the history of welfare provision has been one where it has often been middle-class professional *women* who have controlled their working-class sisters into being 'good' wives and 'good' mothers (see Miriam David's account (1980) of the development of education). This is a significant departure from liberal feminism in particular, with its tendency to assume that the interests of middle-class women are also appropriate to working-class women, and radical feminism, with its assumption of a shared and common experience of oppression by all women. However, socialist feminism's acknowledgement of the differential aspects of Black women's experiences of racism in the welfare state has been patchy. On the one hand, Lesley Doyal's writing on the health service (1979, Doyal et al., 1981) takes into account the role of working-class and immigrant women as workers in the health service, as well as the impact of medical technology on Third World countries. On the other hand, as yet, no feminist social policy texts take on board Black women's struggles or experiences (Wilson, 1977, 1980a; Ungerson, 1985; Dale and Foster, 1986; Pascall, 1986). (See the next section on Black feminism.)

The earlier debate around Engels's work had led to studies by women to extend our understanding of what is biologically given and what is not. Whilst it is true that women have babies and that they menstruate, it is much more debatable whether, for example, physical strength or other physiological differences can explain other forms of division between men and women's work and behaviour. (See Bartels, 1982; Kessler and McKenna, 1982). What emerges from these 'social-constructionist' accounts is that even though biological sex differences exist, what is important *is the way biology interacts with the social and material conditions of women's lives,* and although some aspects of biology may, at present, be unchangeable, the social and material conditions *can* be changed and challenged. Two areas of feminist analysis and action exemplify this point. The first is the recent development of reproductive technologies. Along with earlier developments in medical technology, like contraception and safe abortion, these offer women the possibility of exercising greater control over their lives whilst they simultaneously expose them to the exercise of power by the medical profession who administer such technologies and the state which legislates upon the boundaries of their operation. As Michelle Stanworth points out:

the new reproductive technologies open up to debate matters that formerly belonged in the realm of biological givens: in practices such as surrogacy, the gulf between 'biological motherhood' and 'social motherhood' is vividly exposed, provoking new personal and legal choices, ... By altering the boundaries between the biological and the social – by demanding human decision where previously there was biological destiny – the new technologies politicize issues concerning sexuality, reproduction, parenthood and family. (1987, p. 2)

For the feminist critique the issue has not been technology itself 'but whether we can create the political and cultural conditions in which such technologies can be employed by women to shape the experience of reproduction according to their own definitions' (1987, p, 35). Secondly, studies of the social construction of masculinity and femininity have examined notions of caring and of dependency so central to welfare provisions and have forced a reappraisal of existing divisions between the world of production and that of reproduction. Some socialist feminists have developed psychoanalytic theories in order to understand the dynamic whereby women take on particular caring roles. One direction has been into Lacan's re-reading of Freud (see Mitchell, 1974; Coward, 1984), and another is derived from the object-relations school of psychoanalysis, and concerns itself with the mother–daughter relationship, and how this is at the basis of women's desire/need/capacity to mother, or care for others (see Chowdorow, 1978). This has been popularized by Susie Orbach and Louise Eichenbaum (1983) and their work for the Women's Therapy Centre set up in London in 1976, a feminist-based form of therapeutic provision. There are different views as to the usefulness of psychoanalytic theory (see Sayers, 1982; Segal, 1987). Lynne Segal, for example, suggests that despite intentions to the contrary Chowdorow's work serves those who would wish to suggest that a psychic, if not a biological essentialism exists to separate men and women in relation to the experience and capacity for mothering. More significantly the strategic consequences suggested by Orbach and Eichenbaum are that shared parenting, shared jobs, or shorter hours for both parents, can break into the cycle so that over the generations men as well as women are brought up with a sense of responsibility to care for others. Clearly this strategy is highly idealist, ignoring the economic and structural constraints faced by many women and men who would like to be able to work fewer hours to be able to share equitably the care in their household, but are prevented by their employers or lack of control in employment from doing so. It also is individualist, exhorting individual parents to change their behaviour, and it takes no account of single parents or any parent who does not find him or herself in heterosexual coupledom, nor does it fully acknowledge the importance of state provided socialized childcare. Nevertheless, what is interesting is that the drift of their strategy first recognizes that caring is not a skill tied to biology but can be potentially acquired by either men or women, and secondly inverts the idea of reproduction serving the needs of production, to the notion of 'how people are cared for' determining the way production is organized, or indeed transformed. This idea has been matched by feminists with materially based and collective strategies for achieving this – for example, Anne Phillips writes:

We have to adapt work to fit in with the rest of life and particularly adapt it to fit with children. For the present the adaptation is done by women, the price of having children is paid by mothers. Why not a new approach? If the needs of children do not fit with the demands of full-time work, then jobs must be changed. (1983, p. 5)

She and other feminists propose changes in material conditions to allow for the possiblity to all of shared parenting: a shorter and more flexible working day; parental leave for children's needs (childbirth, sickness, starting school), extensive public provision of day nurseries, after-school and holiday facilities under parents' and careers' control. In demanding a reassessment of the relationship between paid and upaid work, who does it and how, between the organization of production, the organization of reproduction in the family, and the role of the state in balancing this through socialized forms of care, socialist feminism makes three leaps. The first is a methodological leap to recognize the interrelationship between production (the public) and reproduction (the private), the second is to elaborate precisely how the social and material conditions of childcare, and not the biological fact of childbirth contribute to women's oppression, and the third is to create a strategy which spells out the way in which welfare provision and human need are central to the social and economic organization of society.

It is important to add that such a strategy strikes at the very heart of the organization of work and family under capitalism, and it is this that Orbach and Eichenbaum (and Anna Coote) underestimate when they propose such changes as part of economic reforms of individual life-styles. Nevertheless, as an objective which frames immediate demands about hours and conditions of paid employment and forms of childcare it is important and like many of socialist feminism's welfare demands – for example, for free, community-controlled, anti-sexist, anti-racist nursery provision, or for reproductive freedom – they challenge both capitalist and patriarchal social relations. (See the final chapter of Barrett and McIntosh, 1982a for a good summary of such demands.)

A particular tension exists around such demands, between improvements in women's position in the immediate period and those demands not achievable in the short term, but which in the long term are essential to women's liberation. Maxine Molyneux (1984) has called the first *practical gender interests*, and the second, *strategic gender interests*. The distinction is an important one for social policy. Policies for women in relation to income maintenance, like pensions or financial maintenance after divorce, are often caught between the practical reality of a woman's financial dependence here and now on a man's wage, and their own limited job opportunities, and the strategic desirability of financial independence for women, and for women to be eligible to benefits in their own right. In so far as many financial benefits are at present rooted in a contributory system base on paid work, then any moves to make women eligible to such rights as individuals (rather than as wives or mothers) automatically renders them worse off than men by reproducing in the benefit system the inequalities women suffer in paid work. Policies in relation to health, community-care, childcare and custody of children after divorce have to be able to balance the reality of a sexual division of labour in which much of women's time and emotional investment goes into their children and other dependent relatives (and vice versa), with the strategic desirability of involving men in the process of and responsibility of caring. It is vitally important to attempt to weave a relationship between these two types of interests, as Molyneux says:

Thus, the formulation of strategic interests can only be effective as a form of intervention when full account is taken of these practical interests. Indeed it is the politicization of these practical interests and their transformation into strategic interests which constitutes a central aspect of feminist political practice. (1984, p. 63)

Finally, then, in terms of theory and policy socialist feminist theory attempts to integrate biology into a historical-materialist account of capitalist patriarchy or patriarchal capitalism, depending upon the emphasis. Thus, it is not biology which determines women's lives, but the social and material context in which that biology exists. Writers differ over whether partriarchy or capitalism is the more significant force shaping that social and material context. On the onc hand those who have attached importance to capitalism and the mode of production as the key material basis requiring change, have found it less easy to give full acknowledgement to women's experiences of oppressive patriarchal behaviour. On the other hand, those who have attempted to pull patriarchy out as a distinct system have found it difficult to pin down a materialist explanation of why and how men oppress women, which is quite separate from the mode of production. Whilst theoretically socialist feminism is able to recognize that divisions exist between the interests and experiences of women of different class, sexual orientation and 'race', as well as over time, it has to be said that at present it still shares with other feminist theory a blindness to the significance of Black women's experiences, and the implications of this for welfare strategy. Nevertheless, socialist feminism's contribution is, in my view, the most fruitful of the feminist approaches, so far discussed, especially in being able to pursue in strategic terms the significance of the relationship between production – the public sphere – and reproduction – the private sphere – by demanding the reorganization of the sexual division of labour and an end to the divisions between paid and unpaid work. In terms of the welfare state this means recasting the concept of welfare in ways in which it no longer underpins female dependency or the sexual division of labour where caring is seen as women's natural work, and no longer privileges the male-breadwinner nuclear family. This involves two, possibly contradictory, developments: the recognition of women's rights to benefits as *individuals*, as well as the prioritization of a *collective* commitment by society to the care of children, the elderly, the frail and the otherwise dependent, in ways which respect their needs and wishes. It also means providing housing which reflects the varieties of household forms and needs, and it means that welfare provision should be controlled jointly by those who provide it and use it. Many of these objectives cannot be achieved without a substantial reorganization of the social and economic system and a significant challenge to patriarchal capitalism, but they provide an important framework for current struggles over welfare. Some of these involve fighting for the state to devote more resources towards material improvements in women's lives – better funded health services, family allowances, pensions, improved conditions and opportunities for women welfare workers, and so on; some of them aim to advance the rights of women to benenfits in their own right – unemployment benefits, social security, or challenge the assumptions of unpaid care in the home – payments for married women carers; some of them concentrate on forcing society through the state or the local state to take greater responsibility for the care of dependants – socialized forms of nursery and day care and residential provision. A common thread is the emphasis on changing 'the social relations of welfare' – ensuring that provision is organized in non-sexist and non-hierarchical ways and in ways that diminish divisions between providers and users, and create the possibility of greater control by women over that provision (see summary in table 3.1, pp. 82–5). Maintaining these combined objectives is not without problems, even more so since the cutbacks and social policies of the present Conservative government which aim to get the families (i.e. women) to take greater responsibility for their own welfare. For example, discussing alternatives and the present shift to 'community care' for older and disabled people and people with learning difficulties, Janet Finch says:

There are no easy or obvious solutions to the impasse of sexual divisions in caring. 'Community care' as it exists at the moment exploits women's unpaid labour, but alternative forms of community care which could be developed in the practical politics of this decade would do exactly the same. Improvements in the conditions of caring could be achieved, but they will only ameliorate the situation, not make caring non-sexist. (1984, p.16)

Somewhat reluctantly, she concluded that the 'residential route' offers a way out of the impasse for it provides a *collective* solution, it acknowledges the need for caring to be seen as paid work, and it creates jobs. However, whilst this solution recognizes women's needs it may not recognize the needs of those users of services who need care but do not want it in a residential setting.

Black Feminism

Criticisms of white feminism The criticisms of white-dominated feminism emerging over the past decade from Black feminists are important for the development of feminist theory, feminist strategy and therefore, of course, for the feminist critique of the welfare state. Heidi Hartmann (mentioned in the previous section), described the debate about patriarchy and capitalism as the 'Unhappy marriage of Marxism and feminism' (Hartmann, 1981), to which Gloria Joseph, an American Black feminist, has rejoindered that no reference is made in the debate to 'the incestuous child of patriarchy and capitalism. That child, now a full grown adult, is named racism' (Joseph, 1981, p. 92).

A significant amount has been written articulating the experiences of Black women, how their relationship to work, the family, men, sexuality, reproduction, the state, including the welfare state, in structured by '*race*' as well as by gender, and how this renders their experiences different from those of white women. The simultaneous experiences for Black women of racism and sexism not only compounds those oppressions but reconstitutes them in specific ways. Reproduction is a case in point. At a certain level (usually rhetorically, rather than practically, in Britain), within the ideology of familism, the welfare state confers a 'positive' value to women in terms of motherhood. No equivalent conferment exists for being Black – woman or man. Indeed, it is argued that sometimes racism reconstitutes the situation to such an extent that to be a Black mother is not simply negative (Black) plus positive (mother) but it is doubly negative (the reproduction of more Blacks). This is an example of an area where the assumptions of white feminists and their welfare strategies have been challenged by Black feminists. Here the argument has centred around the abortion campaigns of the 1970s. The 'right to choose' an abortion was seen as a demand only appropriate to white women whose fertility was taken for granted and approved. For Black women, the experience was one where their 'right to reproduction' was being questioned and sometimes controlled by a health service operating under a concern about 'Black numbers', a racist view of Black female sexuality and a tradition of eugenicism. This tradition is as strong in the feminist as in other political traditions. (Josephine Butler, Charlotte Perkins Gilman, Eva Hubback, Marie Stopes, Christabel Pankhurst, though not Sylvia, were all infected with eugenicist ideas.) As a response to this challenge some women in the National Abortion Campaign in 1983 broke away to re-form as the Reproductive Rights Campaign with a commitment to the rights of Black and Third World women over issues such as unwarranted abortion and sterilization and testing of potentially harmful contraceptive drugs like Depo-Provera. However, there are still other unresolved problems in both the theory and practice of white feminism which Black feminists have pointed to.

At a theoretical level these problems stem from the use of the concept 'patriarchy', from the critique of the family, from the omission of Black women's struggles against slavery, colonialism, imperialism and racism in the writing of feminist history (or 'herstory'), and from the tendency to see racial oppression and sex oppression and the struggles against them as parallel but separate forms. This latter tendency came, in part, out of the development in the 1960s in the United States of the movement against Black oppression which provided some of the stimulus for the development of the women's movement, not just in that women involved in the civil rights movement felt they were not recognized as equals in political activism, but that both movements were involved in struggling against oppression, the basis of which is *power* and the experience of which is subjective: the domination of Black by white, of women by men. The subjectivity of these oppressions sets them apart, theoretically, from class struggle and exploitation, for class and exploitation, in Marxist terms, are assessed *objectively*, in terms of a person's relation to the means of production (as either working class or capitalist class). This has led some Black feminists to claim, with some justification, that 'the personal is political' was a principle first set in motion by the Black Pride movement. A further apparent similarity of the two types of oppression arises from the fact that existing explanations for both oppressions resort to unsatisfactory forms of reductionism – either biological reductionism, where it is argued in different ways that Blacks and women are 'naturally' inferior, or on the other hand, an economic reductionism which says that the oppression of women and Blacks is functional to, and therefore caused by, capitalism. However much there are similarities, the tendency to see 'race' and gender as parallel has obscured the experience of Black women whose experiences are mediated *simultaneously* through race *and* gender and also class. The failure, in the United States, of the male-oriented Black Power movement and the white-oriented women's movement to deal with, or recognize this simultaneity led, in part, to the need for Black feminists to organize autonomously.

Black feminists have criticized the use of the concept 'patriarchy' in a number of ways. First, the way the concept is used by many radical feminists emphasizes women being oppressed *as women* and therefore suggests, first, that universal solidarity exists between women as women, and, secondly, that stressing *men* as oppressors implies a collective sense of power used by *all* men. It is argued that this interpretation has led to a blindness of differences of power between *women*, particularly the racism of some white women and the specific experience by Black women of the racism of the state as well as its sexism. For example, the work of the Brent Asian Women's Refuge, run for and by Asian women, is explained like this:

The last thing a woman wants when she seeks shelter in a refuge is to have her cultural traditions and values attacked by women who feel they know and understand what is best for her. The experience of being subjected to violence by men, although uniting women, can also form the basis for racist assumptions and stereotyping about men in general and black women in particular. (Brent Asian Women's Refuge and Resource Centre, 1984)

Black feminists have suggested that white women can assume to have *some* recourse to a white power structure (the courts) in a way that Black women cannot. (Lorde, 1984). By a similar token, it is argued that it is not possible to equate the patriarchy of white men with that of Black men. This is not to deny that Black men oppress women in patriarchal ways, but, as Joseph (1981), Hooks (1982) and Carby (1982b) have each pointed out: 'Capitalism and patriarchy simply do not offer to share with Black males the seat of power in their regal solidarity. ... there is more solidarity between white males and females than there is between white males and Black males' (Joseph, 1981, p. 101).

In similar ways Black feminists have also criticized the feminist idea of the family as the 'site of oppression' as not appropriate to Black history and experience. The Black family has been a site of resistance in struggles against slavery and in contemporary struggles, for example, strikes by Asian women at the Chix and Grunwick factories in the 1970s drew important support from the families and communities, as have struggles against police racism, or deportations: 'We struggle together with Black men against racism, while we also struggle with Black men about sexism' (Moraga and Anzadua, 1981, p. 213).

For these reasons, and for other differences to do with aspects of dependency, domesticity and femininity discussed further below, the concept of patriarchy is problematic, as Hazel Carby explains: 'We can point to no single source for our oppression. When white feminists emphasize patriarchy alone, we want to redefine the term and make it a more complex concept. Racism ensures that black men do not have the same relations to patriarchal/capitalist hierarchies as white men' (Carby, 1982b, p. 213). A partial recognition of difference between women has been acknowledged by socialist feminism's attempt to explore the inter-relationship of class with patriarchy, but, in order to take racism into this framework, the framework itself needs to be changed, as Bhavnani and Coulson point out: 'to consider racism as the central issue involves a fundamental and radical transformation of socialist-feminism' (Bhavnani and Coulson, 1986, p. 85). This is because of the need to understand how racism, and its historical progenitors, slavery, colonialism and imperialism, are insinuated into the enmeshed fabric of patriarchal capitalism. An understanding of the position of Black women in Britain requires an internationalist framework of analysis which features imperialism, the role of the Third World workers in the international division of labour and the role of the state in controlling that labour through immigration laws, for all of these aspects affect Black women and their struggles. (This point is elaborated in chapter 4.) And within this there is the need to recognize that the term 'Black' should not imply homogeneity of experience, for the histories and struggles of Afro-Caribbean, Afro-American and Asian women are mediated by different experiences of racism.

Not all Black feminists share the same analysis to explain the interlocking system of oppression and exploitation derived from 'race', class and gender. Angela Davis (1981) uses an analysis which stresses struggles against economic exploitation around the concerns which unite Black and white working-class women – entry into the labour market and the socialization of domestic labour and childcare as the key to change. Gail Lewis and Pratibha Parma argue for an analysis that gives more recognition to the interdependence of factors than to a direct or single cause: 'we would argue that only a synthesis of race and gender within an overall class analysis can lead us forward – for race, class and gender form the matrix of our lives and it is difficult to separate out any one as having primacy'. (1985, pp. 87–8). In a similar way, Bhavnani and Coulson talk of the need to develop an idea of a 'racially structured patriarchal capitalism', (1986, p. 89), whereas Audre Lorde stresses the need for women to recognize differences due to dominations through 'racism, sexism, ageism, heterosexism, elitism and classism': 'difference must not only be tolerated, but seen as a fund of necessary polarities between which our creativity can spark like a dialectic' (1984, p. 111). Her sister-American Bell Hooks argues for a need to develop a 'liberatory radical theory of socialism that would more adequately address interlocking systems of domination like sexism, racism, class oppression, imperialism and so on' (Hooks, 1986, p. 126). Within this Hooks sees race and patriarchy as particularly important: 'Racism is fundamentally a feminist issue because it is so interconnected with sexist oppression' (1986, p. 131). In contrast to Davis, above, Hooks sees issues of sexuality and the rights of women over their own bodies as central for Black and white women. Finally, Gloria Joseph argues for greater recognition to be given to the autonomy of racism and its distinctive pre-capitalist history: 'there is ample evidence to indicate that relations between races have a long and important history which is not reducible to relations between the sexes or classes' (1981, p. 103).

Black women organizing in Britain

What Afro-Caribbeans and Asians in Britain have been concerned to unite around is an experience which is both historical and contemporary, both collective and individual. What unites us is not only the economic basis – rooted in colonialism – for our presence in Britain, but also the ways in which the racism of the British state structures and determines the conditions of our existence. But to work towards such unity is not, of course, to say that our cultural diversity, is not important or significant to us. (Lewis and Parmar, 1985, p. 89)

Afro-Caribbean and Asian women have important separate traditions of struggle, which are linked by opposition to colonialism and imperialism, which have informed their struggles in Britain and stand as important counters to the idea of Third World women as passive or as victims.

The role of West Indian women in the rebellions preceding and during the disturbances in Jamaica in 1938, for example, though known to be significant has still not been thoroughly described. ... women in India have a long and complex history of fighting oppression both in and out of the wage relation. It is clear that many women coming from India to Britain have a shared herstory of struggle, whether in rural areas as agricultural labourers or in urban districts as municipal employees. (Carby, 1982b, pp. 229–30; see also Parmar, 1982; Amos and Parmar, 1984; Trivedi, 1984; Bryan et al., 1985)

Left out of white accounts of history or of struggle are the stories of Black women who fought against the odds. Claudia Jones (1915–64), for example, was a Trinidadian who came to Britian in 1956 having been deported from the United States, where she had been heavily involved in socialist and anti-racist activity. In this country she organized solidarity campaigns amongst workers for Nelson Mandela and for the American Civil Rights movement (see Bryan et al., 1985). In the history of medicine, Florence Nightingale features regularly as the founder of nursing, whilst the name of Mary Seacole is never mentioned. Mary Seacole (1805–81) was a Black woman with a Scottish father and Jamaican mother who travelled in the Bahamas, Cuba, Haiti and Panama gaining a reputation as a 'doctress' for treating cholera and yellow fever. In 1854 she tried to enlist as a nurse in the Crimean War but was turned down because she was Black. Nevertheless, she still went and made an exceptional contribution in treating the sick and wounded. (See her autobiography first published in 1857, and revived by Alexander and Dewjee, 1984.)

However, history is made by the collective rather than the individual. In post-war Britain Afro-Caribbean and Asian women have fought over issues affecting them as Black workers, women, mothers, tenants, patients and claimants: for better pay and conditions (Chix, Grunwick and the health workers strikes of the 70s); with defence committees against police and court racism against their communities and their children; against racist and sexually discriminatory immigration controls and deportations; against homelessness; against the racism of local authorities placing them in the poorest council housing, or by their failing to take action over racial violence against Black families; for the right to organize autonomously against domestic violence (Asian women's refuges); against the practice of the education system, the health service or social services departments of blaming the problems Black families face upon their own cultures or traditions – a racialized form of blaming the victim. Many of these struggles have as their focus the racism of the state and the welfare state, and these are discussed more fully below. But what in the 1980s has become clear is that this racism in various ways has become more intense. This is described by the three authors of *The Heart of the Race: Black Women's Lives in Britian* (1985) in the following way:

As our community came under greater seige Black women would play an increasingly central role in the fight to defend ourselves and our children from the onslaught. As mothers and as workers, we came into daily contact with the institutions which compounded our experience of racism. We were the ones who rushed to the police stations when members of our families got arrested. We were the ones who had to take time off work to confront teachers and the education authorities about the mis-education of our children. We were the ones who cleared up the debris when police entered our homes uninvited to harass and intimidate us. We were the ones who battled it out with the housing authorities, the Social Services and the DHSS as we demanded our right to decent homes and an 'income above subsistence level'. (Bryan et al. 1985, pp. 162-3)

The shooting of Cherry Groce by the police in 1985 when they invaded her home, and the death of Cynthia Jarrett in the same year when they invaded hers, pay testimony to the fact that Black women are on the front-line. Many local Black women's centres appeared in the 1970s. Many of these were created out of the stimulus Black women derived from the Organization of Women of Asian and African Descent (OWAAD), a national organization which ran from 1978 to 1983, held conferences and produced a newsletter, FOWAAD. The significance of this organization was that it recognized the need to develop political unity amongst Black women without minimizing the historical, experiential and cultural differences between them, and also that it placed these experiences whether in the public field of work, or in the private area of the family, sexuality or reproduction – in the international contex of imperialism. This attempt mirrors other areas where Black (and white) women have sought to make organizational, as well as theoretical, links between the struggles of women in the newly developed factories in the Third World who form a pool of insecure and disposable labour, and the struggles of women in the West – often Black women too – who find themselves part of the growing trend of low paid, casual, often home-based labour. The marginalized conditions of both groups of women are a consequence of the trends in the world economy to move capital around the globe to areas of cheap labour. However, this experience for women, as Swasti Mitter (1986) has pointed out, has also forged a common bond where international networks of women workers are challenging both the policies of international capitalism and the male-dominated trade unions.

Black women and the welfare state

Black women as mothers encounter (other) state agencies such as the DHSS, schools and so on in a very particular way; they may be asked to produce their passports before being considered eligible for benefit, or before their children are allowed to be enrolled in schools. Clearly they experience these agencies in a way that white mothers would not. (Bhavnani and Coulson, 1986, p. 84)

Since, as feminists have often pointed out, it is women who encounter the welfare state most, it is appropriate that the first challenges to white approaches to the welfare state should come from Black feminism directed at the feminist critique of the welfare state. These criticisms centre upon the state's relationship to the family, in particular in relation to dependency, domesticity, reproduction and sexuality, and to the role of Black women in the labour market.

One important element of feminists' critique suggests that the state upholds through policy and practice patriarchal relations in the family: it reinforces women as financially dependent on a male partner, as bearers and primary carers and cleaners, and reinforces their role as a reserve army of labour. Black feminists have explained that this 'familism' underpinning the welfare state has never fully appplied to them and their families. Hazel Carby challenges Elizabeth Wilson's interpretation of the immediate post-war period in relation to women and social policy. Wilson's analysis is in terms of the state juggling with is priorities: on the one hand wishing to uphold the ideology of family life and women as mothers, but on the other, aware of the needs of certain industries for female (cheap) labour. The solution, for many working-class women, was found in part-time work which did not interfere with family responsibilities. However, even this was only possible because of the recruitment of Black immigrants to the labour market, many of whom were Caribbean women (a factor often overlooked). Furthermore, these women, as Carby says, 'were recruited into the labour force beyond such considerations. Rather than a concern to protect or preseve the black family in Britain, the state reproduced common-sense notions of its inherent pathology: black women were seen to fail as mothers precisely because of their position as workers' (1982b, p. 219). To relate it to welfare: whilst one arm of the welfare state was busy exploiting Black women's labour in low paid jobs with unsocial hours (auxiliary nursing, for example) another arm was refusing to meet their needs, for childcare for example, and was blaming their difficulties upon the fact that they did such work.

The two significant characteristics of women's involvement as paid workers in the welfare state have been highlighted as being its low pay – in common with much women's work – and its extension of the caring, domestic role women carry out in the home. However, for Black women workers in the welfare state there is an added racial dimension to both these characteristics. The recruitment of Caribbean workers in the mid-1950s into the NHS, as is detailed in the next chapter, was seen by the British government as a cheaper option because the state did not have to bear the social costs it would have to pay for its indigenous workforce – the education and care of the workers, or of their children. Many of the Caribbean women who came initially left their dependants behind. Furthermore, the National Health Service has *continued* to rely on this type of labour (male and female, skilled and unskilled) from India, Ireland, Malaysia, Southern Europe and the Caribbean. In a London hospital study by Doyal, Hunt and Mellor (1981) they found 84 per cent of domestics and 82 per cent of catering workers were from abroad and that the National Health Service had, in spite of the tightened immigration controls on unskilled labour, still managed to recruit such immigrant labour. In this way female immigrant workers have played a crucial role in keeping down the costs of welfare provision. Furthermore, the state has continued to evade responsibilities towards the social costs of maintaining the dependants of these workers even as settlers in Britain, whilst at the same time Black people are presented as 'scroungers' upon the welfare services. Concerns about 'numbers' in immigration policy, particularly the 1962 and 1971 Commonwealth Immigration Acts, were about the admission and maintenance of dependants: children, grandparents and wives (whose dependency was assumed, in spite of evidence about economic activity running counter to this – see below). Although the 1977 Child Benefit Act transferred money for children *in this country* from fathers to mothers, it also, at the same time, effectively withdrew support for the children who live abroad of parents who work in Britain, by changing eligibility to child benefit to tax allowance only. Furthermore, the 'Sole Responsibility' rule of the 1971 Act restricts the opportunity for single parents to bring their children to live with them in Britain unless they can prove they have solely maintained and visited them. Clearly, in these last two cases, the Black and other immigrant woman workers who lose out are precisely those on whom the NHS has depended. Another facet of this state evasion of responsibility to maintain is the abuse of Black women's reproductive rights (see below).

The second characteristic of women welfare workers is described as the continuation in public (low) paid work of their domestic role in the home, as cooks, cleaners, carers, educators and so on. Hazel Carby queries this for its application to Black women. She suggests that the racist image of the *Black woman as servant* is as strong as that of *carer* in the acceptance of Black women in domestic, nursing and cleaning roles (Carby, 1982b, p. 215).

It can also be suggested that the idea of the state *reinforcing dependency* of women upon their husbands, in accordance with the 'family wage' model, has particular inapplicability to Black women in this country (as indeed it does for many white working-class women). Michele Barrett and Mary McIntosh (1985) provide figures drawn from the 1984 Policy Studies Institute survey and the government's 1981 *Labour Force Survey* which show a higher proportion of 'West Indian' and Asian women than white women employed in full-time paid work: 23 per cent of white women, 42 per cent of West Indian women and 25 per cent of Asian women. When it comes to part-time work (the post-war solution, discussed above) the rates are 17 per cent for white women, 14 per cent for West Indian women and 5 per cent for Asian women (Central Statistical Office, 1983 quoted in Barrett and Mcintosh, 1985). The first set of statistics also challenge the prevalent notion of Asian women as passive, retiring and confined to home and family. The 'myth of the male breadwinner' is particularly pertinent to West Indian women: 31 per cent of all West Indian households with children are single-parent units (compared with 10 per cent white and 5 per cent Asian), and 32 per cent of West Indian household are 'female-headed' (compared with 14 per cent white and 6.5 per cent Asian). As Black male unemployment increases these figures can also be expected to rise.

The point was made earlier in this section that Black women's relation to motherhood and reproductive rights was imbued with both racist as well as sexist content. The history of the state's involvement in health care and the 'endowment' of motherhood is infused with eugenicist notions of 'limiting' the children of the unfit or undesirable, and the denial of reproductive rights to Black and Third World women through enforced abortion, sterilization or experimental contraception can be seen as contemporary practice of such ideas. In addition, Hazel Carby points out that the general notion of reproduction, in its meaning of caring and servicing the labour force, has a different meaning for Black women, particularly in the United States, South Africa and the Third World (though increasingly in this country) where they are involved in mothering the children and servicing the members of white families (Carby, 1982b, p. 218).

The operation of racism and sexism does not apply in a uniform manner to Black women as the use of notions of 'Black family pathology' shows. The idea that the cultural characteristics of Black families are the cause of poverty, poor housing, poor schooling and other social problems has long been part of the commonsense practice of social workers, teachers and doctors. However, these are applied in different and contradictory ways to different cultural groups: Black children are seen to fail at school because their Asian mothers are too passive and withdrawn and stay at home, or because their Afro-Caribbean mothers are too assertive and go out to work. Black adolescents' problems are supposed to derive from too much or too little discipline, from being kept in the home or not kept off the streets. Whilst white female sexuality is cast in terms which are *sexist*, Black female sexuality, particularly in the myth of availability, is constructed in *racist* terms. Strategies over the issue of violence to women offer a case of what Black feminists have seen as white women's complacency of the racist nature of law and order and an undue faith in the state. Some of the demands from 'Reclaim the Night' marches in the late 1970s – some of which marched through Black communities – were for greater police protection for women. Not only can this be interepreted as an invitation to exert greater control on Black areas, and as a coupling of Blacks with crime, but it is also a very specific sort of crime which plays into racist notions of Black male sexuality. Again, contradictory commonsense notions of sexuality abound in the experiences of Black women. In 1978 the practice of immigration officials of testing the virginity of Asian women entering the country as the future wives of men settled here was revealed. Not only did this constitute blatant sexual abuse and humiliation of those women but it was born out of a stereotyping of Asian Women as sexually passive and submissive. In contrast, Afro-Caribbean women find that: 'Prevailing stereotypes of Black women as "immoral" or "promiscuous" render social workers hyper-sensitive to the possibility of moral danger, particularly among young Black women who show signs of being sexually active' (Bryan et al., 1985, p. 112).

Since the 1970s there has been a marked increase in the use of repression and control in the Black communities in the greater policing of those communities and the implementation of strict immigration controls. Welfare policies have both mirrored this and, in the case of health and social security in particular, taken on board the policing of suspected 'illegal immigrants' themselves. Factors such as these, combined with the characteristics of racialized social control and pathology already described, and the fact that cuts in services have particularly had consequences for those communities whose access is already severely limited or whose livelihoods depend on the public sector, mean that Black women have a qualitatively different experience of the welfare state compared with white women and one which requires both empirical and theoretical understanding within the feminist critique in social policy.

In the light of our experiences of racism in the field of health, it is little wonder that Black women regard the State's surveillance of our lives through the combined Health and Social Services with growing distrust. Increasingly alienated from potentially beneficial provisions, we have been among the first to question the overall power of the Welfare State to record, control and intervene in our lives. ... There is no single area of our lives which better expose our experience of institutionalised racism than our relationship with the various welfare services ... For Black women, the benign face of capitalism hides a thinly-disguised form of social control. (Bryan et al., 1985, pp. 110–11)

Black women stand on the front-line of the repressive nature of the state, including the welfare state. It is an experience where the distinctions between the benevolent and the repressive sides of the state are far more imperceptible, and this leads to some interesting contrasts in interpretation of the state by Black and white feminists. Jenny Bourne writes, for example:

One can perceive in the WM [Women's Movement] an ambivalence towards the state. Is it an instrument of oppression or is it a welfare state whence concessions can be won? ... In their failure to understand the state, the women fail to side with the blacks; in failing to side with the blacks they play into the hands of the state. (1983, pp. 12–13; the reference is to 'Reclaim the Night' marches)

In contrast, Elizabeth Wilson and Mary McIntosh, constantly urge us not to forget in our criticism of the welfare state the benefits state provision can also bring: social security benefits, day care facilities, etc. (McIntosh 1981, Wilson 1983). At one level, this is an important reminder, but at another it can blind us to the ways in which some provisions which may have been benevolent for white women has not had the same impact for Black women, and that the overriding struggle some Black women have is with the racist and intransigent dimensions of the state. An attempt to reconcile the need Black women have for non-racist, non-sexist welfare provision combined with their present experience of the welfare state is made by Byran et al. in a discussion of health cuts, in this way:

For Black women, who are on the front line when it comes to health service attacks, the implications are very clear. Either we continue to fight tooth and nail for the preservation of the Health Service we have worked so hard to build, *or we risk being ousted from our already unenviable position at the very bottom of the NHS agenda.* (1985, pp. 109–10, my emphasis)

At a more theoretical level, Bhavnani and Coulson suggest that feminism has to recognize that *the state deals with different women differently*: 'we are drawn to the need for fresh analysis of the relationship between the state and "the family" and of how this differs for black and white people. This may lead us to an analysis, and some understanding, that the state may have different strategies for each group' (1986, p. 86). It is in this attempt of Black feminism to grapple much more exhaustively with the notion of difference between women, not just in its subjective sense of culture or experience or struggle, but in its objective sense of how such difference is structured through the interweaving of patriarchy, imperialism and capitalism, and how it is variously reinforced by the state and other institutionalized structures and by ideologies, that Black feminism make a major methodological contribution. Further it makes a connection between the specificity of Black women's experience and the generality of the systems of race, class and gender of which we are all a party. This is through the notion that racism, sexism and class exploitation combine not in incremental fashion, but in such a way as *to reconstitute* the subjective experience and the objective structuring of divisions of labour, elements of family life, sexuality and so on.

Whilst it would be wrong to imply that Black feminism has a single unified theoretical analysis, nevertheless, in terms of the methodological criteria we have been applying, most analyses do not rely on any form of biological, psychological or economic reductionism: the task of explaining the interaction of two different forms of oppression would seem to discourage this. Again, in common with both radical and socialist feminism, most analyses contend with both the private world of the family, sexuality, reproduction and the public world of paid labour and politics in terms of the way the relationship between them is structured by 'race', gender and class. In locating the source of oppression in the interwoven systems of imperialism, patriarchy and capitalism, or more specifically a racially structured patriarchal capitalism, and in identifying its eradication through the struggles against this, then most analyses are materialist in their method. What Black feminism is enriched by is a thorough-going acknowledgement of difference (as against the universalism of some white feminist uses of 'patriarchy') and an international, or global context in which an understanding of slavery, colonialism and imperialism are placed,

The implications for welfare policy are derived from the critique Black feminism presents of the relationship between the welfare state and the Black family in which the state is seen as reinforcing not only elements of women's oppression but of racial oppression too. It is, therefore, necessary to challenge the way the welfare state, as employer, reproduces Black women's subordinated role in the racial and international division of labour, and, as provider of welfare, reproduces the ideology of inferior Black motherhood. Crucially, Black feminism challenges the principles of eligibility to welfare services by unveiling the racist basis of the present and past forms of eligibility through nationality. This concept of nationality, which will be discussed in later chapters, has been employed in such a way as to deny access to welfare provision to immigrant and minority groups and their dependants. Black feminists also demand the right for different cultural household forms to exist, and that control over welfare provision be extended equally to Black women. (See summary in table 3.1, pp. 82–5.)

Conclusion

The feminist critiques of the welfare state, diverse and complex as they are, have been responsible for enriching the analysis of social policy by shedding new light on old concepts, by adding new policy concerns to the agenda of welfare strategy and new analytical and methodological considerations which need to be acknowledged in any account of welfare which aims for theoretical adequacy.

Libertarian feminism does little to advance the analysis of women's oppression or of social policy, being both individualist and biologically determinist in method. The two faces of reformist feminism – liberal feminism and welfare feminism – have highlighted women's inequalities and particular needs and the potential of the welfare state to ameliorate these, but neither has adequately dealt with the division between the private and the public, or the question of women's biology. Liberal feminism is largely concerned about change in the public sphere and fails to acknowledge any aspect of women's biology. Welfare feminism is the converse; it concerns itself with change in the private sphere, for women as wives and mothers, and tends towards a biologically determinist method of analysis. In addition, both are idealist, resting their hopes of change through changing ideas and attitudes and appeals to a neutral state.

Radical feminism has forcefully brought to our attention elements of women's personal lives which deserve political consideration – sexuality, reproduction, the family and the divisions within it – but in its different definitions of male power and its appeals to 'women's special nature' tends to both biological determinism and idealism. Socialist feminism has, however, more adequately provided a consistent theoretical framework for understanding the issues raised by radical feminists, a framework that explores the relationship between the personal and political, between women's biology and its material context, in terms of the social and economic organization of patriarchal capitalism and its implications for change. It has done this in a materialist way, attempting to avoid both economic reductionism or biological determinism. At the same time, Black feminism's contribution and critique of feminism is crucial, for it has highlighted the ways in which, subjectively and objectively, Black women's oppression is different and how not only the sexual division of labour but the racial and international division of labour, not only patriarchy and

Table 3.1 Feminist critiques of welfare

			(A) New dimensions of analysis	
	Women's oppression caused by	*Role of biology in analysis*	*Relationship between public and private sphere*	*Emphasis on universal or differentiated oppression*
Libertarian feminism	State intervention	Some say: none. Some say: determines women's role	Maintains the division between the two	Differences between women understood as result of individual ability or free choice
Liberal feminism	Sex-discrimination and sex-biased laws	No place in analysis: Inconsequential for women's equality	Maintains division between the two. Emphasizes change in public sphere, but takes into account effect of socialization in private	Little acknowledgement of class or 'race' inequalities
Welfare feminism	Devaluation of motherhood	Determines women's family role	Maintains the division between the two. Emphasizes change in the private sphere	Emphasis on universal oppression but with concern for improvements for British working-class women
Radical feminism	Patriarchy: men's power over women's reproduction and sexuality	Determines women's special nature (and men's exercise of power over women)	Links the two spheres by the assertion that the personal *is* political	Universal oppression emphasized

Socialist feminism	Patriarchal capitalism: capitalist patriarchy; or patriarchy and capitalism separately	Emphasis is upon the social material and historical conditions in which women's biology exists	As above, but also sees reorganization of the relationship between reproduction and production as crucial to change	Recognition of differences of class and sexual orientation, but 'race' only latterly
Black feminism	Racially structured patriarchal capitalism, racist and imperialist patriarchy; or imperialism, capitalism and patriarchy separately	Rejection of biological explanations for racial inequalities. Emphasizes the differential experiences of social and material conditions of biological and social reproduction	As above, but stresses that the relationship between reproduction and production be understood in terms of racism, imperialism and the international division of labour	'Race' and class and other differences crucial to analysis

Table 3.1 *cont.*

	(B) New norms for social policy derived from (A)		(C)
	Relationship between state, family and women	*Principles of eligibility and organization of welfare provision*	*Method of analysis derived from (A) and (B)*
Libertarian feminism	Some say: minimal state intervention to allow for greater individualism and acceptance of women in the market on the basis of ability. Others say: minimal state intervention for equal rights in order to foster natural state of motherhood		Biologically determinist and individualist
Liberal feminism	State to provide anti-discrimination laws and reforms to foster women's equality	Women eligible to access in their own right to state-administered welfare system	Abiological and idealist
Welfare feminism	State to 'endow' motherhood with reforms for mothers and children; state respons-ibility for sexually differentiated needs within the family	Women eligible for wide range of benefits as mothers and wives within state-admini-stered welfare system	Biologically determinist and idealist
Radical feminism	Critique of state at present as representing patriarchal interests and values. Need to challenge this, seize means of reproduct-ion, right to own sexuality and foster woman-centred values	Women eligible in own right. Collective responsibility of women to provide welfare under their control and organized along the non-hierarchical, skill-sharing lines of women-centred values	Biologically determinist and idealist

Socialist feminist	Critique of state at present as representing combined but contradictory interests of patriarchy and capitalism which reinforces women's role as dependent and carer within the family, and low paid worker outside it. Need to challenge this by demanding socialization of caring and reorganization of sexual division of labour and division between paid and unpaid work	Women eligible in own right. Control by women and changing the 'social relations of welfare' – breaking down hierarchies and distinction between provider and user and sexual division of caring – becomes the model for all welfare practice	Materialist, neither biologically determinist nor abiological
Black feminism	Critique of state at present as representing the interests of patriarchy, capitalism and imperialism in maintaining Black women's subordinated position as carer/servant and low paid/migrant worker. Need to challenge this by demanding socialization of caring, reorganization of the sexual division of labour and division between paid and unpaid work and end to international and racial divisions in production and reproduction	Women eligible in own right, regardless of country of origin, or migrant status. Control over non-racist and non-sexist welfare provision with right to autonomous Black provision, changing the social relations of welfare and the racial and sexual divisions of labour	Overall materialist, internationalist, neither biologically determinist nor abiological

capitalism but imperialism too, have to be brought into the analysis of social policy to understand the relationship between the state, the family and women. Whilst the welfare state plays an important role in defining the boundaries of women's lives, in underpinning female dependency and the sexual division of labour within and outside the home, Black feminist analysis forces us to acknowledge that the state nevertheless treats different groups of women in different ways. In demanding a changed basis to the relationship between the welfare state and women, feminists have also made the issues of *who* controls welfare and how it is organized – questions of immediate concern and political priority. Together these critiques have shown that women are as central to the welfare state (and thus to social policy analysis) as the welfare state is to them.

Table 3.1 summarizes the discussion in this chapter, indicating the new policy norms and methods derived from feminist approaches to welfare and also applying the methodological criterion derived from the discussion of existing approaches to welfare which were summarized in table 2.4. These new norms and methods are summarized in table 3.1 as:

(A)   New dimensions of analysis for social policy:
- What causes women's oppression?
- The role given to biology in the explanation.
- The relationship between the public sphere and the private sphere.
- The emphasis on universal or differential forms of women's oppression.

(B)   New normative concerns for policy:
- The relationship between the state, the family, women and sexual division of labour.
- The principles of women's eligibility to welfare provision.
- The principle of the organization of welfare provision.

(C)   New methodological concerns for social policy:
- Whether theories are not only materialist, idealist, individualist, but also biological-determinist or abiological.

In addition, Black feminism highlights the importance of an internationalist analysis. This issue is picked up in the next chapter.

4 The Basis for an Anti-racist Critique of the Welfare State

Introduction

Whilst there are an increasing number of studies of 'race' and racism in relation to the welfare state, and more recognition is being given to struggles against Black oppression and anti-racist policies, these have not coalesced in the same way as happened within the feminist movement and the feminist critiques, to form a distinct anti-racist critique of the welfare state. One reason for this is that from the 1950s until the 1970s much of this work centred upon studies of 'race relations' and associated policy recommendations. In this way, 'race' and racism was very much a discrete and separate area of study and policy-making, which made few connections to the overall nature of social policy. The assertion and evidence of 'institutionalized racism' in the 1970s began to change this. This is the recognition of racism not as an individual prejudice but as a material and ideological force permeating in different ways the major institutions of society, schools, workplaces, police and so on. This was accompanied by a revival of theoretical work on the relationship of 'race' to class and racism to capitalism. Much of the empirical work associated with this development has focused, with good reasons, more on the repressive side of state policy towards Black people – racist immigration policy, law and order policy and practice – than upon state welfare policies traditionally the concern of social policy. In addition, some of this work has found more fertile ground for development in disciplines other than social policy, such as in cultural studies, or education studies. Nevertheless, theoretical and empirical work does exist on aspects of the relation between 'race', racism and the welfare state from which we can begin to construct an anti-racist critique, and to examine some of the challenges this poses to existing approaches within the discipline of social policy. The aim of this chapter is to examine this work.

'Anti-racist' may be too scanty a term to describe the major import of some of the work described in this and the following chapters, for the term has recently acquired a restricted meaning associated with equal opportunities and the policies of local authorities. While these represent an element of anti-racism, I intend to convey, as will be explained, a much broader meaning based on a historical and internationalist (i.e. anti-imperialist) conception of the development of racism.

The discussion of Black feminism in chapter 3 began to indicate some of the dimensions of racism and the welfare state: ideas of Black family 'pathology'; role of Black women as cheap labour in the welfare state; the linking of immigration controls to welfare policy. It also began to extend the context of social policy analysis from patriarchal capitalism to an international context which offered an understanding of imperialism and the international division of labour. In the following discussion we are concerned to examine the way different perspectives on 'race' and racism approach the following questions. To what extent do the dynamics of racism in the welfare state concentrate on personal racism, on institutionalized racism in welfare practice and processes, or on state policy and ideology as manifested, for example, through racist immigration controls or nationalist ideology? Secondly, what are the types of explanations offered for racism – are they individualist, idealist or materialist in their explanations and remedies for racism, and how far they see racism determined by other phenomena – capitalism or 'cultural differences' for example? A third and associated issue is in what context should racism be viewed – the national context of post-war British society or the historical and contemporary international context which draws upon colonialism, imperialism, the global divisions between North and South and the international division of labour? All these issues lead to different views about the relationship between the state and racism, and therefore, between the welfare state and racism, particularly about the extent to which state welfare produces or alleviates racism. These in their turn lead to the question: what welfare policy and practices will serve to eradicate racism and what is the motor of change to produce these? Finally, we might now feel justified, in the wake of the previous chapter on feminism, in asking to what extent these approaches acknowledge gender and the oppression of women.

Table 4.1 on pp. 113–15 summarizes the application of these questions to the different approaches to 'race' and racism that will be discussed.

Approaches to 'Race' and Racism

The approaches examined here are those that have greatest relevance to welfare theory and policy, and fall into two main groups: first, the approaches associated with the sociology of race relations – assimilation theory and cultural pluralism – and secondly, those approaches emerging from studies of 'race' and class – the 'relative autonomy' and 'autonomy' approaches and the 'racialized class fraction' approach. I have included John Rex's work, which in many ways straddles the two camps. For more detailed studies and critiques of these approaches the reader is referred to Miles (1982), Lawrence, Solomos and Carby, in CCCS (1982), Bourne (1980), Hall (1980a), and especially to Robinson (1983) for an account of Black radical thought; and also to the work of Du Bois, C. L. R. James and Richard Wright.

Assimilation and Integration

The development of studies into race relations which aimed at encouraging the assimilation and integration of Black immigrants into British culture took place in the context of the post-war British government's response to its labour shortage problems. The 1945–51 Labour government debated the desirability of importing workers from the Black Commonwealth in terms of their economic cheapness compared with other foreign workers (for example, Italians or Poles). Somewhat ironically Commonwealth workers were deemed 'cheaper' *because* they had British citizenship rights and would need no formal arrangements for their arrival, or accommodation or welfare provision. As Aneurin Bevan said in 1948, 'If colonial subjects come here on their own responsibility and initiative we do all we can to fit them into useful jobs, but they cannot complain if all is not plain sailing' (quoted in Joshi and Carter, 1984, p. 60). At the same time, some problems were envisaged in terms of political and social unrest, particularly by way of the racist and protectionist response of the white working class and trade unions, in the face of the presence of 'uncivilized' and 'culturally backward coloured Colonials'. Neither the Labour nor the subsequent Conservative governments had the weapons or the will within their ideological armoury to attack manifestations of white racism. Nationalism, colonial superiority had been their mobilizing themes during and after the war. So, in so far as the mass immigration of Black workers might bring problems then responsibility for such problems was seen to lie with the immigrant him or herself: he or she would have to adapt, make out or go home.

The immediate response to the arrival of Black immigrants has been described as '*laissez-faire*' (Sivanandan, 1976): no state intervention to provide for housing and welfare needs, and the treatment of immigrants simply as units of labour. What welfare provision did exist was from the voluntary sector: the National Council for Commonwealth Immigrants whose policy was to help immigrants adapt to their circumstances. The general assumptions behind these two responses were that the immigrants in general had few requirements, and secondly, in so far as they did then these would be met as soon as they were assimilated – spoke the language, understood British culture and knew the values of democracy. However, events from the 1950s, like the uprisings in Notting Hill in 1958, revealed the extent of white racism (and also Black resistance to it – see Sivanandan, 1982). The reaction of the state's policy-makers, as well as those who studied policy, was to identify the *numbers* of Black immigrants along with their characteristics – their culture, language and so on – as the social problem requiring action. It was within this framework that the subsequent debate on policies for Black immigrants took place. Official policies combined *integration with Black immigration control;* as Roy Hattersley said in 1965, 'without integration, limitation is inexcusable; without limitation, integration is impossible'. This emphasis on the desirability of integration suggested that there was something about the immigrants – their 'colour', 'culture' or their 'concentration' with other immigrants in particular areas – which posed problems. The consequent policies shockingly reinforced this, especially *dispersal*, whether in education, or housing. A DES circular in 1965 suggested schools should have no more than 30 per cent immigrant children because of the 'serious strains' they caused, and recommended that the surplus Black children be bussed to other schools. The study by Flett, Henderson and Brown (1979) of racial dispersal in council housing in Birmingham shows that such a policy was only possible by systematically ignoring the housing preferences of Black tenants in order to maintain a 'one-in-six' allocation rule. In all these different ways, white racism was appeased and not challenged.

Academic work in the 1960s centred upon the Institute of Race Relations, an independent body whose studies followed Fabian lines – strongly empirical, rather than analytical, problem- and policy-orientated and concerned with influencing government policy and public opinion. Their concern was 'racial harmony'. In *Colour and Citizenship* (1969) Rose and Deakin identified what they called 'the real problems of the adjustment process': 'discrimination' in the form of irrational prejudices and intolerances of individual employers and landlords. The elimination of this through the law was the aim of the Race Relations Acts. The first Race Relations Act of 1965 was limited to 'public' places. The 1968 Act extended the law to housing and employment. Its powers of implementation and redress were weak, however, and it identified Black people's poor housing and employment position as the consequence of prejudice rather than lying within the structure of society, 'not an act, but an attitude' as Sivanandan describes it (1982, p. 117). The 1976 Act was stronger in recognizing the existence of 'indirect' as well as direct discrimination, that is, where a universal practice puts a particular group at a disadvantage. It created the Commission of Racial Equality to carry out its campaigns and investigations, and it permitted, under Section 71 (though it does not require), local authorities to implement equal opportunities policies.

The 1960s also uncovered fears of political instability and outbreaks of racial violence of the sort that had occurred in the United States in the declining urban areas. Urban aid policies followed, such as Section 11 of the 1966 Local Government Act, which allows local authorities to claim grant aid from central government when they have 'substantial numbers of immigrants from the Commonwealth' in their area, as well as the 1968 Urban Programme and the 1977 Inner City Programme. This development represented an offshoot in the conceptualization of 'race problems' and this was the notion of *disadvantage*. Not only did it hide structural racism under problems of and policies for the 'disadvantaged', but it identified the presence of Black people as being an indicator of disadvantage, rather than racism as a factor of poverty, poor housing and low pay.

The quest for assimilation and integration assumed that *cultural*, not *power* differences were the problem: the cultural 'strangeness' of Black people and the quirksome intolerance of whites. The institutions of welfare were taken for granted: if children 'underachieved' at school then it was seen as a problem of language, of different childcare patterns, of different cultural values attached to the meaning of education. If Black families had poor housing then it may have been the prejudices of landlords and housing workers, but it was also seen in terms of the unusual characteristics of those families – they were larger, they were disadvantaged. Such an approach to 'race' and racism ignores the historical dimensions of racism and the structural position of Black people in the development of capitalism. In terms of welfare provision, then, Black people's access to such provision is assumed to be straightforward once they have assimilated into the British way of life. Its recommendations for change shift between a cultural pathology approach often associated with *individualism*, that is a tendency to see individuals, or in this case cultural groups as bearing a responsibility for thier own social problems, and an *idealism* derived from their emphasis on anti-discriminatory reforms. Here, state intervention through education and law to change ideas and attitudes is seen as the way, alongside assimilation, to end racism. Finally, their construction of the problem of racism is set very firmly within *nationalist* boundaries in espousing British democracy and way of life as the framework for assimilation and integration, and issues of class or gender play no part in this analysis. (See summary in Table 4.1, pp. 113 15.)

Cultural Pluralism

Racial harmony never came, but the National Front did and so did economic crisis. In the early 1970s race relations parted company with the policy-oriented researchers and part of it went off with sociology. The sociologists took with them the concept of 'culture', put it under the microscope and fused it with the concept of 'ethnicity'. The emphasis on integration shifted to one of cultural differences and upon encouraging cultural understanding and diversity. 'Cultural conflict' – being between two cultures – was identified as the root of young Black people's problems, their low educational achievement, poor job prospects and increasing unemployment and 'alienation' (for example, *Between two Cultures*, Community Relations Commission, 1970). Although the step forward taken by ethnicity researchers was to examine culture from the immigrant's point of view and in a positive light (for example Khan's study of Mipuri villagers in Bradford, 1979) and to establish the reality of a multi-racial society, nevertheless, looking at 'minority – majority' relationships in a cultural framework excludes vital elements in the relation of 'race' to class and power, and institutionalized racism. This means, however sympathetic the cultural appreciation, it can still skew the analysis and 'blame the victim': Khan, for example, suggests that Asian people do not use welfare provision because they are 'unskilled in informal, matter-of-fact, distance-maintaining interaction typical of urban and Western life-styles' (Khan, quoted in Lawrence, 1982), or because by custom they are able to use their own informal networks. Some multiculturalists have attempted to incorporate the issue of power and resistance and argue that maintenance of cultural norms is a form of 'reactive ethnicity' to white culture (C. Ballard, 1970; R. Ballard, 1979). Jenny Bourne, however, sees this as mistaken. She comments: '"Reactive ethnicity" or cultural resistance can only be a resistance to racialism in British society. Racialism is not about power but about cultural superiority. Racism is not about cultural superiority but about power; and the resistance to racism must in the final analysis be political resistance, expressed perhaps in cultural forms' (Bourne, 1980, p. 345).

Nevertheless, multiculturalism has recently been the dominant approach favoured by social policy writers and policy-makers. The approach has been used especially in education, focusing on linguistic pluralism – the teaching of mother-tongue in schools – on the understanding and celebration of different life-styles, on the exposing of racialist stereotypes in books. The aims of multicultural education are usually framed in humanistic terms: encouraging tolerance and respect. However, the impetus behind multiculturalism and the assumptions about its potential throw some scepticism on the significance it has for improving the education of Black children. It is possible to see multicultural education as developing from two concerns. First, from educational studies which identified Black children's lack of achievement to a poor self-esteem which results from the negative stereotyping of white society (see Milner, 1973, and the critiques of this by Stone, 1981, and Sarup, 1986). The solution to this is seen as encouraging white children's appreciation of Black cultures, and fostering a positive sense of cultural identity among Black children. There are two main problems with this: the assumption that Black children have poor images of themselves and their cultures is not born out by research done by Black researchers (Stone, 1981), by the development of Black pride and Black consciousness, or by the fact that if any group of oppressed people absorbed wholesale the negative attitudes of their oppressors there would exist no history of resistance. The other problem is that in finding a psychological reason for Black underachievement the cause of the problem is deflected from questions of social and economic power in the wider society which schools themselves reflect, and, in addition, it locates the solution within the psyche of the Black child – another way of blaming the victim.

The second impetus for the development of multiculturalism was rather different. This was an official acknowledgement of dissatisfaction amongst Black parents and pupils evidenced by their demand for Black Studies to be part of the school curriculum, and by the development in the 1970s of Saturday schools run on a voluntary basis by Black teachers for Black children in the community. A report from the Select Committee on Race Relations and Immigration in 1973 made it clear that whilst it recognized a need for the teaching of the history and geography and cultures of the 'large minorities', this was not the same as Black Studies for Black children nor would it involve 'turning the curricula upside down' (quoted by Carby, 1982a). This situation led to the criticism that multiculturalism represented an attempt to contain rising dissatisfactions from the Black community as well as further marginalization of Black children from the learning of basic skills for educational achievement (Stone, 1981).

There are further problems associated with multiculturalism. Firstly, seeing the solution to racism as the acceptance of cultural diversity fails to recognize how the existing hierarchy of cultures has a long history, particularly through imperialism, of the imposition of the superiority of white culture. Secondly, particularly since 98 per cent of teachers are white, there is the danger that their teaching of cultural awareness, without reference to racism, may serve to reinforce stereotypes rather than remove them: 'the "steel bands, saris and samosas" approach of cultural pluralism' (Bhavnani, 1986, p. 105). Thirdly, by focusing upon *culture* and not power and inequality, multiculturalism has been unable to hold its ground against the attack from the New Right, who have equated it with the lowering of educational standards, and the demand for a reassertion of British cultural traditions in education. None of this means that the teaching of cultural sensitivity has no place: it has, but as part of the development of a critical awareness in children of the historical development of racism and the meaning of culture within this; an awareness of the reproduction of racism not only at the personal level but within schools, the labour market and state policies; and an awareness of the need to resist these.

The preoccupation with cultural difference within health studies and policies has led to a concentration on the 'exotic' or unusual aspects of Black people's illnesses – rickets, TB, hepatitis – and often special initiatives directed at Black groups have been to the exclusion of not only the way 'race' and racism contribute to ill-health and access to good health care, but the exclusion also of the positive elements of their cultural knowledge and traditional health practices.

The majority of these 'special' health initiatives have met with fierce criticism from some of the communities which they purport to help ... Moreover, the research agendas have been defined by professionals and their perceived priorities of health problems, which are not necessarily those of black people using the Health Service. The emphasis on black pathology in increased morbidity and mortality is mirrored by an emphasis on perceived cultural deficits which policies have presumed to try and rectify. (Pearson, 1986, p. 102)

The influence of this culture-orientated approach can be seen in other ways. Since the 1960s various sets of monies have been available to improve the lives and opportunities of Black people. These include provision under Section 11 of 1966 Local Government Act (though the terms under which this money is available is more by way of 'compensation' for local authorities for the 'problems' incurred by the presence of Black immigrants); Sections 37 and 71 of the 1976 Race Relations Act, which rather ambiguously allows for promotion of equal opportunities programmes, and the Inner Cities Policy of 1977. However, use of these monies by local authorities is heavily influenced by cultural pluralist notions. So, for example, Section 11 money has generally provided for specialist teachers of English as a second language or remedial skills (Ben-Tovim et al., 1986, p. 133). It has not increased the employment levels of Black teachers and in some cases it has simply been used to supplement mainstream education budgets. Money injected into the inner cities has also often, initially, given rise to tokenistic gestures such as the funding of cultural centres. Ben-Tovim et al. document how Wolverhampton in the late 1970s was marked by the 'high profile, albeit gestural response of funding one-off cultural projects' (p. 142). The other response to inner cities money has been to concentrate on general economic and environmental schemes which may, but do not necessarily have any relevance to the needs of the Black community. As Ben-Tovim et al. comment, the irony of the 1977 policy for the Inner Cities (Department of the Environment, 1977) is that for the first time economic and environmental factors were emphasized in an explanation for the cause of urban decline, but at the same time the only race-related initiatives emerging came 'from the remnant philosophy of the old urban programme, with its emphasis on "problem" groups, or group pathology' (p. 141). In addition, as Cross (1982) points out in 1979–80, 62 per cent of the Black population lived outside the areas designated for urban aid under the 1977 Inner Cities Policy. Even where Black groups apply for funds, local authorities do not necessarily allocate the money accordingly. For example, in Birmingham in 1980–1 Black groups applied for one-third of the funds – a figure proportionate to their population in that area. However, they only received 3.9 per cent of what they asked for, compared with 20.6 per cent for other groups and 16 per cent for multicultural groups. Furthermore, Cross (1982) and Solomos (1985) point to the way in which the concept of *'special needs'* or 'special treatment' when imbued with connotations of 'culture' reinforces racism and lack of opportunities. For example, it is acknowledged that unemployment amongst Black youth is disproportionately high, but the 'special needs' programmes offered by the Manpower Services Commission concentrate on 'cultural deficiencies' – language, attitudes – rather than on the racism of teachers, career and training officers and employers. It thus reinforces the process whereby employers believe Black youths on Youth Training Schemes are second-class workers.

Cultural pluralist approaches draw attention to the facts of linguistic or cultural differences, and the need for sensitivity, but at the same time they obscure, with this emphasis, the historical and contemporary differences of *power* between the white and Black populations. The solution to racism becomes cultural understanding and tolerance, and this is seen as the mechanism for change. In this way this approach is idealist: it rests on the assumption that change can come from education or rational argument. Although it attempts to recognize the worth of other cultures, its framework of analysis and prescription for change remains firmly within contemporary and nationalist boundaries (see table 4.1, pp. 113–15). Finally, in so far as women and the family are acknowledged, it is generally in terms of their different cultural patterns, rather than in terms of gender and gender roles.

From Race Relations to 'Race' and Racism

The main challenges to the policy-oriented study of British 'race relations' came in three developments in the early 1970s from mainly Black and Marxist radicals. First, an interpretation of the Black experience in Britain emerged from those who experienced it, rather than those who observed it. This located the problem as stemming from a white society and its institutions steeped in racism, and it transposed Black people from problems and victims, to a people with a history of struggle against imperialism, colonialism and racism in its various forms (see Bernard Coard's 1971 study *How the West-Indian Child is Made Educationally Sub-normal in the British School System*, John and Humphrey's *Because They're Black* (1971) and Sivanandan's essay 'From Resistance to Rebellion', 1982).

Secondly, the study of 'race' was widened by those Marxists who examined the wider context of Black immigration: international capitalism and the movement of labour was the subject of Castles and Kosack's *Immigrant Workers and Class Structure in Western Europe* (1973), Sivanandan's work analysed the 'race' and immigration policies of post-war British governments in terms of the accumulation needs of capital, and identified repatriation not simply as a political slogan of the right but as a possible economic strategy in the context of the new imperialism in Third World countries and the movement of capital from the centre to the periphery (Sivanandan, 1976, 1979).

The third development combined the first two to examine the roots of race oppression and its relation to class exploitation and capitalism. This is an important debate with significant implications for the nature of struggles against Black oppression. It is not, however, an altogether new area of study; these had also been the concerns of earlier Black radical writers like Du Bois, C. L. R. James and Richard Wright in works written from 1915 onwards (see here Cedric Robinson's magisterial account of *Black Marxism* (1983).

In addition to these theoretical developments there were increased levels of resistance by Black people in Britain. The inner-city riots of 1981 in particular pushed many of the local authorities to institute more rigorous equal opportunities policies and anti-racist strategies. The debate about racism was, therefore, also marked by different views on the usefulness or otherwise of these policies.

The 'race' and class debates emerged to deal with basic problems: it is not only social reformist writing which has subsumed the dimension of 'race' and gender, but Marxist writing too. Westergaard and Resler (1975) for example, identify 'race' and gender as variables which simply compound class inequalities. Such an approach hides the ways in which 'race' and racism may operate both *independently* of and at the same time *articulated with* class and the effects of the class structure. Secondly, the coupling of racism with capitalism in some Marxist works, for example the work of Castles and Kosack, appeared to suggest that ultimately the disappearance of capitalism would herald the eradication of racism. This tendency to explain phenomena by reducing their existence to the workings and requirements of capital (for example, racism as a capitalist strategy of divide and rule), known as the sin of *economic* determinism or reductionism, is an aspect of early Marxist writings which has been increasingly criticized by neo-Marxist writers since the late 1960s. In many ways, feminism and works on 'race' and class have added extra strength to these criticisms though there has not always been a reciprocal acknowledgement of this. In relation to 'race' and racism these two problems, the elision of 'race' under class and economic determinism, carry a number of difficulties. First, there are significant studies which identify racism as pre-existing capitalism (Robinson, 1983; Fryer, 1984); second, economic reductionism does not account for other forms of racism, like anti-semitism; third, it tends to a functionalist account of the ruling class's use of Black labour to extract surplus value, and racism to divide and rule, and does not account for why and how the white working class – except through false consciousness – become racist themselves (or even resist it). Black consciousness and resistance is similarly dispraised. And fourth, both the white and Black working class are treated as homogenous groups – little acknowledgement is given to the different histories and varied forms of struggle against, say, colonialism, of Asian, Afro-Caribbean or Afro-Asian groups.

There have been a number of attempts to cope with these problems. My concern here is to examine those approaches which have a *particular relevance or application to the study of the welfare state*, rather than to sift through the varieties of positions on 'race' and class. I begin with John Rex's work. In chronological and theoretical terms this belongs more properly to the former 'race relations' school, but at the same time Rex offers a critique of economic reductionism, an analysis of Black workers as a separate class and, importantly, an analysis where the welfare state is central.

'Race' and the Underclass

Rex's work (1973, 1983; Rex and Moore, 1967; Rex and Tomlinson, 1979) is important because it is one of the few contributions to make the connection between racism and the welfare state, and it also attempts to avoid the economic reductionism of classical Marxism. Central to Rex's analysis is the idea that European industrialized societies are marked by the rights that the working class have won through the trade unions to security of employment, welfare benefits and rights to housing, health and education. These represent a 'truce situation', a political stability to whose maintenance both ruling class and working class are committed. Furthermore, the working class are as much, if not more committed to the maintenance of their welfare rights as they are to their job rights, because housing and education confer their own class/status positions and possibilities. However, the Black immigrant worker (predominantly male in Rex's accounts) is excluded not only from the rights at work, but, within the context of the city, from the housing and education opportunities afforded to the whites. Whilst the working class are incorporated into the welfare state, Black immigrant groups are not, and constitute an *underclass* – a separate class, which may develop its own underclass-consciousness and organize for itself. This use of the concept of the 'underclass' is Rex's attempt to refine the Marxist concept of class, that is, a position measured by one's relation to the means of production (whether you work for a wage, or whether you own capital and employ others). He sees this as too narrow to account for other forms of domination – he is concerned not only with Black workers in post-war Britain, but also with how to explain the differences between Black and white labour in South Africa and the preservation of segregation within capitalism. As far as Britain is concerned, he employs a tool, derived from Weber, of measuring class (or status) in relation to other circumstances – here, one's situation in the housing market and access to welfare benefits. More recently Rex has added 'the right to protection by the primary institutions of law and order' as a further right from which Blacks are excluded, and he sees the move toward equal opportunities policies by some local authorities as an important outcome of underclass political organization (Rex, 1984b).

Rex's analysis has been criticized on a number of accounts – some suggest he moves 'class' too far from the means of production (Bourne, 1980); Miles (1982) questions Rex's implication that the underclass is homogenous and, secondly, his uncritical use of the concept of 'race' and failure to identify it as a social construct; suspicion has been thrown by Gilroy (1980) on his emphasis upon the manageability of the truce situation, compared with the inflammability of the 'underclass'; and Hall, in an important essay discussed below (Hall, 1980a), suggests that while Rex's attempts to refine class are important, he has too readily rejected a 'too-simple' interpretation of Marxism. The concern here is to look more closely at his concept of the welfare state.

Rex's emphasis is on the benefits that accrue to the white working class from welfare, and the process of exclusion of Black people. However, the gap that needs filling is *how* and *why* that exclusion takes place. The suggestion by Rex is that a number of ideas operate together.

The memory, and sometimes the actual experience, of prolonged unemployment, together with the clear understanding of the inferior position of the colonial, can only mean that labour will resist uncontrolled immigration ... if there are limited housing, education and health resources, the appearance of immigrants, even if their arrival is accompanied by equivalent emigration, will seem to lessen the chances of the metropolitan native worker enjoying these benefits. (1973, pp. 85–6)

As an example of this attitude, he quotes the general secretary of the Amalgamated Engineering Union, William Carron, who in 1967, said to his members:

it would be interesting to obtain detailed statistics applying to the grand total that is consumed by educational grants, National Health expenses and subsistence payments that become immediately available by the ever-growing number of individuals who were not born in the country and who in no way contributed towards setting up a fund into which they so willingly dip their fingers. (Rex, 1973, p. 104).

This attitude was not, as Rex suggests, just born out of the post-war coincidence of working class self-interest combined with the colonial heritage, for support by the labour movement for the exclusion of 'aliens' (as well as other groups, like women) from welfare benefits was built into demands for reforms, as well as the platforms of political parties, from the early twentieth century. Defence of welfare benefits also became a basis for trade union support for immigration controls. Exclusion from pensions, unemployment and education grants was written into pre-war social policies, as was the duty of the beneficiary agencies to investigate the nationality of the claimants. The post-war welfare reforms reinforced these through, for example, the 1953 Aliens Act and the 1949 NHS Act which excluded free treatment to people 'not ordinarily resident' in the United Kingdom (Cohen, 1985, p. 90). This intertwining of the ideologies of national efficiency and national chauvinism with the materialism of welfare reforms at the beginning of the twentieth century is a key to understanding the development of labourism and welfare.

Although Rex acknowledges that 'the services of the welfare state are, for the most part, based upon some test of worthiness' (1973, p. 131), in general, the concept of the *truce* emphasizes the welfare state as a gain or concession to the working class, in return for political stability, and, in so far as these benefits are denied to Black people, this happens through racially discriminatory practices which prevent access to such gains. Whilst this conflict model of welfare avoids the difficulties posed by a determinist or functionalist model, it nevertheless obscures the extent to which the welfare state *itself* also reproduces labour power in a gendered and racially stratified form, and maintains social control which at specific times focuses on certain groups. It is not simply a question of those who allocate resources or gatekeep the system. As Black people have gained access to council housing they have found themselves allocated to the 'problem estates' and to those forms of social control and management previously reserved for poor whites and single parents. The education system espoused equal opportunities whilst reproducing the class, 'race' and gender specifications of the labour market. The problem is as much the racism of the welfare state as it is exclusion from it. And that racism results not just in racial inequality and injustice but is part of ongoing relations of power and domination. It is for this reason that some critics have seen Rex's theory as idealist because, ultimately, it reduces racism to the racially discriminatory practices of those who allocate welfare provision and thereby prevent the access of Black people to that provision; that is, it reduces racism to attitudes and personal behaviour (Brittan and Maynard, 1984, pp. 66–7).

However, Rex's analysis *does* offer a historical dimension of the development of 'pre-colonial, colonial and post-colonial' society, although this is rather limited when applied to the welfare state. Secondly, he attempts to avoid any form of economic determinism, first by his insistence that 'race' and racial stratification can operate independently of class, for example, through exclusion from welfare benefits and services, and secondly, by his reference to the subjective – the human agent in change – whether it be white working-class struggle which results in provision through the truce of welfare, or the community-based struggles of the 'underclass', which as he observes, are organized not simply over trade union issues but against imperialism and 'four hundred years of slavery'. He also acknowledges that racism is not just a prejudice but is built into the structure of 'post-colonial societies'. However, Rex's account makes no concession to the concept of gender, and gives the impression that the entire underclass is male. Above all, Rex's analysis lacks coherence, because it is not altogether clear what the relations between class and 'race' are, or what the links between class struggle and underclass struggle are, how they can be forged, or where they are going. Nor, as I pointed out, is there any link made between the structural or historical aspects of racism and the welfare state itself. (See summary in table 4.1, pp. 113–15.)

The Relative Autonomy of Racism

The publication of the essays in *The Empire Strikes Back* by authors from Birmingham's Centre for Contemporary Cultural Studies (CCCS) in 1982 crystallized a theoretical development in ideas about the relationship of 'race' to class. The intellectual roots of this analysis can be traced to an earlier *UNESCO* publication by Stuart Hall in 1980, 'Race, Articulation and Societies Structured in Dominance', (Hall, 1980a) and also to Hall et al.'s *Policing the Crisis: Mugging, the State, Law and Order* (1978). There are some divergences between Hall's work and *The Empire Strikes Back*, particularly in relation to the latter's emphasis on the racist nature of the state and on political strategy; this divergence is pursued most vigorously by Paul Gilroy in *There Ain't No Black in the Union Jack* (1987a), which amongst other things examines the political nature of Black expressive culture.

Nevertheless, these writers have a common intellectual concern which may be summarized as an attempt to give full recognition to the material and ideological ways in which 'race' and racism are experienced and struggled over by people, both Black and white, and as members of a particular class and gender. They attempt not to fall into the trap of economic reductionism on the one hand, where everything is analytically reduced to the needs of capitalism, or into the trap of sociological pluralism on the other, where society is analysed in terms of different counterbalancing forces – whites, Blacks, women, men, bosses, trade unions, and so on – amongst which 'race' and racism take on a free-floating and independent form. Hall describes these positions as, 'the Scylla of a reductionism which must deny almost everything in order to explain something, and the Charybdis of pluralism which is so mesmerised by "everything" that it cannot explain anything' (1980a, p. 343). A further refinement to avoid economic determinism is the stress these writers give to 'historical specificity', that is, the different historical variations in the relationship between capitalism (and earlier forms of production) and 'race'.

In these terms then racism is seen as *relatively autonomous* from the social relations of capitalism – neither totally dependent upon them nor totally abstracted from them. The relationship of 'race' to class is described by Hall in this way: 'Race is thus, also, the modality in which class is "lived", the medium, through which class relations are experienced, the form in which it is appropriated and "fought through". This has consequences for the whole class, not specifically for its "racially defined" segment' (1980a, p. 341). In other words, 'race' affects the way class struggle is experienced and then formulated both in the present and historically. Commercial colonial exploitation, military and economic imperialism, decline of the Empire, rise of independence movements, the importation of immigrant labour to Britain – all of these periods are marked by specific ways in which 'race' was transformed by and reformulated production, exploitation and social relations. Not class, class struggle nor racism are fixed phenomena. But at the same time, it is within this history that the material and ideological roots of racism lie. This, then, is a 'moving picture' analysis of 'race' and racism in its relationship to capitalism. 'Race' is not reduced to the needs of capital but is a 'modality' interacting in a complex way with class, and with gender. Racism is not an autonomous ideology nor an ahistorical constant, but a materially rooted and changing set of ideas.

The authors of these works use this framework to analyse a number of aspects of post-war Britain. An analysis of the way 'race' has become central to the explanations and policies for Britain's economic crisis from the late 1970s onwards is offered by Hall et al. (1978) and also by Solomos et al. (1982). They describe the 'racialization of state policies' – how the themes of British 'nation' and 'culture' have been harnessed to an explanation of economic crisis with moral and political dimensions, in which the presence of Black people threatens national unity, Black cultures threaten British culture and Black youth threaten social stability and British democracy. Black communities, cultures and families are thus seen as pathological, bringing upon themselves the poverty and unemployment and racial violence they endure. The trickle of Black immigrants are identified as 'swamping' the country. These ideas pick up 'commonsense' racism and thread them into a justification for racist policies and heavier social control – the increased policing of immigrants and of Black communities. Solomos (1985) has shown how the image of Black unemployed youth as a 'threat', as 'potentially violent' and as 'alienated' has been a central concern in race-related policies of the 1980s. As such, policies directed at unemployed Black youths have been ineffective through locating the cause of their unemployment not in the institutionalized racism of school and the labour market, but in the supposed 'racial disadvantages' or cultural handicaps (language, attitudes, skills) of Black youth themselves. And, in fearing that the threat of continued racial inequalities will lead to disorder, policies of control and discipline have been sanctioned. Hazel Carby (1982a) examines how post-war schooling for Black children has been constructed around the idea of the Black child as a 'problem' and how the response to this has moved from remedial policies to compensatory policies, and with the crisis, to more coercive schooling. Carby (1982b) and Lawrence (1982) also both offer critiques of feminism and of the sociology of race relations as constructions of dominant white ideas (see previous chapter).

In terms of political strategy Carby and Gilroy both emphasize the importance of autonomous Black community organization and resistance finding expression in struggles over racism in schools, racial violence or harassment on housing estates or from the police. Gilroy (1987a) has elaborated the significance that the anti-capitalist, anti-state and anti-work imperatives of Black expressive culture have for class struggle. He sees them as class struggles experienced and expressed in Black terms. In this way he challenges the Marxist notion that anti-capitalist consciousness develops amongst the working class by virtue of their relation to the means of production (the working class as the historic agent of socialism). This clearly has implications for other social movements like the womens' movement, but there remains a tension between the way Gilroy almost imputes these social movements an element of vanguardism, yet holds tenaciously on to the importance of class struggle (see Stubbs, 1987).

With good reason, reflecting the reality of many Black British peoples' lives today, these writers have concentrated on the more overt manifestations of state racism and less on the local state or welfare state, and struggles within and against them. However, Gilroy (1987a) offers a critical analysis of the Greater London Council's municipal anti-racist strategy of the early 1980s which sets out the problems with this sort of strategy. First, he examines the extent to which such strategies, following as they did the 1981 riots, represent an attempt to incorporate leaders of the Black communities, to transform their struggles into more manageable bureaucratic procedures and to hijack the site of struggle away from those communities to the town hall. Secondly, he questions how far the good anti-racist employment practices within the town hall can be a blueprint for other less bureaucratic and formal institutions. And thirdly, he suggests that the GLC's public awareness campaign assumed a consensus of popular 'anti-racist sensibility' which does not exist. What is less forthcoming in his account is any possible strategy for community-based anti-racist and Black groups or equal opportunities personnel who operate with a clear understanding of these limitations.

Such strategies are more forthcoming from educational policy writers and activists. For example, in her account of the attempt to get Avon County Council to adopt an anti-racist strategy, Reena Bhavnani (1986) stresses the need to shift the local education authority's (LEA) agenda from their multicultural concerns with, for example, Hindu/Sikh and Caribbean studies, monitoring what languages children spoke and talks on why Sikhs wear turbans, to procedures to deal with 'racial abuse, over-representation of Black children in special classes, anti-racist curriculum development, a coherent multilingual policy, the racism of teachers, and why schools fail Black children' (p. 105). This involved the setting up of campaign groups based on Black and white parents, trade unionists and anti-racists in the community which would be 'consulted but not coopted'. Avtar Brah also outlines a strategy for anti-racism in schools, LEAs and as national policy, which is set in an analysis of racism not dissimilar to Hall's and others described above, but with greater stress on gender (Brah and Deem, 1986). She argues for the study of racism to be compulsory in teacher training; the challenging of 'cultural explanations'; eradicating racism in the 'hidden curriculum'; challenging racist elements in assessment and selection procedures; arguing against the perpetuation of a white male hierarchy within teaching; supporting Black teachers and pupils subjected to racist abuse; involving white pupils in an understanding of racism and fostering a non-sexist and non-racist environment. In addition Madan Sarup (1986) uses an anlaysis for 'multiracial' strategies in education which spans personal racism, institutional racism (policies and practices of schools etc.) and state racism, e.g. immigration policies. He sees the need for teaching about and challenging racism in schools to be linked to 'the struggle for a socialist transformation of education', which is about challenging the *forms* and *hierarchies* of education and creating a critical consciousness in children (1986, p. 41).

A final area is the controversy over development of Black professionalism. This has been a significant development in social service departments, with the Association of Black Social Workers and Allied Professionals (ABSWAP), who have made a major intervention in response to the high numbers of Black children in care, and in response to Black family pathology by demanding the right and need for Black children in care to be fostered with Black foster parents, or remain in children's homes where there are Black residential workers (see ABSWAP, 1983; Small, 1984). Small's argument, put briefly, is that in a society structured in racial domination a Black child can only acquire a positive Black identity from a Black parent who has learned to cope with day-to-day racism. Clearly in this argument Blackness or 'race' is seen as the most fundamental division in both the child and the parents' world and in shaping identity. This is a view contested by Gilroy (1987a, pp. 64–8), who suggests that, first, it ignores other divisions that may affect a child's identity – class, gender, neighbourhood – and secondly, that such race essentialism, or 'ethnic absolutism' does not counter but only mirrors the nationalism and cultural essentialism of the New Right, whilst denying the diversity of the histories of the Black populations within Africa, Asia and the Caribbean. He sees no future for Black separatism in a country where the 'black population is too small, too diverse and too fragmented to be conceptualised as a single cohesive nation' (1987a, p. 66). Paul Stubbs's analysis (1985) of the recruitment by social service departments of Black social workers suggests that equal opportunities policy commitments to recruit Black staff have dovetailed with a management concern to use Black social workers as part of a policy of ethno-sensitivity to respond to the needs of Black clients. However, hidden within this is an attempt at greater 'cultural effectiveness in social control', that is, to reach those 'alienated' parts of the community which white social workers cannot reach. It is in response to this that some Black social workers have set up autonomous Black worker groups. Stubbs suggests that those groups that connect their challenge to the reproduction of racism within social work to the social control element of social work and the professional/client divisions, have a greater chance of achieving change. Gilroy takes this further and sees the move against transracial adoption and fostering as misguided: 'The variety of ethnic absolutism which is produced, banishes, or at least salves, the pain which grows in the tension of trying to be black and professional at the same time' (1987a, p. 67). What this question of Black fostering reveals is the contradictions Black professionals face in working 'in and against' the state: on the one hand the promotion of Black fostering stands in danger of giving cultural mileage to the New Right; on the other hand, it provides an opportunity for Black social workers to mobilize, to counter the ideas of Black family pathology and to expose the racist processes by which Black children are taken into care.

Hall's groundwork (1980a) points out the need to have a materialist explanation of 'race' and racism which does not simply reduce the explanation to the economic level but which recognizes the historical specificity of different phases of colonial and imperialist development. He does this by defining racism as relatively autonomous to capitalism, and 'race' as articulating with class, both of these being subject to historical variation. The CCCS authors have applied this to give us a picture of the forms and intensity of state racism, and the significance and historical diversity of autonomous Black struggle, marked out not only by its opposition to capitalism but by an internationalist consciousness derived from its struggles against slavery, colonialism and imperialism, and they have also acknowledged gender as a further dimension. We have, then, in this approach a sensitivity to *historical specificity* and to a *non-reductionist materialism*, as well as an acknowledgement of the internationalist context and of the internationalism which informs some forms of Black resistance: it is a moving picture of 'race', class and gender, or racism, capitalism and patriarchy. If this were to be applied to the welfare state it would clearly take us far beyond the approaches described in chapter 2. However, the authors of the *The Empire Strikes Back* do not address themselves fully to the welfare state or the local state, and in addition, they make little reference in their accounts to another feature of racism which we noted earlier was important for the welfare state: the use of cheap migrant labour which keeps down the cost of welfare provision (Hazel Carby's work is something of an exception here). What they do offer is a thorough-going critique of the way the institutions of the state (including the welfare institutions) reproduce in different ways the subordination of Black people in our society. Whilst this approach recognizes the need for equal opportunities policies, for the provision of more resources to the Black community and the need for the employment of Blacks in significant positions within the local authority to argue for this, it also stresses the limits of such reforms, and places its hope for change on Black organized resistance. Writers differ over the relationship this resistance has to the organized white working class, but certainly it is clear that if this relationship is to be a progressive one then the priorities of the white working class would have to change significantly to begin to take on board the specific demands of the Black community as well as its emphasis on anti-imperialist struggle. (See summary in table 4.1, pp. 113–15.)

The Autonomy of Racism

John Gabriel and Gideon Ben-Tovim (1978, 1979; Ben-Tovim and Gabriel, 1981; Ben-Tovim et al., 1986) argue that the relative autonomy approach described above still does not, in the end, avoid a determinist trap of reducing 'race' to class and racism to capitalism. The only guarantee against this is firstly to see racism as having its own *autonomous* formation as complex and contradictory as its repercussions, and secondly by having, as the starting-point of theory, a concrete analysis of the way racism and struggles against racism operate at any particular historical moment and in any given situation. What is particularly significant for social policy is that, with Kathleen Stredder and Ian Law (Ben-Tovim et al., 1986) and unlike the Relative Autonomy Group, these authors have directed more of their attention at the 'racisms' which operate at the level of local government and local statutory welfare services. They suggest that a deconstruction of racism at this level opens up the possible spaces in which local anti-racist struggles can manoeuvre. This, in their view, is a necessary corrective to the accounts of racism which link it solely to the needs of capital, or which concentrate on the 'high profile' state racism of immigration and law-and-order policies, which offer little hope for the here-and-now struggles against racism. Their view is that the actions of the state are more contradictory and therefore open to pressure and reform. They thus indentify a number of different ideologies which operate to reinforce racial inequalities.

In their study of Wolverhampton and Liverpool (Ben-Tovim et al., 1986), they identify the ideology of *universalism* in the operation of the statutory social services in which housing officers, teachers, youth leaders and local councillors obscure the needs of Black people by emphasizing the need for provision to be seen as fair and equal. However, the ideology of *labourism* operates in different ways. First there is the labourism of Militant socialism, which maintains the supremacy of *class* struggle over any other forms of struggle – race or gender – which are seen as dividing the working class, and thus in a different way obscures the specific forms of racism suffered by the Black working class (Ben-Tovim et al. provide a very readable and worthwhile documentation of the struggle to get a Race Relations Unit and Equal Opportunities Policy in Liverpool). Secondly, there is also the labourism of Wolverhampton's Labour Group which stems from its roots in the white male trade union movement of the 'black country' (i.e. North Midlands), which historically has been protective towards its own priorities. Cutbacks in local expenditure have provided the rationalization to marginalize the meeting of Black demands. The strength of Ben-Tovim and his co-authors' work is to identify in well-ordered detail the sets of racist assumptions which operate through these ideologies, and how anti-racist struggle can be organized to attack such assumptions. However, in distancing themselves from the 'grand' materialist approach which links racism to class exploitation, and which sees many state policies as implacably racist, it can be argued that they move too far in the other direction, and fail to analyse the links between racism at the local level and the high-profile racism of immigration and law and order policies. In fact they suggest: 'Although these ideologies do not originate within the institution itself they have become an integral part of the traditions and mores of institutional practice' (Ben-Tovim et al., 1986, p. 64). But this still leaves the question: where *do* these ideologies originate? Furthermore, where does anti-racist ideology spring from? Doesn't a historical account of state housing provision show some very tenacious links between council housing, race and empire (see Jacobs,

1985) even though these take different forms of expression? Was not the ideology of nationalism a central feature of the popular democratic propaganda of the post-war welfare state? While Gabriel and Ben-Tovim recognize the historical specificity of racism at different periods of time (though, in fact, they do not offer a historical account), their tendency is to see these forms of racism as *so* specific as to be suspended in time, unattached from the cause and effect of any economic structure. Whilst the details of local racist practice fill an important gap, and the authors' ability to relate theory to practice is important, the account limits the explanations of the racism of the welfare state to the practices themselves, rather than the historical basis of social imperialism, eugenics and nationalism in both welfarism and labourism. Their emphasis on the dynamics of struggle within the local state is important, but they have moved over in this to an idealist notion of change where human action, fuelled by anti-racist ideas, determines all. It is not clear where this anti-racist consciousness springs from, how it is related to class-consciousness, nor how these struggles within the local state may relate to the sorts of struggles in the Black community detailed, for example, in *Heart of the Race* by Bryan et al. (1985), mentioned in the previous chapter. Indeed, the complexity of 'race' and gender does not feature strongly in their work. Further, the emphasis on policy changes, without the backcloth of the dimensions of (high profile) race oppression, suggests that these policy changes are solutions themselves, rather than fragile toe-holds in a struggle against the complex form of class exploitation and race and gender oppressions.

These authors *do* address the problems of economic determination, and they *do* attempt to provide an analysis of racism and anti-racist struggle in the local state. In their view, intervention by Black and white groups committed to anti-racism at the local level, in political parties, local authorities, community organizations, can significantly reduce racial inequalities in the local and welfare state, and bring about 'the institutionalization of anti-racism'. By demanding the implementation of equal opportunities policies, the use of, for example, Section 11 monies, and the employment of Black professionals, it is possible to challenge the racism of the ideologies of universalism and labourism. On the other side, however, it can be argued that the framework in which they rest their analysis demands such a degree of specificity and autonomy of racism as to render the analysis, in the end, ahistorical and idealist. Futhermore, by distancing themselves so far from the racism of such state policies as immigration control, which can only be understood in an internationalist context, they provide, like much social policy analysis, a framework limited by national boundaries and national prescriptions. (See summary in table 4.1, pp. 113–15.)

The Political Economy of Migrant Labour

It was noted earlier that one of the important elements in an anti-racist critique of welfare should be a recognition of the role of Black workers *within* the welfare state, particularly as a source of cheap labour aimed at keeping down welfare costs. Of all these approaches discussed so far, perhaps only the Black feminist critique outlined in the previous chapter gives due recognition to this aspect (see for example Amina Mama's (1984) use of Doyal et al.'s (1981) work). There are, however, two sets of writers in the 'race' and class group who *do* make this aspect the centre of their analysis (although theoretically they differ) and therefore have relevance to the study of the welfare state. They are, first, A. Sivanandan, and secondly, Robert Miles and Annie Phizacklea. The latter have also been concerned to provide a non-reductionist analysis of racism.

Sivanandan's writings are mainly to be found in the journal of the Institute of Race Relations, *Race and Class*, and the three essays of particular relevance here are all to be found in *A Different Hunger* (1982): *'Race, Class and the State',* (1976); 'From Immigration Control to Induced Repatriation', (1978); and *'Imperialism and Disorganic Development in the Silicon Age'* (1979). The first two essays (1976, 1978) take the exploitation of labour and resources from the colonies and ex-colonies for the maintenance of British capitalism as central to an analysis of the British post-war state's 'race relations' and immigration policies. In the 1950s 'Colonialism had already underdeveloped these countries and thrown up a reserve army of labour which now waited in readiness to serve the needs of the metropolitan economy' (see 1982, p. 102). The cheapness of this labour force lay in their restriction to low paid work and also in the fact that their social costs (their own education, and often the welfare of their dependents) was borne by the countries from which they came. The introduction of immigration controls from 1962 is analysed as an attempt to maintain a political stability threatened by white racism, as well as to diminish the rights of immigrant workers in line with other West European countries' use of short-term contract migrant labour, which was more suited to the new capital-intensive development of Britain's economy which had absorbed all the unskilled labour it needed. The third essay (1980b) examines the political and economic implication of the new economic developments in imperialism. Earlier imperialism was marked by a shift of labour from the Third World to the centres of capital in the West. The new shift is for capital and production, particularly the new micro-chip production, to move away from the West to the areas of cheap labour in the Third World, like the Free Trade Zones of Sri Lanka. The social costs of these developments are the massive super-exploitation of Third World workers (often young women) and high unemployment of workers in the West, and it is, as Sivanandan points out, the former who will provide the 'living dole' of the latter. The political costs of this are the move towards the 'corporate state maintained by surveillance for the developed countries, and authoritarian regimes and gun law for the developing' (see 1982, p. 156).

The heavily functionalist overtones of these analyses (Black labour fulfilling capitalism's needs) has been the main criticism directed at Sivanandan's work (see Miles, 1982; Gilroy, 1987a). Nevertheless what he draws our attention to is the use of cheap Black labour in post-war Britain; this clearly has implications for who has borne and who will bear the costs of the welfare state. He also sets the actions of the British state in implementing immigration controls into the context of the development of international capitalism. Finally, though he offers no specific prescriptions for welfare strategy, he sees the agent of change as the working class – especially the anti-racist, anti-imperialist Black working class, within which he attributes as much resistance to Black women as to Black men.

In a very different way Miles and Phizacklea (Miles, 1982; Miles and Phizacklea, 1979, 1984; Phizacklea and Miles, 1980) have raised the issue of migrant labour in terms of its theoretical centrality to racism. Briefly, then, for these authors the concept of 'race', particularly as used by the sociologists of 'race relations' or even by the CCCS authors, is ultimately a reactionary and problematic concept. Its use as an analytical starting-point is misguided and idealist because 'race' as such does not exist, it is merely a construction, and a reactionary construction at that, used by politicians, policy-makers and others as an indication that the problem is 'race' (i.e. Black people) when in fact the problem is racism. The object of study, according to Miles and Phizacklea, should be racism, and the understanding of racism must be set in terms of the historical and material conditions which give rise to it through *the process of racialization.* In contemporary society, the specific historical and material condition associated with this process is the use of migrant labour by capitalist societies. This is at the root of the racialization process and has resulted in what they call the formation of Black people as a *racialized fraction* of the working class (or any other class). However, whilst this economic dynamic is at the root of the racialization process, and also at the root of resistance to this process, it does not prevent racism from taking on independent forms at the political or ideological level (that is, racisms based on ideas of culture or law-breaking). At the same time the effect of these racisms is still circumscribed by the material structure in which they operate. Miles also qualifies two aspects of his analysis. First, he suggests that whilst the state in Britain has done little to alleviate racial inequalites, it does not follow that racism is *necessarily* funtional or beneficial to the state, For example, violent racist or anti-racist protests shake political stability and unmask the ideology of liberal democracy. However, it could also be argued back that the way the state intervenes to quell such protest itself reinforces racist ideas; for example, assimilation after Notting Hill in 1958, or the exercise of greater police control of the community after Tottenham in 1985 (see Stubbs, 1987). Secondly, he maintains that the experience of racism must not be seen as identical for all Black groups: the threat of repatriation has been met with greater resistance by 'second generation' British-born Blacks than by the first generation of immigrants, for example.

Clearly, Miles and Phizacklea attempt to provide a thorough historical materialist understanding of racism which is clearly distinct from the idealism of the 'race relations' school and authors like Ben-Tovim and Gabriel. They try hard to avoid determinism by acknowledging the relative autonomy that racism takes. In addition, they weave gender into their explanation (see Phizacklea, 1984). For all these points their work has theoretical significance. For social policy it has significance because, like Sivanandan, they provide a political economy of migrant labour and draw our attention to the international context of capitalism which gives rise, in this and other countries, to the use of migrant labour for specific purposes. Though they are not concerned with welfare policy implicitly, they point to the ways in which the state *devises different strategies to deal with the social reproduction costs and welfare needs of its labour force, and how these may be additionally influenced by racist and nationalist ideologies of welfare.* However, criticism has been levelled at Miles and Phizacklea, first of not sufficiently avoiding the determinist trap (Brittan and Maynard, 1984) 'since ... racial categorization ... in the final analysis will be determined by those productive conditions' (p. 46). The case against accepting some kind of determination is a difficult one, as we saw with the 'autonomy' approach. A more significant criticism for our concerns is that it is not clear how some of the forms of Black community-based struggles around, for example, racial violence in schools or on housing estates fit into their analysis, for little reference is made to these, yet these are significant forms of welfare struggle. (See summary in table 4.1, pp. 113–15.)

Conclusion

The first part of this chapter looked at aspects of racism and the Black experience of the welfare state which find little mention in either descriptive or analytical accounts of social policy. The second part looked at the range of theoretical explanations for racism which might help to provide a framework to understand and explain these aspects. Having discounted two approaches derived from 'race relations' studies, for their idealism and their failure to give attention to the structural context of racism, I began to suggest that the approaches derived from the explorations of the relations of 'race' to class might be more fruitful. To summarize: Rex's concept of the underclass provides an important study of the exclusion of Black people from welfare rights, the significance of which social policy writers have consistently failed to acknowledge. He offers a limited historical approach, but is uncritical about, and fails to explain, the racism of the political and welfare institutions from which Black people are excluded. Ben-Tovim and Gabriel's contribution is the application of their theory to the complexity and variety of racisms, and possible struggles against them, operating within the welfare and local state; this is an area badly neglected by writers on both social policy and 'race' and racism. However, in terms of their analysis, they insist on such a degree of historical specificity for racism as to leave no room for an understanding of its historical development, and secondly, they insist on such a degree of autonomy for racism as to leave no room for any materialist explanation, which leaves us to suppose that racism exists as a result of the practices consequent upon wrongful ideas and policies. In addition, both these analyses have little to say about the relationship of race to gender oppression. We are left with the theories of relative autonomy and of migrant labour and the process of racialization. These would seem to provide a better theoretical basis for an understanding of 'race', racism and the welfare state, though none of these writers have sought to apply their analyses to the welfare state. Both the 'relative autonomy' group and Miles and Phizacklea attempt to provide an explanation for racism which neither reduces it totally to the dynamics of capitalism, nor fails to acknowledge the different historical and materialist contexts of its development and the struggles against it. In the end, any resolution of this problem of the autonomy of racism can only be made by applying the analysis to the real world, and here John Solomos's conclusion seems to be sensible:

It seems to me that it is important to insist on the complexity of 'dermination of the last instance', while accepting that there is some form of determination of racism of other social relations. For example, within the context of economic decline and political crises-management during the post-war period, can one really talk of the autonomy of 'race' from other social relations? Or can one separate out the political meanings which are attached to 'race' today from the actions of successive governments defining and redefining decades? Or can one understand the long-term patterns of inclusion and exclusion of black workers in the labour market without an analysis of the restructuring of British industry during this period? (Solomos, 1986, p. 105)

What these two sets of approaches and Black feminism offer in their analyses is the room to understand the historical development of racism and its changing relationship with patriarchal capitalism, the economic, political and cultural expressions of racism, the 'racialization' of 'state' policies and the importance of Black resistance in this process, and the international context of migrant labour and the global divisions of labour.

All these aspects are crucial in my view to understand the links between social imperialism, neo-imperialism, immigration control and nationalism in the development of both labourism and welfare capitalism. In addition, these provide a broader framework in which to understand the sometimes contradictory (and sometimes not) relationship between the repressive areas of law and order on the one hand and the administration of welfare benefits and services on the other, *and* the range of struggles over them. Drawing from these two sets of analyses, as well as from Black feminism, we might begin to have an approach to welfare which is formulated according to the experiences of Black men and women as workers (including welfare workers), as consumers of welfare, and as those engaged in struggles over welfare. It has to be based on a historical analysis of racism, imperialism and neo-imperialism, and their articulation with the main goals of the welfare state: accumulation, reproduction, control, legitimation/repression. Class struggle, women's struggles and class conflict too must be deconstructed to understand their relationship – ideological and material – to racism, imperialism and neo-imperialism, patriarchy and other forms of oppression. And our strategy for welfare must be informed and regenerated by the needs articulated by Black people themselves, both in Britain and internationally.

Clearly this provides a major challenge to existing approaches to welfare. How far do they provide the basis for a historical account of the welfare state in terms of capitalism's relationship to the specific aspects of racial domination? How far do they provide a materialist explanation for racism which does not simply reduce it to the economics of capitalism, nor loosens it so much from this structure that it becomes a free-floating idea? And finally how far do they recognize the importance of the international economic context? In short, we want an analytical framework for the study of the welfare state which is not just historical-materialist but historically specific, materialist but not reductionist, and internationalist.

Table 4.1 summarizes this discussion and indicates the different explanations offered for racism; the consequential actions necessary to eradicate racism; the extent to which gender is an acknowledged part of the analysis; the national or international context of the analysis; and the method of analysis. This summary may be interpreted as contributing new policy, theoretical and analytical concerns for social policy. These are:

(A)   New dimensions of analysis for social policy:
- What is the cause of racism?
- What is the relationship of racism to the economic organization of society?
- In what context should racism be understood: national or international?
- What is the impact of racism upon Black women and the Black family?

Table 4.1 Explanations for racism and Black oppression

	Racism caused by	Racism eradicated by
Assimilation and integration	Failure of immigrants to assimilate plus white prejudices	Policies which encourage integration in housing, education etc. and laws which discourage discrimination
Cultural pluralism	Lack of cultural awareness from host community	Policies and practices which encourage the acceptance of a multicultural society
Race and the 'under-class' (Rex)	Colonial heritage and protectionism of white working class closes off access to housing and welfare rights for Blacks	Effective policies to ensure equality of opportunities in welfare and employment services, plus full involvement of Black people in democratic and political processes (TUs, political parties etc.)
Relative autonomy (CCCS)	Racism takes different forms according to specific historical conditions. Rooted in the shifting historical relations of capitalism to colonial domination, but takes on a relatively autonomous ideological form, permeating all areas of life and being a site of struggle	Confrontation of racism at all levels, with particular emphasis on separate cultural/political organization of Black people and its potential to reformulate class struggle in an opposition to an imperialist and patriarchial capitalism and state racism
Autonomy (Gabriel and Ben-Tovim)	While racism today is the produce of very specific historical and contemporary conditions and struggle, it is neither caused nor determined by these but has its own autonomous formation and dynamics	Anti-racist campaigns and struggles in local, political, and community organizations for policies aimed at racial equality

Table 4.1 cont.

	Racism caused by	Racism eradicated by
International division of labour		
Sivanandan	An ideology rooted in colonialism and used by modern international capitalism and the capitalist state as a justification for exploitation, but discarded when the social costs are too high, leading to immigration controls and repatriation	Struggles by Black workers and communities deepening and broadening class struggle to be anti-imperialist and anti-racist as well as anti-capitalist
Miles and Phizacklea	Racism is a product of, and reproduced by, the 'racalization process' and whilst this is determined by the historical development of the relationship of capitalism with colonialism, it nevertheless becomes part of political and ideological as well as economic relations	Struggles by the Black working class which are struggles against racism in the context of capitalism, and which aim to win the support of the labour movement

	Acknowledgement of impact of gender	Context of analysis	Method of analysis
Assimilation and integration	None	Nationalist (Britain)	Individualist, idealist and ahistorical
Cultural pluralism	None	Nationalist (Britain)	Idealist, ahistorical
Race and the 'under-class' (Rex)	None	Internationalist	Historical and materialist but with broader and non-economic definition of class
Relative autonomy (CCCS)	Recognition mainly by Black feminists in this group (i.e. Carby, Parmar) of entwining of specificities of race and gender	Internationalist	Historical, materialist, non-reductionist
Autonomy (Gabriel and Ben-Tovim)	None	Nationalist	Idealist, recognizes structure but strictly non-determinist
International division of labour Sivanandan	Recognition of struggles of Black women and women workers	Internationalist	Historical materialist
Mies and Phizacklea	Recognition of divisions in working class, along both racialized and gender lines	Internationalist	Historical materialist and non-reductionist

(B)   New policy concerns for social policy:
- What is the relationship between the state, the welfare state and the political economy of migrant labour?
- Should there be a nationalist basis to welfare eligibility, and what is the meaning of 'nation' and 'national' in welfare policy?
- What racisms exist in welfare policy and practice, and what policies and practices would eradicate them?

(C)   New methodological concerns for social policy:
- Whether theories are not only individualist, idealist, functionalist or materialist, but also reductionist or non-reductionist, and nationalist or internationalist.

5 The Perspectives Revisted: a Reassessment of Anti-collectivism, Social Reformism and Political Economy of Welfare in Terms of Gender and 'Race'

Introduction

New questions from the feminist and anti-racist critiques emerged in chapters 4 and 5 about the role of the welfare state in relation to women and the family, women and paid work, and the sexual division of labour as well as racism and the Black family, immigration control and the racial and international division of labour. These questions cover areas of which the existing perspectives of welfare, described in chapter 3, make little mention, and which do not feature in most welfare analyses. Yet it is clear that these are issues that have been integral to the development of state welfare in Britain (and indeed in other Western capitalist countries) and are central to the welfare experiences of women and Black people. It also began to be evident in the preceding chapters that new conceptual tools were needed to understand the oppressions of women and Black people, tools which have not been part of the intellectual kit of most welfare thinkers. Amongst these are ways of understanding the distinction and relationship between the private sphere and home and family and the public sphere of paid work and production; of understanding the distinction between biology and its social and economic context, to avoid biological, 'race', or cultural determinism or essentialism; of understanding divisions and differential experiences of welfare beyond class divisions to avoid a false universalism; of understanding the welfare state in an international context of imperialism and the global political economy of migrant labour. The aim of this chapter is to explore to what extent the existing welfare perspectives deal with the welfare issues pertinent to 'race' and gender, and, in so far as they do, to evaluate the conceptual tools they use, and, in so far as they do not, to suggest why not. The argument here is that it is not simply that some of these perspectives have *omitted* to mention 'race' and gender but that for the most part, the cast of their thinking inhibits a full understanding of the welfare experiences of women and Black people. We return to the five perspectives outlined in the conventional classification of chapter 2: anti-collectivism, non-socialist welfare collectivism, Fabian socialism, radical social administration and political economy of welfare. Their understanding and, where appropriate, their policy, on women and the family and on 'race' and racism are now examined.

Anti-collectivism

It was pointed out in chapter 2 that the strands of anti-collectivist thinking have shifted over time. First there is the economic liberalism of writers like Hayek and Friedman derived from nineteenth-century *laissez-faire* philosophy, which is labelled *neo-liberalism*, and secondly, a new form of conservative thinking, *neo-conservatism*, which places more emphasis on maintaining authority, morality and law and order, if necessary through a strong state (this is sometimes referred to as social authoritarianism – see Gordon and Klug, 1986). The ideology of the New Right administration of Margaret Thatcher is made up of both strands.

Women and the Family

In relation to women and the family neo-liberals and neo-conservatives have both a similarity and a difference. They are similar in that in both philosophy and practice women as a category are subsumed under the family unit, there to fulfil what are seen as natural, biologically determined roles: bearing, rearing and caring. They are different in that neo-liberals such as Friedman and Hayek say little about women or the family – they appear as 'an occasional appendage to the world of production' (Pascall, 1986). By contrast, the articulation and model of family life has been the linchpin of the New Right's economic and social policies. Central to the philosophy of Friedman and Hayek is the *liberty of the individual*, though the two writers arrive at the concept via different routes; Friedman's emphasis is on liberty (or freedom) in the market place, and Hayek's on freedom from coercion, and thus economic freedom. However, it can be argued that neither liberty nor individualism in this context has any relevance for women: they are men-only concepts. Hayek and Friedman depict the family as a 'natural', basic and private unit to be preserved from state interference particularly in the form of welfare provision. As such the implication is that it is women who will carry out the domestic and caring roles within the family, and men as wage-earners and heads of household will engage in the market place. What this means is that only men are individuals, and liberty is only attainable by them in the public sphere, and not by women, who are not individuals but part of the family unit in the private sphere.

Another writer on the right gives greater attention to the family and women: Ferdinand Mount's book *The Subversive Family* (1982) claims that the family's historical resistance to outside interference by the Church, state, or welfare state and its insistence on privacy render it an important guarantor of liberty. He goes further than Hayek and Friedman when he acknowledges that 'Women's rights to equality are unassailable because women are human beings' (1982, p. 241). However, like Hayek and Friedman, Mount insists that biology and 'natural instincts' play a major role in determining differences in men and women's behaviour; he reinforces the separation of the private sphere of the home and the public sphere of work; he idealizes the private sphere and relations within it, and he fails to identify the ways in which the private and the public spheres are closely interlinked, particularly in maintaining women's inequality. All this means that these writers cannot come to grips with one of the basic contradictions of neo-liberalism: while women are subsumed in the private sphere of the family, then its promise of liberty can only apply to men (Wayler, 1986).

Many of the policies of the New Right follow a neo-conservative view of the family as upholder of decent values of law and order, a characteristic it shares with a strong state. The family is, nevertheless, still a 'natural' form, as Roger Scruton argues: 'the family, then, is a small social unit which shares with civil society the singular quality of being non-contractual, of arising (both for the children and the parents) not out of choice but out of natural necessity' (1980, p. 31). The irony of this situation, in terms of New Right policies, is that in spite of the philosophy that state intervention interferes with the 'naturalness of family functions', in fact the New Right has resorted to state policies and legalization to reinforce families' responsibilities. One example is in the removal of householder status from unemployed under-25s which forces them back into dependence on their families. Scruton argues, in contrast to Mount and Hayek who see the family as a domain to be preserved from state interference, that state intervention is necessary to strengthen the role that the family plays in fostering hierarchy, authority and loyalty. He therefore sees 'family-law' as inevitable (see Levitas, 1986, chapter 3).

In general, neo-conservative policy the family and the traditional sexual division of labour are not assumed as they are in Hayek and Friedman's writings, but spelt out as part of a programme of social and economic policy. The family has become a central theme in welfare policies, law and order, monetarism and morality. The welfare state, the New Right argues, has divested the family of its role, and by the same token the cutting back of state provision will lead to the restoration of care of old and young to the family, will give the family greater spending freedom and choice and will strengthen it in its traditional caring role. Also part of the traditional role is one of transmitter of discipline, morality and order, a role whose reinforcement may ironically, require state legislative intervention. Thus football hooliganism, riots, promiscuity, drug abuse are often blamed on the lack of parental authority. The (failed) attempt in 1985 by Victoria Gillick to prevent the provision of contraception to girls under 16 years of age was a reassertion of that parental authority (see David, 1986). In addition, the family serves as an organizing model for monetarism and the 'nation'. The family and nation are seen as parallel: self-contained and private, looking after their own, earning its own money and spending its own money, shopping wisely in the market place of health and education. It has been suggested that this is even reflected in Mrs Thatcher's presentation of herself as disciplinarian mother of the Family/Nation and prudent housewife budgeting for the Family/Nation:

The people who give everything to their children because they don't like to exercise family discipline, don't get it right. And its the same in politics. You've got to do the things you believe to be right and explain them. Some of them will hurt. But you just can't retreat. (Margaret Thatcher, 1981, quoted in Fitzgerald, 1983)

The form that this family takes is a patriarchial one in which father is breadwinner and mother is dependent but economic consumer on behalf of her family as well as engaged full-time in care and nurturance of her dependent children and husband. An Institute of Economic Affairs document summarizes this as 'men will expect to specialise in market work and women will expect to specialise in household work' (Papps, *For Love or Money*, quoted by Levitas, 1986, p. 98). Both neo-liberals and neo-conservatives suggest that women's traditional role in the family as carer and preserver of moral order is biologically, or God-given. Even though neo-conservatives draw parallels between the family and the state, the distinction between the private and the public is maintained, in the sense that, apart from exceptional cases like Margaret Thatcher, the place of the majority of women is seen to be in the private realm of family. On the other hand, the neo-conservatives, in contrast to neo-liberals and other dominant political philosophers, elevate the family and morality to issues of public debate rather than consigning them to the recesses of taken-for-grantedness.

'Race' and Racism

Again, some differentation should be made between the neo-liberal and neo-conservative positions. The former's emphasis on the freedom of the market might lead them to disfavour immigration controls as restricting the free movement of labour, and their individualism would have no place for legislating against the discriminatory practices of individuals. Friedman argues the the impersonality of the market overrides personal discrimination: people do not question the colour of the hand that grew the wheat in their bread (Friedman, 1962). The issue of 'race' remained relatively hidden in neo-liberalism until the overt racism of Powell's speeches against Black immigrants in the 1960s. David Edgar (1986) argues that the emergence of new racist ideas cloaked in ideas of nation and culture was partly an attempt to dissociate the New Right from the spread of virulently racist fascism which Powell's speeches encouraged.

These ideas from neo-conservatives such as Scruton, Casey and Honeyford, have a particular theory of nation and 'race' which focuses on cultural difference. The proof of this theory is a belief that social cohesion lies in national unity. The 'sense of nation' derives from a shared history, way of live, custom and overall sense of loyalty to 'one's own kind'. Ultimately, however, this loyalty is explained in biological reductionist terms as natural or instinctive. Thus, cultural differences are seen as inevitably producing conflict. But, Barker (1981) points out that this ideology relies far less on ideas of an innate or genetic superiority of one group over another. In effect, however, given that most adherents to this ideology are arguing for their white British culture in a society where power lies with the white British, they are reinforcing and justifying that domination. For Scruton, Casey and others, the threat to national unity comes from the cultural differences of the Black communities and their resistance to assimilation into British culture. Thus in Casey's view (discussed in Seidel, 1986) West Indians are undisciplined, resent authority, have low educational standards, a different family structure and are predisposed towards crime. Asians' 'problem' is in the strength of their culture, in their large numbers and 'their profound differences' which inhibit assimilation. The answer can only be forced assimilation or repatriation. The case in Bradford, where Ray Honeyford attacked multicultural education (Honeyford 1983, 1984, cited in Seidel, 1986) is an example. Here, Honeyford takes issue with mother-tongue teaching and the removing of textbooks with negative Black stereotypes as a threat to culture and national identity. The methodological individualism of the neo-conservatives' approach rejects a structuralist view of racism, and attempts to give intellectual respectability to racist ideas by representing such ideas as patriotism. Sherman makes the distinction in these terms: 'Racism is largely a New World phenomenon deriving from the aftermath of slavery ... Nationhood and natural consciousness are a positive force, providing a sense of belonging, social cohesiveness, patriotism and civic consciousness' (Sherman, 1979, quoted in Barker, 1981; Seidel, 1986).

This defence of nationhood as untainted by racism ignores the fact that such concepts or forces do not exist in isolation from British imperialist history or from present power relationships in British society, but are very much part of it. Whilst the neo-conservatives deny the existence of institutionalized racism, their concepts of culture and nation are part of it, and reinforce the material and ideological processes of racial domination. As Seidel comments, 'Power helps to construct the concept which can be used to consolidate the legitimate power, and the concept of nation, predicted on race, is one such concept' (1986, p. 130).

Elements of both the neo-liberalism and neo-conservatism are reflected in the policies of the New Right. On the one hand there was, until the riots in 1981, a playing down of any intervention to stop racism, in line with free market thinking. So, for example, the Commission for Racial Equality was cut back in spite of mounting evidence of inequalities. On the other hand, immigration controls have been more harshly instituted to preserve the 'British way of life', to avoid the country being 'swamped' as Mrs Thatcher described it. This has been backed up by greater policing of Black communities and the association of Black people as a threat to British culture, to law and order and democracy. There have also been attempts to discredit and weaken anti-racist strategies, by accusing anti-racists of being the real racists by demanding special privileges for Blacks at the expense of whites, or by disempowering or abolishing local authorities where Black organizations had found funding support or where equal opportunities policies had been promoted (see chapter 6).

In general, then, in the ideology of some of the New Right 'racism' is identified as a natural defence of, and loyalty to culture and nation, unlike the liberal position of Friedman who saw competition and market-freedom as a universal concept privileging neither nation nor colour. Like the family, the theme of British culture and defence of the nation has been a principal motif in the composition which attempts to win popular support for social and economic policies, and has served not simply to appease white racism, but in many ways, to support it.

Social Reformism

In describing the development of the social reformist mainstream social administration in chapter 1. I have already indicated how a number of features of the mainstream led to its 'race' and gender blindness. Its empirical and atheoretical nature led it to take certain things for granted, amongst them the family and the sexual division of labour, immigration control and racial division of labour. Its government and policy orientation meant that debates centred upon the role of the state as against the market; upon public power and public dependency and not the private power and dependency relationships between men and women, or the power relationships between whites and Blacks. The concern was equality and redistribution *between* families and not *within* them. The concentration on the statutory social services meant that most of the unpaid caring work done by women within the family was overlooked, and their needs were subsumed under their families or their husbands. The emphasis upon the benefits of *state* provision also inhibited a critical approach first to the sexist and racist manner in which such provision was delivered, and secondly to the ways in which the welfare state, as employer, reinforced a sexual and racial division of labour amongst its own welfare workers. The historical perspective of the welfare state in relation to women had been to see them primarily as mothers and wives, in other words, both their biology and their economic dependency were facts of life. It was this perspective the mainstream took for granted. In addition, social imperialism, which had been a strong mobilizing theme for welfare reforms at the beginning of the century, as well as a sense of the British welfare state as a *nationalist* achievement, contributed to social administration's parochial, British-bound concerns. This, amongst other things, meant that 'race' and racism were not seen as having any direct relevance in the study of the welfare state. Within this general context of the social reformist approach, we will now pick up on the contributions of writers and policy-makers representing the streams identified earlier: non-socialist welfare collectivism, Fabian socialism and the more recent radical social administration.

Non-socialist Welfare Collectivism

Women and the Family

Beveridge is the arch-villain in much feminist writing (see Land, 1976; Wilson, 1977, 1980a). His vision of the welfare state, embodied in the *Report on the Social Insurance and Allied Services* (the Beveridge Report) in 1942, placed women firmly in the home serving their husband's and children's needs, doing 'work', 'vital though unpaid, without which their husbands could not do their paid work and without which the nation could not continue' (1942, p. 49). Thus man and wife were treated as a team, a single administrative unit: in national insurance terms a married women was to be treated as a dependant of her husband, or if she worked, as eligible for a lower rate of benefit. Elizabeth Wilson characterizes the Beveridge Report as 'one of the most crudely ideological documents of its kind ever written', embodying 'the principle of insurance; the principle of the subsistence income; and the principle of the sanctity of the family' (1977, p. 148). She suggests that policies stemming from his two incorrect assumptions and predictions about the nature of post-war family life have caused suffering for women ever since. These were that most married women would not do waged work and could remain dependent on their husbands' incomes and benefits, and secondly that the numbers of unsupported mothers would remain minimal and required no special provision. The consequence now being that lone mothers, on supplementary benefit, represent a significant group of those in poverty.

In many ways, with regard to women Beveridge simply institutionalized the national insurance policies of Liberal and Labour governments since 1906. Health insurance policies from 1911 were deemed to apply only to men, in accordance with the belief that it was their wage, or the loss of it, upon which women and children depended. Even though many women did work and many worked in traditional male occupations throughout the First World War, policies during the 1920s and 1930s sought to exclude women's – particularly *married* women's – eligibility to unemployment benefit. At the same time this period was marked by state intervention in the form of infant welfare centres and domestic instruction for girls in schools which reinforced women's domestic role in the home, encouraged her role as breeder of the British race, but at the same time supervised closely her activity in both these respects (see chapter 6). In this way Beveridge's ideas about women assumed a natural place for them in the home looking after their husband and children, and assumed a natural separation between paid work and home. Even where Beveridge came under pressure from women's organizations and included a family allowance for women and their children, the idea was acceptable with the ideological drift of the new welfare provisions because it was seen as assistance for mothers to carry out their mothering role more ably.

Contemporary proponents of non-socialist collectivism can be identified as those who argue for a 'mixed economy of welfare' or 'welfare pluralism', that is to say, that welfare provision should not just come from the state but from the informal and voluntary sectors and the private market. Generally speaking, proponents of these ideas make little reference to the specific needs or rights of women, instead they are included as part of the family unit. This emerges in the pluralist approach to welfare described by Hadley and Hatch (1981). Taking on board the criticisms that the institutions and welfare state are remote, bureaucratic, authoritarian and paternalistic, they propose democratized, decentralized, accountable welfare provision, with a significant role being given to informal care (i.e. care within the family) by linking it up to statutory and voluntary agencies. The statutory agency's role would be to identify informal networks of care in a neighbourhood and support them through use of voluntary services like meals-on-wheels or local domiciliary services. As feminists have pointed out, written into this scenario is the assumption of the availability of women to provide not only the unpaid informal care, but probably the voluntary work and the low paid domiciliary work too. As Norman Johnson comments: 'The exploitative nature of family care has constantly to be borne in mind. It is fatuous to talk about equality of opportunity for women in employment if the sexual division of labour persists in the home. This feature of family care is not given much attention in the welfare pluralist literature' (Johnson, 1987, p. 93). In this strand of thinking then, the distinction between the public and the private is maintained and in so far as women's interests are improved by the welfare state, they also reinforce her role as wife and mother.

'Race' and Racism

Beveridge's welfare policies were firmly grounded in terms that related them to the advancement of national efficiency and racial supremacy: 'housewives as mothers have vital work to do in ensuring the adequate continuance of the British race and British ideals in the world' (Beveridge, 1942, para. 117). In an essay on 'Children's Allowances and the Race' he stated, 'Pride of race is a reality for the British as for other peoples' (quoted in Cohen, 1985). The sense of pride in the *British* welfare state stemmed partly from the idea of its being a reward for the self-sacrifice of the war effort as well as a protraction of the ideology of nationalist collectivism felt during the war. At the same time, the introduction of forms of collectivism especially in welfare provision had, since the turn of the century, mobilized around a strongly nationalist theme. The promotion by all the major political parties of the sense of solidarity through '*nation*' vied, relatively successfully by the First World War, with the sense of solidarity through *class* which political organizations like the Social Democratic Federation had mobilized in the 1880s. Furthermore, this sense of nation was strongly tied to Britain as an imperialist power. The justification for imperial war and conquest and colonialism was rooted in ideas derived from Social Darwinism of the cultural and moral superiority of the Anglo-Saxon Christian European over all colonialized and oppressed peoples – Jews, the Irish, Muslims, Africans, Caribbeans, Asians. British nationalism was thus historically set in a racist mould, a mould which had a significant effect upon the cast of welfare reforms. The Conservatives under Chamberlain pushed the line that the maintenance of the empire and its markets was essential to provide employment and welfare reforms for the working class. The Liberals, whose programme of reforms of unemployment and sickness benefit and old age pensions in 1906–14 was the framework upon which Beveridge built his National Insurance system, integrated imperialism into welfare reforms in a particular form of *social imperialism* which stressed the necessity for social reforms, including provisions for mothers and children, to assist in breeding the Imperial Race in Britain to defend and maintain the Empire. An offshoot of this line of thinking was the eugenics movement, which saw the need to encourage the breeding of the fit and intelligent and discourage the reproduction of the weak of body and intellect. This conception of fitness and intellect, however, was based on a racist, classist and sexist model with most oppressed peoples at the lowest range. Support for a flat-rate universal family allowance was argued on the grounds that any sliding scale might encourage the poor to reproduce disproportionately. In addition, the combination of nationalist outlook with the contributory principle, upon which most forms of benefit were based (the worker contributing to her/his own national insurance), created a clear view of the limits of welfare obligation: the beneficiaries should be British nationals who worked full-time. This meant that there was intense hostility to the idea that non-Britons – particularly immigrants – might have access to welfare. Paranoia that immigrants might scrounge from 'our welfare' were written into many of the policies of the welfare reforms of the 1920s, 1930s and 1940s. As well as denial of access to immigrants and aliens, welfare agencies historically played a role in assisting immigration authorities by reporting suspected immigrants (see chapter 6).

But what of contemporary non-socialist welfare collectivist writers? In general, hardly any reference at all is made to strategies for racial equality or racism in welfare provision. However, the role of welfare in promoting 'national efficiency' is a strong theme of such writers. Particularly interesting here is the work of Rober Pinker, who sets out to defend the nationalist basis of welfare reform.

In *The Idea of Welfare* (1979) Pinker suggests there are boundaries to obligation and entitlement in social welfare; Titmuss's 'altruism' is confined for most people to kith and kin and nation in that order, and the sense of internationalism in Titmuss's concept of the 'universal stranger' is misconceived. Indeed, it is also the *internationalism* underlying Marxism and its concept of working-class solidarity, and the *internationalism* of classical economic theory and *laissez-faire* in the form of free trade between nations, which also flaw these doctrines. Quoting Letwin, Pinker says the reality is that 'the ordinary citizen naturally concentrates on a selected number of persons who are closest to him (sic) in a moral sense, his family, old friends, neighbours and compatriots, in descending order' (Preface to Reisman, 1977 p. xiv). In contrast to the internationalism of left and right, he proposes a third model for welfare based on the seventeenth-century system of mercantilism: *mercantile collectivism*. This was a *nationalist* doctrine, where economic policies were aimed at national wealth creation (tariffs, import and export restraints, etc.) necessary for the benefit of all citizens. Nation and welfare are thus interdependent. This concept of interdependence found its modern form in the policies of

Keynes and Beveridge, of which Pinker approves. As we have seen, Beveridge's welfare policies were firmly grounded in terms which related to national efficiency and racial supremacy.

But what of this nationalism and patriotism Pinker attests to? He proposes that there is no 'convincing reason why, in treating the subect of patriotism we should equate it with jingoistic intolerance' (1979, p. 29) (A rather similar distinction to the one made by Sherman, above.) He suggests it is this question which has led liberal and socialist intellectuals to reject it – 'Nationalism became a noble cause only when it was practised by foreigners – notably those engaged in ways of liberation against imperialist powers' (p. 29). It was imperialism, he suggests, that gave nationalism its racist name. However, Peter Fryer's book *Staying Power* (1984) points to a far deeper and more lasting relationship of British nationalism with racism directed at Black people. Describing this same mercantilist era, he says:

> The primary functions of racism are economical and political. Racism emerged in the oral tradition in Barbados in the seventeenth century, and crystallized in print in Britain in the eighteenth, as the ideology of plantocracy, the class of sugar-planters and slave-merchants that dominated England's Caribbean colonies. It emerged, above all, as a largely defensive ideology, the weapon of a class whose wealth, way of life, and power were under mounting attack. (p. 134)

Nationalism and racism have been frequent bedfellows in European history; though their relationship has not always been constant, they have none the less come to each other's aid at specific times. Whilst Pinker draws attention to the historical link between nationalism and welfare policy, his uncritical defence of nationalism, as a basis for entitlement and obligation is social policy, must be severely questioned.

This strident nationalism is not confined to this strand of thinking, it also affected the Fabians, to whom we now turn.

Fabian Socialism

Women and the Family

The underlying familism in Fabian thinking and policy, particularly in the inter-war and early post-war years, was noted in chapter 1. This represented a strong commitment to maintaining and supporting through state intervention the family in its privatized form with a strict division of labour in which a woman's primary responsibilities were to care for her family and home. Early Fabian writers on social policy like the Webbs and Shaw and Annie Besant were, in some ways, more explicit about improvements for women's lives, though this was confined to their role as mothers, than were the post-war male Fabian social administrators for whom the social divisions between rich and poor were the more central theme in their writings. At the same time the framework on which this support rested was one which emphasized the *method* of collectivized welfare provision through centralized state intervention and the *aim* of national (i.e. British) development. The major role women could play in national development was again that of mother, and therefore, the priority of state intervention for women was in terms of her maternal role. Like the Liberal Imperialists the early Fabians were influenced by eugenicist arguments about the need maintain the Imperial Race and to encourage reproduction of the 'abler' classes. The configuration of these different ideas came together from the early years of the century in the form of the Fabians' proposals for the Endowment of Motherhood (family allowances): 'once the production of health, moral and intelligent citizens is revered as a social service and made the subject of deliberate praise and encouragement on the part of the government it will, we may be sure, attract the best and most patriotic of the citizens' (S. Webb, 1907, p. 19).

However, the contradiction between the aims of some Fabians (especially Fabian women) for woman's economic independence and her relegation to the care of children was not resolved in Fabian policies or writing. Only in the writing of the social eugenicist Karl Pearson (of whom the Webbs, Shaw and H. G. Wells all approved) do we see an attempt at resolution. Bernard Semmel (1960) describes Pearson's views in this way:

Women under socialism would have the duty to labour outside the home – until the coming of children – [and] would be able to contract 'free sexual union' as sex-relationships would be separated from child-bearing, with the state taking an interest in child-bearing to prevent economic dependence on the part of the mother and regulating both the 'quantity and quality' of children since this had such an important bearing upon 'the happiness of society as a whole'. (Semmel, 1960, p. 47, quoting from Pearson, 1886, pp. 418–27)

Richard Titmuss was also influenced by this line of thinking, as we discuss in the next section, but his writing has also come under close feminist scrutiny because of its influence on mainstream social administration in the 1960s and 1970s (Rose, 1981; Pascall, 1986), and because much of Titmuss's area of study directly concerns women – population control, demographic changes, childbearing, the elderly, female dependence – especially in the essays 'The Position of Women' and 'Industrialization and the Family' (Titmuss, 1958). Although Titmuss wrote about women, he nevertheless cast them in a particular family mould which was derived from a contemporary sociological 'functionalist' view of the family. Thus Gillian Pascall (1986) notes that when Titmuss wrote about demographic changes in family life, or the greater involvement of men in childbearing, he was displaying a concern with the *form* rather than the content of family life: that is, how far the communal values of family life balanced and were functional for the competitive values of the public world of work. In this way he also perpetuated the distinction between the public and the private, a distinction which not only tends to an idealization of relations within the 'private sphere' but also a blindness to, first, some of the darker sides of relations of power, control and violence within the family, and secondly, to the role the family plays in bolstering, rather than balancing the economy. Pascall also suggests that Titmuss's model of family life to be supported by welfare policies was a bread-winner/dependant model.

Although Titmuss shares many of the characteristics of the mainstream outlined in the previous chapter, Hilary Rose argues that Titmuss's conception of social policy, 'his preoccupation with the micro, with the intimate social relations of redistribution, has a specific relevance to a feminist anlaysis' (1981, p. 478). She proposes that Titmuss's framework in *Social Divison of Welfare* (1958), which analyses the social inequalities in the distribution of benefits from fiscal welfare (taxes), occupational welfare and state welfare, could be applied to other forms of division and inequality, such as sex, age and 'race'. Rose suggests that while the political economy approach offers a larger-scale, more comprehensive and more historical approach to the study of social policy, the danger is that it ignores the small-scale analyses of distribution which were not only a feature associated with Titmuss, but also with feminist studies, for example, Hilary Land's intensive examination of the social security system and its impact on women (Land, 1978).

A more theoretical treatment of the development of the welfare state is offered by Marshall in his elaboration of citizenship rights. In his view, these are attainable upon the granting of civil rights – liberty and equality before the law; political rights – the right to vote and hold office won through suffrage; and social rights – a right to a minimum social and economic security, won through the welfare state. Although Marshall devotes space to an analysis of the relationship between *Citizenship and Social Class* (1949), and although he examines women's suffrage, he does not face a fundamental contradiction that although women developed their political rights as individuals, a woman's eligibility to many social rights through welfare policies is as a dependant of her husband or the man with whom she lives. Like individualism, citizenship is very much a man-only concept. Pascall comments: 'If women, too, claim rights as individuals (as they have often done) it offers a threat to the fabric of interdependence on which men's rights depend' (1986, p. 9).

'Race' and Racism

It was noted in chapter 1 that the discipline of social policy, which was dominated by a Fabian socialist outlook, had largely ignored or marginalized the issue of racism in the welfare state. This was the result of a number of different aspects: its empiricism and atheoreticalness, which meant that certain conditions were taken for granted, including imperialism, racist immigration control and institutionalized racism; a tendency to view problems from the 'perspective of the state' which had seen Black immigrants in terms of cheap labour and not in terms of providing for their welfare needs; a belief in the welfare state as inherently integrative and universalistic; and a concentration on particular issues: poverty, state and market, universalism and selectivity, redistribution between rich and poor, which meant that the problems of racism became hidden under the problems of poverty; and an idealism which, in so far as it did recognize racism, categorized it as a separate issue of race relations to do with changing people's behaviour and attitudes. At the same time, Fabian social administrators' concerns had a *nationalist* focus, a concern with the social conditions of Britain, a pride in the British welfare state which was not incidental, but rooted in Fabian socialism's own historical commitment to nationalism. The cluster of ideas around this theme and their influence on later Fabian social administrators have remained a relatively unexamined element in social policy.

It was noted earlier that the Fabians shared with the Liberal Imperialists and the eugenicists a belief in the importance of maintaining imperial supremacy. The collective state provision of welfare was seen as a major contribution to what Sidney Webb described as the 'race struggle'. It was a collectivism directed towards the benefit of the British nation rather than the international working class. State intervention to provide welfare therefore was not coincidental with British imperialism, with ideas of racialist supremancy and with immigration control, but crucially part of these. In 1900 the Fabian Society split over its attitude towards imperialism but the majority, led by George Bernard Shaw, voted for a pro-imperialist line, for, as Shaw wrote, 'the effective social organization of the whole Empire, and its rescue from the strife of classes and private interest' (Shaw, 1900, p. 6). (Indeed, the Fabians' ardour for militarism led them to become the first political group to argue for compulsory military training – see Semmel, 1960, p. 72.) Ideas of racial and cultural supremacy were bound up in the acceptance of Social Darwinist and eugenicist ideas of hierarchy of races and intellects. These ideas harboured and justified racist biogtry. In his concern about the fall in the birth rate, particularly amongst the middle classes – which led to support for family allowances – Sidney Webb wrote: 'This can hardly result in anything but national deterioration; or, as an alternative, in this country gradually falling to the Irish and the Jews' (Webb, 1907, pp. 16–17). Socialist collectivism, then, was seen as the highest social, economic and moral condition within the grasp of the fortunate Britons but alas, as Graham Wallas lamented in 1890, 'impossible in a nation of individualist savages like the Australian blacks, and could not, perhaps be introduced except by external authority among a people like the peasants of Brittany' (Wallas, 1890, p. 147). By the same token, it was also feared that its achievement in Britain would attract scroungers from other countries,

It does not seem necessary to conclude that Socialism must be established over the whole globe if it is to be established anywhere. What is necessary is that we face the fact, every day becoming plainer, that the condition of the proletariat in any single European country must be accompanied by a law of aliens considerate enough to avoid cruelty to refugees, or obstruction to those whose presence would raise our intellectual or industrial average, but stringent enough to exclude the unhappy 'diluvies gentium', the human rubbish which the military empires of the continent are so ready to shoot upon any open space. (Wallas, 1890, pp. 137–8)

Wallas regretted this possibility but concluded that there was no argument to reject the necessity of such control. In fact, exclusion of welfare benefits to 'aliens' became written into the Liberals' reforms of 1906 onwards, and the concern was once again raised in the establishment of post-war welfare state that it would be abused by 'immigrant scroungers'. A 1950 Labour Cabinet Review Committee on immigration saw as the main problem of immigration from the colonies that 'they are tempted to come to the United Kingdom by better prospects of employment and in the knowledge that if they fail to find work they will be supported by the Social Services at a higher standard of living than many of them had in the Colonies' (quoted in Joshi and Carter, 1984, p. 62). Even Aneurin Bevan, on the left wing of the Labour Party, and considered to be an internationalist who as the first Minister of Health had said in 1949 that he supported 'the right of aliens to make use of the National Health Service' (Hansard 2.6.1949, quoted in Cohen, 1985, p. 89), said in response to claims of scrounging later that year that he had 'arranged for immigration officers to turn back aliens who were coming into this country to secure benefits off the health service' (Hansard 19.9.1949).

Bevan was not a Fabian but the contradiction in his statement is reflected in Fabian approaches to the welfare state in the 1940s, 1950s and 1960s. The blatant racial bigotry of the Webbs and Shaw, their belief in a hierarchy of races and their defence of imperialism was not carried wholesale into later Fabian thinking but shifted in a number of ways. The concern in the 1940s and 1950s by some Fabians for a 'positive colonial policy' combined an evangelical and a pragmatic concern. On the one hand it was the duty of British collectivism and democracy to set a good example for self-management and economic development in the colonies, but on the other hand, granting of independence should be seen as an opportunity to concentrate resources on the 'national interest' – the development of a planned economy and egalitarian welfare programme in Britain. These shifts mark the changes in imperialism. The main doctrines of imperialism had been power, profit and civilization; as power and profit began to decline, only civilization remained. Paul Rich (1987) has commented how some on the left, like John Strachey, hoped that the welfare state could replace the old imperial ideal in sustaining national cohesion. In effect the 'new socialism' of the mid-1950s eschewed any notion of international class solidarity.

In 1958 Richard Crossmann wrote 'what strikes me is that this new Socialism has been shaped by two men whose names are largely unknown to the general public. They are Dr Thomas Balogh and Professor Richard Titmuss' (1958, p. 751). Titmuss's work represented some aspects of the shift in Fabianism from social imperialism as well as the paradox in Bevan's ideas. On the one hand Titmuss passionately believed that the welfare state stood to serve the 'universal stranger' regardless of 'race, religion, colour or class' (unlike the residualized welfare system in the United States where the poor received third-rate stigmatized public welfare whilst only those who could afford it received any decent form of health care, insurance and so on). At the same time, the theme of nationalist pride and even superiority picks its way through his writings. Titmuss's earlier concern in *Problems of Population* in 1943 to 'guide the teeming millions of Africa and India to a more abundant life' has already been noted. For Titmuss, *altruism* as represented by the voluntary blood-donation service in Britain ('the gift of blood') was the essence of the redistributive welfare ideal, yet as well he wrote 'Altruism, the highest moment in the social relation of redistribution, is English' (quoted in Rose, 1981, p. 488).

Titmuss's strong belief in the power of the welfare state through *universalism* – that is, access to all equally – to harmonize and integrate different groups in society, inhibited an acknowledgement that this same ideal could be used to deny to certain groups access to welfare to meet specific needs. The view that everyone should be treated equally, that there should be no 'special privileges', ignores already existing inequalities, and furthermore can and has reinforced such inequalities and, in the case of Black people's needs, served as a defence of racist welfare practices. In the 1950s Black people were denied access to council housing because of failing the residency qualifications and racist allocation procedures. After the Notting Hill uprisings in 1958 *The Economist*, in the spirit of encouraging both selective welfare provision *and* retaining immigrants as a pool of cheap labour, suggested Black workers be given 'special privileges' on council house waiting lists. Of course such a strategy was based on a mean market evaluation of Black workers and would only have made sense within a massive council house building programme for *all*, which is *not* what *The Economist* supported, rather the opposite. Nevertheless, Titmuss saw in their suggestion *only* an attack on the principles of universalism and dismissed it, concluding that *The Economist* was 'unlikely to appeal to many Commonwealth citizens looking to Britain for moral leadership' (first written in 1959, and revised in Abel-Smith and Titmuss, 1987, p. 71). However, in the 1960s Fabians generally approved of one particular form of selectivity – positive discrimination. At that time this referred to attempts to divert extra resources into needy areas, for example, schemes like Educational Priority Areas, or the Community Development Projects. These projects, through money, resources and personnel, attempted to raise the standards, educational and environmental, in these areas to put them on a par with others. The limitations of such schemes lay in their inability to solve some of the structural causes of the existence of pockets of poverty and deprivation.

Some Fabians *did* concern themselves with racism, or 'race relations' and, as was described in the previous chapter, applied the same pragmatic idealism to securing the assimilation and integration of the new immigrants. But this was seen as an entirely separate issue and not the concern of social policy-makers and thinkers. This externalization of the problem of white racism reflected thinking at the political level, where debate about racial discrimination in the Labour Party in the immediate post-war years was confined to the members of the Movement for Colonial Freedom. 'Racism was viewed as the proper concern of those involved with colonial affairs; it was something external, not germane, to the mainstream of the labour movement' (Joshi and Carter, 1984, p. 55).

The traditional polarities within Fabian social administration studies of universalism versus selectivity, the state versus the market, poverty and wealth, provided the framework for an extensive analysis of poverty, redistribution, the social division of welfare, but inhibited any acknowledgement of the issues of oppression – of 'race' or sex – whose constituents were woven into the fabric of that framework. This failure was reinforced by the high profile of familism and nationalism in Fabianism. In so far as the problems of Black people became visible they were submerged under genuine problems of poverty, deprivation and urban decline, or ghettoized into the policy studies of race relations. Contemporary social policy writers in the Fabian tradition have had to give recognition to the documented experiences of women and Black people in relation to the welfare state, but this recognition barely touches upon the magnitude of the problem. In *The Future of the Welfare State* (1983) Howard Glennerster calls for a reappraisal of social policy and its priorities which includes examining 'social assumptions' about the family and 'minorities'. Each of these issues according to Glennerster raises the problem of a mismatch between provisions offfered and the expectations of rights by women and Blacks, and each is cast by him as a post-war problem (p. 3). And, in spite of a thorough-going radical analysis offered by Miriam David and Hilary Land within the chapters of the book, Glennerster concludes with a strategy to dispel discrimination against women and Black people who have been denied full citizenship because of 'social custom, values and prejudices. To give them full access and rights of citizenship will involve changing our laws which, by changing behaviour, may begin to modify built-in, barely appreciated prejudices' (1983, p. 223). To reduce, in this way, the experiences of Black people and women to a post-war parochial problem of discrimination fails to comprehend the historical and international context which gives rise to those experiences of discrimination, and limits the solution to an idealist strategy of the modification of behaviours and attitudes.

Radical Social Administration

This growing group within the discipline of writers and policy-makers whose analytical framework draws from the empiricism of Fabianism and the structuralism of Marxism, have begun to question some of the assumptions of familism, though they give less ready acknowledgement to racism. Though the writers grouped in this category show considerable variations, a particular paradox is noticeable in their handling of these issues, perhaps resulting the discomfort of having one foot in the Fabian camp and the other in the Marxist camp. On the one hand there is an acknowledgement of sexism and racism as institutionalized, as structural problems in society, but on the other hand, some of the solutions offered, whilst *improving* the lot of women and Black people, make no clear attempt to change the structural problems which give rise to these institutionalized forms of oppression. The spelling out of the ways immediate demands or reforms can be linked to transitional demands (i.e. fundamental changes required to liberate the oppressed) is crucial in social policy and has been one of the significant contributions of feminism (see the reference to Maxine Molyneux in chapter 3). This point will be elaborated below.

Women and the Family

Peter Townsend's work follows the Fabian tradition in so far as its object of scrutiny is poverty and its strategy is redistribution, but at the same time it goes beyond the tradition in identifying structural problems whose solution requires structural transformations. How then do women feature in Townsend's theories and strategies for welfare? In his large study, *Poverty in the United Kingdom* (1979) and in his later essay, *Why are the Many Poor* (1984), Townsend indicates that it is those on Supplementary Benefit who make up a large part of the poor. These include, as a majority, *women*, as lone parents or elderly. It is this evidence, combined with the evidence from feminist writers of the poverty of wives without an income of their own, or deprived of their income through obligations to care for the young, disabled or older people, that has been identified as the 'feminization of poverty'. Hilda Scott argues, for example

It is impossible to attack the problem of poverty in the industrialized or the developing world unless the extent to which poverty is a woman's problem is recognized. This is not to underestimate the importance of class, race, national and international divisions. The fact is that feminist research during the past twenty years has revealed that all these divisions affect women in special ways, ways that have been largely ignored. (1984, p. 14)

Townsend sets his analysis of poverty clearly in *class* terms: the creation of a mass 'underclass' dependent on inadequate state income, and made up of different groups – the unemployed, disabled people, the low paid, lone parents, older people (1984, pp. 17–23). Many of those in the last three groups are women, which suggests a complex interaction of class with gender, an aspect overlooked by Townsend.

In *Poverty in the United Kingdom* (1979) Townsend documents the financial dependence of women in marriage, their lack of access to decently paid work, but again he tends to subsume sex inequalities under those of social class. For example, he says 'inequalities between the sexes in marriage, social policy and the labour market reflect class inequalities' (1979, p. 782, quoted in Gough, 1981). And although he sees radical social administration involving transformations which include 'welfare as the reorganization of private relationships' (1983, p. 62), he does not spell out how the relationship between the two strategies for women that he mentions – greater recognition of employment rights (the public sphere) and the unpaid responsibilities of women (the private sphere) – would achieve this goal.

Alan Walker goes much further in incorporating a feminist approach into his analysis. For example, in *Social Planning* (1984) Walker argues for a democratic form of social planning which places economic policy subservient to the meeting of need through social policy, and not vice versa, as historically has been the case. He sees this democratic process and its outcome injected with the demands of the women's movement, which gives priority to the question of who cares for the children and other dependants. In *Community Care* (1982) Walker also sees the sexual division of labour, in which it is women who are expected and obliged to do most of the caring, whether low paid or unpaid, as a central problem in the development of community care policies. He suggests that this has to be changed, along with, amongst other things, the expansion of domiciliary services, the reorientation of professional attitudes and changes in the relationships between the statutory, voluntary and informal sectors. At the same time, he recommends that radical action on employment, the labour market, housing and incomes is necessary to change the fundamental assumptions about who does the caring and where. What he does not do, however, is spell out the relationship between these two sets of policies, in particular the fact that they appear to be heading in different directions. It is not surprising therefore that the feminist writer Janet Finch suggests that the first set of policies are unlikely to alter the sexual division of labour in the home whilst the second are at too grand a level to formulate demands for the here and now (Finch, 1984). She counterposes Elizabeth Wilson's suggestion that it is the concept of 'community' which has to be abandoned before we can develop caring policies that do not exploit women. In contrast to Walker, then, Wilson says: 'The "community" is an ideological portmanteau word for a reactionary, conservative ideology that oppresses women by silently confirming them to the private sphere without so much as ever mentioning them' (1982, p. 55). Finch suggests a different approach from Walker's, she suggests a 'residential route' which can combine *collective* solutions with a recognition of caring as labour, deserving of pay. However, as we noted in chapter 3, this solution may conflict with the wishes of people who need care and support.

Ramesh Mishra, whose work is concerned to develop the discipline of social policy as well as to elaborate welfare strategies, did acknowledge the significance of the feminist critique in social policy in work written in 1986 (Mishra, 1986a, b). In a spirited defence of welfare capitalism as the lesser of two evils (the other being Thatcherism), he notes that in spite of their critique of the sexist forms of welfare provision feminists still, in general, agree that collective welfare provision is favourable to the promotion of women's interests and therefore agree that the defence of the welfare state under capitalism is important (1986b). He then goes on to outline a necessarily defensive strategy for the present period against the deteriorization of living standards imposed by the New Right. This consists of defending the welfare state in its original conception, that is, as part of an economic strategy for full employment. A non-sexist welfare state and full employment, then, represent the best strategy for the working class, including women. What Mishra does not make clear, as with Townsend and Walker, is what *exactly* this means when it has been precisely the traditional organization for full employment which has contributed to the maintenance of a distinction between work and family and the sexual division of labour within it. It may be considered that the satisfactory resolution of this problem is one to be left to the organizations defending these interests. But it is precisely the organizations of the labour and trade union movement which have also maintained the distinctions between home and work (although there are signs that with significant women's interventions this is beginning to change).

Not all writers in this group fail to spell out the implications for employment of the feminist critique. Malcolm Wicks's book *A Future for All* (1987), again a defence of the welfare state, shows a sensitivity to these issues.

Looking to the future, much will of course depend on policy, both the success of economic policies designed to stimulate the economy and hence tackle unemployment and also the effect of social policies which will help determine the pattern of work and the distribution of resources and tasks between men and women. The question of work therefore looms large and must fundamentally shape any future social strategy. (1987, p. 162)

When it comes to the question of racism and racial inequalities Wicks does not, however, offer such an integrated approach.

'Race' and Racism

Both Wicks and Townsend, in different ways, call for an international strategy in social and economic policy. In *Why Are the Many Poor?*, the 500th Fabian Tract written in 1984, Townsend gives significant attention to the international context of poverty in Britain and the Third World, and the necessity to see solutions in terms of 'joint action internationally by trades unions, democratic socialist parties, professions, pressure groups' (p. 34). Wicks also notes that 'a socialist concern to eradicate poverty and inequality has to adopt an internationalist stance' (1987, p. 184). This means taking 'full account of our obligations to the Third World', and as an example he suggests that import controls should not discriminate against poor nations whose economic survival rests on export. At the same time both authors acknowledge, though very minimally, racial inequalities and what Wicks calls 'racial discord' (p. 251), but no strategies are offered which spell out the specific material and ideological dimensions of racial oppression in Britain, or which make the links between this and the international context of the movement of capital and labour which are outlined in the previous chapter. It is not clear how either Wicks's general strategy of equality and social integration ('only through socialism can we build one nation; in the sense of an equal society', p. 175) or Townsend's stress on transferring planning and redistributive policies from a national to an international level are going to tackle white racism or cut the ties between immigration control and access to welfare. Alan Walker (1984) also attempts to create a framework for the study of social and economic policy which, amongst other things, focuses on differences of status, power and rewards not just between classes, but sexes and 'races' too. However, the strategy makes no reference to, for example, white racism or the racial divisions of labour in the welfare services. We can conclude therefore that whilst some of the radical social administrators have begun to acknowledge racial inequalities and have begun also to assert the need for an internationalist social and economic strategy to eradicate poverty, the specific dimensions and causes of those racial equalities remain quite unaccounted for, and any connection these inequalities may have with an international division of labour, with international movement of capital, with immigration control, or with the legacy of imperialism and nationalism within and outside the British welfare state, pass them by.

Political Economy of Welfare

So far I have argued that there are elements of both gender- and 'race'-insensibility, as well as inherent theoretical limitations in anti-collectivism and the varieties of reformism which limit a full understanding of the experiences of Black people in the welfare state. Earlier, in chapter 2, it was suggested that the political economy approach provides a more theoretically coherent and comprehensive analysis of the welfare state, but also at the same time it does not have a lot to say about women or Black people. Why is this? Is it another case of insensibility or are there theoretical flaws in the political economy approach? Chapters 3 and 4 indicated some of the theoretical issues in debates between Marxism and feminism and 'race' and class theories; these issues are pursued further here.

Women and the Family

Here it is more a case of partial-sensibility. The work of two main proponents of this approach, Ginsburg (1979) and Gough (1979), makes reference to the family and women. Thus, Gough lays emphasis on the role of the welfare state in, first, regulating the reproduction of labour power in which not only schools and health services but also 'the family and the labour of housewives is still all-important' (1979, p. 46), and secondly, in maintaining the non-working population – children, elderly, sick, disabled, and people with learning difficulties. Ginsburg's analysis of the social security system describes the way in which it reinforces women's dependence on men, supports the ideology of domesticity and sustains their position as low paid casual workers, and as 'a unique stratum of the reserve army of labour' (1979, p. 80). Both writers draw our attention to the ways in which women's work, unpaid and paid, mediated through the welfare state, benefits capitalism by maintaining at no cost, except to themselves, a fit and healthy workforce. But, as both Hilary Rose (1981) and Gillian Pascall (1986) have pointed out, these analyses, in common with much Marxist writing, leave other questions unanswered: *why* and *how* do women do this unpaid and low paid labour, why is it *women*, and how far do *men* as well as capital benefit from this situation? This process of 'economic reductionism' – of reducing the causes of women's subordination to the workings of the economy – has foreclosed an investigation of these questions. As Pascall notes:

What is unsatisfactory about these accounts for some feminists is that they treat women's relationship to capital at the expense of women's relationship to men ...

the political economy of welfare makes productive relations the key to understanding; everything else is a reflection of productive relationships and therefore of secondary importance. (1986, p. 14–15)

This focus on production is not just a question of theoretical emphasis, but a question of the traditions of the left having given far greater validity to those struggles that directly challenge capital – struggles in the workplace for better wages, for example – than to those based in the community, often led by women, which are concerned with the meeting of welfare needs. As chapter 3 showed, it has largely been left to feminists to examine the importance of power relations between men and women and the interplay between this and capitalism and welfare provision, and also to argue that the family, the relations and distribution of resources within it are central to an understanding of how the state through welfare regulates the reproduction of labour power and maintains the non-working population. In other words, who earns what, who does what work and why, and who is dependent upon whom are crucial issues in understanding the system of how those who work and those who do not are looked after and maintained. Some writers using a political economy framework have attempted to draw in these questions too. One work that extends a Marxist analysis to look at the relationship between medicine, medical ideology and oppression of women, and the contribution of women's struggles over health care, is Doyal's *Political Economy of Health* (1979).

A further criticism of political economy's approach centres upon its theoretical formulation of the role of the welfare state. As was described earlier, Gough contends that the Marxist analysis argues that the welfare state results from *both* the need of capital and class struggle, and in doing so avoids the static determinism of a functionalist analysis (the welfare state only serving capitalism's requirements) or of a conspiracy analysis (the welfare state as a ruling class 'con-trick'). However, there are difficulties with this for the feminist critique of welfare (and also for an anti-racist critique). Feminism's emphasis has been on the ways in which reforms that are identified as benefiting the working class – the Factory Acts, the Beveridge Report, the National Health Service – have *reinforced* women's dependency, the sexual division of labour and circumscribed and controlled biological and social reproduction. Gough's generalized concept of class struggle and the implicit unitariness of the working class obscures a view suggested by feminist history that what were seen as gains for some sections of the working class (often the male white skilled sections) can also be seen as losses for other sections – women, the poor, Black people. The contribution of feminists has been to unpick the strands that make up class struggle, to reveal the role of women's struggles and to examine the ways in which particular demands from particular sections have met with a greater or lesser response from capital and the state.

A different argument which has a bearing on this question is advanced by Peter Taylor-Gooby (1981, 1985). He suggests that there is, in the discipline of social policy, a tendency for the theoretical base to 'revert to type', particularly in relation to a perspective which emphasizes the *reforming* nature of the state.

In practice those traditions which offer a radical critique of the status quo, in particular those which challenge the possibility of the welfare state enhancing welfare, tend not to be assimilated so readily as those which do not. Such perspectives are often reduced to a partial critique, which is more readily absorbed; partial critiques document shortcomings in the welfare state and set out strategies of amelioration. (1981, pp. 433–4)

In this way, he argues that the predominant approach taken by political economy writers, like Gough, or interpreters, like George and Wilding, has been one which stresses the potential reformability of the state. Such an approach, however, is less easy to sustain in the face of a feminist critique which depicts the state as upholding not simply capitalism, but patriarchy too. Taylor-Gooby suggests that the more radical changes implied in the feminist critique have become watered down to policies to counter gender discrimination and not women's oppression.

For example, it is possible to distinguish strands in feminism which link patriarchy to the state as an institution from those which focus on gender discrimination in access to social resources. The former perspective offers a radical critique of the possibility of the welfare state enhancing welfare in this area, it is the latter that has been developed in the subject. (1981, p. 434)

Some writers have pointed to the history and legacy of Marxism to explain how Marxist analysis has concentrated on the 'public' world of production and exploitation and less on the 'private' world of the family and oppression. Barbara Taylor's study of the early nineteenth-century movement of utopian socialism shows how 'personal' issues of family life, free love, reproduction were all central to their debates and visions. The development of a socialism with its emphasis on the materialist conception of struggle and change based on the conflict between capital and labour led to a rejection not only of utopian, 'unscientific' socialism, but the concerns that went with them. 'As the boundaries of the socialist project thus narrowed, so women's independent aspirations became stranded outside them – to be ignored, attacked as bourgeois deviationism, or relegated to the category of secondary issues which would be tackled once the primary battle against capitalist exploitation had been won' (Taylor, 1983, pp. 285–6). The reawakening of some of these concerns within the women's movement of the 1960s has led to a greater recognition of the importance of struggles over 'private' issues, such as domestic violence. It has also influenced others to insist upon the need for prefigurative politics, that is, the necessity to have a vision of future welfare based upon non-hierarchical, collective, non-sexist and non-racist relations as well as a materialist strategy to achieve it (LEWRG, 1979; Deacon, 1983). This shift has proved an important counterbalance to the more heavily 'economistic' concerns of some political economy of welfare theorists. Without returning to idealism, this shift can also create the space to argue for the centrality of policies to do with caring, dependency and reproduction to strategies for socialist welfare.

'Race' and Racism

Since the political economy approach offers an analysis of welfare based on the relations between class, capital and the state, as such it should be theoretically more capable than the approaches already discussed of doing justice to the concept of institutionalized racism, at least in terms of the role of welfare in reproducing a reserve army of labour. In fact, there is little mention made of this, or of racism, in the Marxist theory of welfare standards (Ginsburg, 1979; Gough, 1979; Offe, 1984). Thus, although Gough states:

Colonialism was used to open up [the] markets to capitalist competition to protect them against depredations from other imperialist countries. In this way then a *world* capitalist system was established in the late nineteenth century. *Note that this too impinges directly on many aspects of the welfare state.* To take one example, since the war millions of migrant workers have been drawn to the industrial centres of Europe, so that now one in seven of all manual workers are immigrants. (1979, p. 29, my emphasis)

Here the analysis stops. We never get to know the 'many aspects'.

One writer in the political economy vein who has drawn attention to two particular ways in which welfare, imperialism and immigration are linked is Lesley Doyal (1979; Doyal et al. 1981). First, her analysis in *The Political Economy of Health* (1979) examines the role of Western medical technology and investment in the underdevelopment of health in the Third World and concludes that 'the historical form of capitalist expansion in the Third World has not only systematically undermined the health of the population, but has also created obstacles to the realization of effective health policies' (p. 137). Secondly, she examines the role that Black immigrants and workers play in providing a cost-effective source of labour in the NHS: 'these workers provide a critical source of cheap labour and their utilisation has always been an important component both in keeping down costs and in rationalizing the labour process in health care' (Doyal et al., 1981, p. 54). So far, then, two aspects are identified: the role of Black workers as cheap labour in the welfare state, and the role of imperialism and neo-colonialism in the development of the welfare state. But there are many other welfare issues that a reading of Black and anti-racist writers reveals, issues that find no mention in political economy: the historical role of nationalism and welfare; the systematic neglect of the welfare needs of Black people; reproduction of a racial division of labour not only within the welfare state, but through the institutions of welfare, like education; the pathologizing of Black families and cultures; the racial harassment of Black households; use of the heavier forms of social control in welfare-sterilization, disruptive units, taking into care and incarceration, as well as through law and order, and the use of welfare institutions to police the state immigration controls; and not least, the role of Black and anti-racist welfare struggles.

It might be suggested that these writings have only emerged recently. It is also true, however, that Sivanandan wrote his article on 'race', class and the state more than ten years ago (Sivanandan, 1976). On the one hand, it is likely that Black radicals are justifiably suspicious of academic social policy, after all, the policy-orientated studies of the 1960s and 1970s have, if anything, tended to reinforce not alleviate racism and the welcome given by white radicals to such ground-breaking books as *The Empire Strikes Back* (CCCS, 1982) was less than enthusiastic. On the other hand, I would also suggest that some emphases in the political economy approach inhibit an acknowledgement of the Black experience of the welfare state: these cluster around the issues of class struggle, the state, reforms and the international division of labour, and they also reiterate some criticism made by the feminist critique.

As we noted above, Gough's analysis attempts to avoid the evils of a functionalist or conspiracy analysis of the welfare state as a tool of ruling-class domination by taking into account the role of working-class struggle for welfare reforms, but in doing so he implies a unity of working-class struggle and purpose which fails to explain why many welfare struggles have resulted in gains for some sections rather than or even at the expense of others. The white skilled male working class in the 1920s gained from National Insurance, for example, whilst 'aliens' and women were denied access. Jews, Irish, Black people, and women and the undeserving share a history of welfare either being denied from them or controlling them. The state's power to divide and rule and its need for an army of reserve labour is clearly one part of this, but it is not enough of an explanation, for it merely returns us to a functionalist analysis. What is also necessary is to examine more closely these class struggles, to deconstruct them and understand them in terms of the role of racism and nationalism in moulding the demands of the working class and in formulating the response from state and capital. Often racism and nationalism have only been taken seriously by the white left when exhibited by fascists or the far right. At the same time, there is a need to assert the historical importance of all types of struggle against racial domination. Too often the theory and practice of the left in Britain has ignored the political, trade union or anti-colonial traditions that Black immigrants (as well as Irish and Jewish immigrants before them) brought with them, and the challenges posed by contemporary anti-racist struggles in the community.

Many accounts of the Black experience of welfare and the state give a clear picture of the state and capital continuing to oppress and exploit Black people, with the welfare state giving them a helping hand. The intertwining of immigration control and welfare agencies is one example. Most emphasize the controlling and repressive features of welfare (Amos and Parmar, 1984; Mama, 1984; Trivedi, 1984; Bryan et al., 1985). Furthermore, it is often the *limitations* of reform, especially in the present period, which Black accounts point to: 'We argue that in a context of emerging authoritarianism and a strengthening of repressive agencies, there is little hope that reformist strategies will fundamentally improve the material conditions which confront Black people in their daily struggle to survive in British society' (CCCS, 1982, p. 35). Some analyses of reforms in 'race' politics in the post-war period cast doubt on the supposition that they might have achieved *anything* at all for Black people (Bridges, 1975; Bourne, 1980; Lawrence, 1982; Jacobs, 1985; Solomos, 1985). All of these emphases sit uneasily with a discipline whose subject matter is reform and whose political economy approach insists upon a careful balancing of the gains of the welfare state with its controlling and bureaucratic features. This is not to say that Black people do not need or do not benefit from the welfare state, they do; but the nature of the contradictions they face is qualitatively different and perhaps more stark, compared with the experiences of many white people. Thus, whilst Black people are amongst those who fight to retain the welfare state, they do so, as Bryan et al. (1985) point out, from an unenviable position at the bottom of the welfare state's agenda. These contradictions are qualitatively different because of the specific ways in which racism is woven into welfare provision.

Ginsburg is one writer to go some way in recognizing these difficulties. He examines in a detailed way the precise role played by sections of the working class and ruling class in struggles over housing and social security. Secondly, he begins an explanation of the 'duality' of the welfare state which connects the struggle, gains and capital more clearly: 'the demands of the welfare state have produced important gains; but those demands have been processed and responded to in such a form that, far from posing a threat to capital, they have deepened its acceptance and extended its survival' (1979, p. 19). This is taken further by the authors of *In and Against the State* (LEWRG, 1979), who include racism as one of the ways in which the state reproduces the social relations of capitalism through the institutions of welfare. For them the important point is that class struggle has to be capable in itself of visions and struggles which incorporate quite opposing social relations – collectivist, anti-sexist, anti-racist.

To begin to raise questions about racism means examining imperialism, neo-imperialism and international movements of labour. Bourne writes that 'the struggle against racism today has also to be a struggle against imperialism' (1980, p. 350). Most political economy analyses rest within the confines of Western Europe, perhaps influenced by a nostalgia among Marxists for a Euro-Centric Internationale. Anti-racist analysis must be able to relate welfare strategy to immigration controls. Is the political economy approach for or against immigration controls? What is the relationship between economic growth in this country and the continuing global divisions between North and South? What role does the welfare state play in relation to the international division of labour? Apart from Lesley Doyal, who deals with the last point (1979), the political economy approach has not been particularly forthcoming on these issues. Whilst the political economy approach offers a historical-materialist analysis of the welfare state which can provide a framework for understanding the role of women and Black people in relation to capitalism, the tendency has been to ignore many of those specific aspects of these oppressions which are not part of, or explicable in terms of, capital accumulation or a particular view of class struggle. In addition, both the Black experience of welfare and the feminist critique of the welfare state suggests that the symmetrical model of the welfare state as the outcome of pressure from above (bad) with pressure from below (good) needs further clarification: the unified concept of class struggle needs to be opened up, the nature and impact of welfare reforms to be re-examined and its net of contradictions to be cast wider. Its focus upon production needs to be extended to encompass the dynamics of reproduction and its scope enlarged to situate the British welfare state in the context of imperialism, neo-imperialism and the international division of labour.

Conclusion

To sum up: the individualism of anti-collectivism combined with its acceptance of women's 'natural' role within the family means that its values and freedom are contrary to women's interests. Furthermore, neo-conservativism has used the ideal of the traditional patriarchal family as a central theme in its social and economic policies. This same individualism fails to register institutionalized racism, and this, in tandem with the neo-conservatives' articulation of theories of nation and 'race' which stress the importance of cultural essentialism, and the identification of Black people as a threat to law and order and British culture, all means that this approach is entirely unable to account for the experiences of women and Black people or present a strategy which furthers their interests. The influences of familism and nationalism, and history of social imperialism upon non-socialist welfare collectivism and Fabian social policy thinking also limits the understanding of these approaches to the oppressions of gender and 'race'. In so far as women's interests have been represented, it has been in terms that have emphasized their role as wife and mother. And in so far as, more recently, sex and racial inequalities are acknowledged, they have been identified as the result of post-war discrepancies and discriminations, whose eradication is possible through legislation. Of the two remaining radical approaches, the radical social administration and the political economy approach, both acknowledge sex inequalities and the latter offers an approach which sets the oppression of women within the context of the historical role of the family under capitalism, but both fall short on elaborating the specific nature of women's oppression and the implications of this for a strategy which attempts to break down the separation of production and reproduction, and the sexual division of labour. Neither of these approaches has much to say about the dynamics of 'race' and welfare, and although both ascribe in different ways to an international approach, the crucial link between the history and development of the international economy and domestic social policy and ideology is missing. I suggested earlier that the concern of the political economy approach to present a dialectical analysis of the welfare state has had the effect of taking for granted the 'unitariness' of class struggle as well as the progressive nature of some welfare reforms, and of underplaying some of the more repressive and controlling aspects of state welfare as experienced by women and Black people.

In the preceding chapters elaborating the feminist and anti-racist critiques of the welfare state it was concluded that an adequate welfare theory should be able first to offer a historical and materialist account for the relationship between the state, the family and women without recourse to either biological determinism or crude economism, and secondly, to offer a materialist analysis of 'race' and racism and its relation to welfare which is grounded in the economic structure but does not simply reduce these phenomena to the economic level. At the same time such a theory has to recognize the historical specificity of different phases of development of imperialism and international capitalism.

In more practical terms this means that the political economy of welfare is an important but insufficient basis on which to build an understanding of 'race', class and gender in the welfare state. However, if we combine with it the import of socialist feminism's critique of welfare – taking into account the important criticisms from Black feminism – and the contribution of the 'moving picture' approach to 'race' and class offered by Hall, Gilroy and others *and* the political economy of migrant labour approach offered by Miles and Phizacklea, *then* it is possible to provide a framework which takes much greater account of the issues of 'race' and gender and class in the welfare state. Such a framework would have to recognize the role that women and Black people have played in relation to the welfare state as workers, paid and unpaid, as consumers and as people struggling for their needs to be met. It would have to be based on a historical analysis of the shifting relationship of the state to the family, women, capitalism and patriarchy as well as racism, nationalism, imperialism and neo-imperialism. It should attempt to examine how the welfare state articulated these relationships and the role class struggles have had in challenging or otherwise the oppression of women and racially oppressed groups. The next two chapters attempt to provide such a framework.

PART III The Welfare State: an Analysis

6 The Historical Cast of Welfare Reforms: Family and Nation

Introduction

Chapters 3, 4 and 5 have shown that whilst significant empirical and analytical accounts and critiques testify to the racism and sexism, and its variously contested forms, operating historically and today in the welfare state, major theoretical works on the welfare state have made little or limited acknowledgement of these. What is needed is an approach which examines the development and operation of the welfare state in the light of the shifting constellation of capitalism with imperialism and patriarchy, that is to say, the welfare state as part of a racially structured and patriarchal capitalism. This and the subsequent chapter begin the attempt to do that, to highlight the issues which are important for such an understanding and to point in the direction of others which require further examination. As a first step this discussion is necessarily selective.

A structure for understanding the welfare state as part of capitalism is offered by Gough (1979) (see chapter 2). Gough makes three major points: firstly, that the major aim of the welfare state is the organization of *social reproduction*, that is to say, the reproduction of labour power and the maintenance and control of the non-working population (through, for example, ensuring a minimum level of consumption, as well as shaping the behaviour and skills that people develop, both by reward and sanction). Secondly, in doing this the welfare state fulfils two further functions – *accumulation*, the maintenance of conditions favourable to capital accumulation, and *legitimation or repression*, the preservation of social harmony or the containment or control of dissent. Thirdly, this process has to be understood as the result of conflict between two main political forces – on the one hand, pressure from the organized working class, and on the other, reforms from 'above', the state working directly or indirectly in the interests of capital, or sections of it. Now, once we begin to inject this model with an understanding of capitalism as both patriarchal and racially structured we find that elements of the analysis need unpacking to discover where the interests of women and of Black people can be found, and that further, both the focus of the analysis and its context have to be broadened. Its production focus has to be broadened to include social reproduction, an understanding of the family from the point of view of those most central to it, women; and its context has to be broadened to an internationalist understanding of imperialism and its impact on the lives of Black and immigrant welfare users and workers. Put simply, we require an analysis which identifies not just work but also Family and 'Race'/Nation as the key organizing principles of welfare development.

The following attempt to do this is in two sections. In this chapter we begin to sketch out the development of the welfare state from the 1830s to the present day in terms of the shifting relations of imperialism, patriarchy and capitalism, and the ways these relations affect not only the reforms from above, but also the demands and struggles of 'pressure from below'. It is suggested that the construction of the welfare state around the consolidating themes of Family and Nation, largely endorsed by powerful sections of the labour movement, served to marginalize the struggles and interests of women, Black and other immigrants and workers. The following chapter examines elements of the contemporary welfare state which illuminate the role that women and Black people play in the welfare state, as paid and unpaid workers and as people involved in welfare struggles, and the impact upon them of a welfare state as part of a racially structured and patriarchal capitalism. The final part of that chapter looks at the implications of struggles around these issues for welfare analyses and strategy and suggests that these struggles and issues are central to the development of a future welfare strategy.

It is important to stress that, although the objective here is to understand the development of the welfare state in terms of imperialism and patriarchy as well as capitalism, the relationship between these three has not been constant nor always mutually accommodating. The nature of the relationship of 'race', class and gender to the workers and consumers of the welfare state is, and has been, a complex one.

1830s to 1880s: Early State Intervention

State intervention in the nineteenth century, from the 1830s, followed in the wake of the expansion of industrial capitalism and was directed by the liberal philosophy of *laissez-faire*. Thus, rather than intervene in the workings of the free market of domestic capitalism or the free flow of trade and immigrant labour of higher imperialism (mainly from Ireland at this point), the state stepped in to create the conditions favourable to the maintenance of the freedom of the market through, for example, the 1834 Poor Law. At the same time, by the end of the nineteenth century, capitalism had sealed the separation of home life from work life, and established women in the home as responsible for social reproduction – nurturing and caring for both wage-earners and dependants. Both these processes rendered women more or less dependent upon the wage of the male 'breadwinner', even though for many of the working class this wage was insufficient and many women were forced to take low paid casual or home-based work. Nevertheless a forceful ideology of women as subordinate to men, mentally and physically, was reinforced through religion, science and medicine (Ehrenreich and English, 1979). In these ways, the social relations of capitalism – individualism, exploitation and antagonistic class interests – became welded on to and reconstituted the already existing relations of patriarchy, of male authority over women at home and at work. In this situation the role of state intervention defined the boundaries of what was 'public' and what was 'private' and relegated women's lives to the private, particularly by the reinforcement of women's financial dependence on their husbands and their restriction from areas of paid work. The Factory Acts of 1844 onwards, whilst partly a victory for the male-dominated trade unions for shorter hours, represented at the same time an attempt by the state, Victorian moralists, sections of the ruling class and ordinary working men to exclude women from significant areas of work and ensure their presence in the home as bearers and carers under patriarchal authority (Walby, 1986, pp. 100–26). The combination of the exclusion of children from work and the introduction of state education began also to define their responsibility as mothers, and the period of welfare reforms from the turn of the century to the 1930s marked the second phase of much more direct state intervention which for women meant an attempt to regulate and supervise their domestic lives. In addition to reinforcing material dependency and regulating motherhood, the state, through medicine and law, also became a powerful executor over women's sexuality in the second half of the nineteenth century. One way it did this was in its identification of women's sexuality, through prostitution, as responsible for the spread of veneral disease. The Contagious Diseases Acts between 1864 and 1886 allowed detention by force and medical examination of women suspected to be prostitutes in major seaports and garrison towns.

None of these state manifestations of patriarchal capitalism can be separated from Britain's imperialist role and imperialist ideology. Myths of the inherent superiority of the northern white Christian world were longstanding and found their way into state legislation. In 1813 Asian seamen, known as 'lascars' were denied any form of subsistence in Britain through the East India Act which forced the East India Company to provide the necessary subsistence for these men until they returned to India. This proved costly to the company and the act was changed in 1849. However, controls were introduced to ensure lascars did not stay in Britain or have recourse to public funds. If they did the first their ship's master was fined £30; if they did the second they were subject to repatriation. This law was only finally repealed in 1970 (Gordon, 1985). Such policies found justification in the pseudo-scientific racism of the 1850s of Herbert Spencer and Charles Darwin. These ideas of 'survival of the fittest' identified white skins and 'Anglo-Saxon' civilization as the culmination of the evolutionary process; Spencer believed that dominant races were able to conquer inferior races by virtue of their greater 'mental mass'. Such scientific and sociological expositions unleashed a backlog of expressions of cultural, religious and racial superiority, as well as male superiority, and gave justification to some of the worst forms of exploitation and barbarianism performed in the name of England's 'civilizing mission'. In 1862, for example, John Arthur Roebuck, MP for Sheffield, told the House of Commons that in New Zealand 'the Englishmen would destroy the Maori, the sooner the Maori was destroyed the better' (quoted in Fryer, 1984, p. 180). By 1869 the last Black inhabitant of Tasmania was hunted down and killed. As Fryer comments 'Social darwinism taught white people that the Tasmanians were their brothers and sisters. It also taught them that the extermination of those brothers and sisters was an inevitable part of the struggle for existence, in which their own 'superior' race alone was destined to survive' (p. 181).

This exposition of 'races' meant that the Irish too were designated a different 'race'. Even Engels wrote of the Irishman in 1844 'his crudity places him little above the savage' (quoted in Foot, 1965, p. 82). This too found reflection in state policies for the relief of poverty. Two centuries of British political domination in Ireland were sealed in 1800, two years after the Irish Rebellion, by dissolving the Irish Parliament and creating an Act of Union between Ireland and the United Kingdom. Over this time, through restrictions in trade which threatened the indigenous economy, Ireland became a dependent sector of the British economy, a pattern which was repeated in many of the British colonies. Poverty, and particularly the 1847 famine, pushed many Irish people to Britain in search of work. By 1841 400,000 Irish-born immigrants were living in Britain. Many of these workers were active in the radical and revolutionary organizations of the working class of the early nineteenth century, especially the Chartist movement of the 1830s and 1840s, to which they brought their own experiences of struggle against political domination. One of the main Chartist leaders was the Irishman Feargus O'Connor. At the same time strong anti-Irish sentiment existed, rooted in the anti-Catholicism of the Reformation, as well as the belief that the Irish were a separate and inferior 'race'. This justified for many employers the employment of Irish people in cheap, unskilled and back-breaking work. With the failure of Chartism by the mid-nineteenth century this ideology became stronger in the working class and the trade unions who began to see the Irish as undercutting wages, as unorganizable and lacking in political traditions. This found reinforcement and sustenance in the 1834 Poor Law. This Poor Law created a system of poor relief based on 'less eligibility' – that none receiving relief should be better off than the lowest paid labourer – and also a system of deterrence – that the conditions of accepting relief, particularly entry into the workhouse, would be so shaming as to deter people from applying for it and push them instead into the labour market. As it was, the workhouse system proved too costly and difficult to contain all the existing paupers, and in many areas outdoor relief was given. A further aspect of the Poor Law was its connection to the laws of settlement which form the origins of the test of residence status which operates in several areas of the welfare state today. The settlement laws made the cost of relief the responsibility of the claimant's parish of settlement, that is, where he or she came from. This became a problem when people moved to the towns and then became unemployed, ill or old. The 'power of removal' gave the host parish power to send a person and family back to where they had come from if they applied for relief. Clearly, fear of removal deterred many from claiming, but in many cases the towns simply charged the parishes of settlement for the relief they were distributing. Eventually, in 1846, the law created a five-year rule which allowed a claimant right to freedom from removal if he or she had resided in the parish for five years. The power of removal affected the Irish most, deterring them from applying for relief for fear of deportation, and forcing them into low paid jobs. Indeed, when it was argued that the settlement laws should be abolished because they prevented the free flow of labour and were costly to administer, one of the main arguments given in their favour was that they prevented widespread availability of relief to the Irish (Rose, 1971, p. 193). By the late 1840s more Irish were being forced out of Ireland because of the potato famine, which killed more than one million people. They found themselves caught between the exigencies of the lowest paid work in Britain and dire poverty in Ireland and thus provided a pool of cheap labour for employers. The vagrancy laws were also punitive and degrading and affected the Irish immigrants in particular, pushing them from pillar to post, and identifying them as criminals.

As far as women were concerned the Poor Law shifted between accepting the rights of women with no male breadwinner partner (widows, deserted and separated wives, and unmarried mothers) to poor relief, forcing women to become dependent on a man or liable relative, insisting they support themselves through their low paid work, and discouraging 'immortality' with punitive and deterrent practices. As ever the system found itself caught between reinforcing the ideology of family life and female dependency, and facing the reality of the existence of many women who were forced to maintain themselves and their children from a position of marginalization from the labour market. The 1834 Poor Law aimed to shift the responsibility for maintenance of the children of unmarried mothers from the father and the parish to the mother. Many such women had to work and submit their children to the 'care' of the workhouse, but ten years later, with increasing concerns about the costs of the workhouse system, they were given the right to outdoor relief (Ginsburg, 1979, p. 82). Widows were granted the right to outdoor relief from the beginning, but efforts were often made to find a relative who would accept liability for their maintenance, or to get the women to take on casual women's work – washing, taking in lodgers, fostering workhouse children. By 1871 all widows with only one child were required to take paid work and not relief (Lewis, 1984, p. 63). Deserted and separated wives were treated with particular suspicion and not considered eligible for relief until a year after the separation or desertion. This eligibility, however, was strictly circumscribed by the attempts by the Poor Law authorities to shift a woman's financial dependence back on to her errant and often unreliable husband or another liable relative. The obligation of a man to maintain his wife and children became law in 1878. The 'obligation to maintain' imposed by the state through its institutions of welfare was the other side of the coin of the family wage system which formed the basis of trade union bargaining. Both were premised upon the woman's financial dependency and marginalized her needs and contributions within the household. This was challenged in different ways by organizations of working-class and middle-class women (see chapter 3) who demanded economic, political and legal rights, but the conflict between these demands and the family wage system was not resolved.

By 1891, according to Halèvy (quoted in Robinson, 1983, p. 351), the number of subjects under some form of British rule amounted to more than 394 million, more than ten times the population of Britain. The British Empire covered almost one-quarter of the entire land surface of the globe. The countries within the Empire, particularly the undeveloped ones, provided Britain with raw materials and cheap labour and increasingly, by the end of the century, with markets for the export of manufactured goods. The Empire permeated every area of social, economic and political life: the institutions of industry, of government, of religion, of science and of education all justified and sustained its existence.

1880s to 1930s: Motherhood, Imperialism and Welfare Reforms

The first major period of welfare reforms was from the 1880s to the 1930s and the complex and varied interaction of capitalist, patriarchial and imperialist social relations is perhaps best shown by reference to two examples of policy-making during this period: policies for motherhood and policies for unemployment. (Other areas too afford good examples; see for instance Lucy Bland's study of the policies around venereal disease which 'represented a lurking, undefined threat to stability, the family, the British race and empire', Bland, 1985, p. 192.) These two examples, of motherhood and unemployment policies, show five different and important facets: first, the ideological dimensions of imperialism (a 'racism abroad') in the construction of domestic (in both senses) social policy around the family; secondly, the implications of this in unemployment policy for a 'racism at home', particularly in the exclusion of 'foreigners' and the use of welfare agencies as a form of immigration control; thirdly, in relation to women, the state's role in defining and supervising motherhood, as well as, fourthly, the state's role through welfare of restricting and marginalizing women's access to paid work. Finally, an analysis of struggles around these issues also indicates the extent, by the time of the defeat of the General Strike in 1926, to which internationalism and feminism were marginalized issues in the labour movement and the demands for welfare reforms were constructed within a reformist, nationalist and familist framework which offered little defence to the interests of women and the subsequent interests of Black immigrants, and little inclination towards solidarity with either. Before examining these two examples a picture of the political and economic background is necessary.

The 1880s onwards marked an important political and economic shift. The certainties of the old *laissez-faire* liberalism were shaken by a number of developments. Britain's industrial supremacy in the world markets was being challenged by the United States and Japan, her imperial power was rivalled by Germany and its legitimation challenged by the strengthening demand for Irish Home Rule. The Boer War had revealed the poor state of physical health of British soldiers, and furthermore there was concern about the decline in the birth rate. Policies were required to produce the soldiers and sailors with the necessary fitness and skills to defend Britain's economic and imperial power. The certainties of the old regime were further challenged by important political movements. First there was the strength of the 'new unionism', the mass organization of increasing numbers of workers. In the mid-1870s trade union membership was about half a million, by 1914 it was four million (Hinton, 1983, chapter 3). The strength of these unions is best marked by the successful five-week Dock Strike in London of 1889, led by Ben Tillett, which gave enormous confidence to marginalized sections of the working class, although it still left sections of the urban poor – the residuum – untouched. Nevertheless, fear of organized rebellion from the former, or unorganized riots from the latter, haunted the ruling class. This fear was highlighted by two further factors. First, the free market of capitalism, rather than running smoothly, was subject to a succession of booms and slumps which undermined the belief in the inevitable logic and progress of the market economy and furthermore gave rise to periods of unemployment which threatened political stability. Secondly, there was a revival of a whole spread of socialist organizations: the Marxist-based Social Democratic Federation and the Socialist League with commitments to international solidarity amongst workers to overthrow capitalism; the anarchists based in London's East End Jewish community; the Independent Labour Party which spawned the Labour Party and from that the first representation of the working class in Parliament in 1906, and the first Labour government in 1924. Also important were the political demands of universal adult suffrage and in particular the feminist campaigns which were focused on the vote through the Women's Social and Political Union and the National Union of Women's Suffrage Society. Feminist activity also included an attempt to repeal the Contagious Diseases Acts and expose men's double moral standard, attempts to secure admission to the professions for middle-class women and to push the trade unions to take up the demand of equal pay for working-class women. The feminist militancy of this period was cut across with differences of class interest and political objectives, marked particularly by the split at the outbreak of war in 1914 between those who urged patriotism and backed the war effort and those like Sylvia Pankhurst who maintained an anti-imperialist and class view of the war. More significantly any potential for a merging of the socialist and feminist goals was never reached at any level, not among the revolutionaries, the trade unions or the Labour Party. 'Feminism challenged the apparent unity of the male labour movement, just as the impact of socialism disrupted the women's organisations' (Hall and Schwarz, 1985, p. 15).

What then was the resolution of these threats to the old liberalism? It combined two forces: collectivism under the rubric of social imperialism. Social imperialism was a solution supported by all political parties to the threat posed in the 1880s and 1890s by an increasingly organized and socialist working class. It aimed to subordinate class interests to those of nation and empire, and it succeeded by linking these issues to social reform and by suggesting a necessary interdependence. In this way trade unions pressing for welfare reforms came to believe that such reforms were the fruits of imperialist policy and were necessary to create national efficiency upon which imperial power depended (Semmel, 1960). This combined with a strong influence of Darwinism and eugenics. There was thus an *apparent* material as well as ideological basis for the working class to believe in imperialism and racial supremacy. It also created a principled belief in entitlement to welfare benefits *by nationality*, which became written into all the early benefits – 1908 and 1911 Old Age Pensions Acts, 1918 National Insurance Act, municipal education and housing in the 1920s (see Cohen, 1985).

Policies around motherhood combined these issues and illustrate the nature of a collectivism which urged state intervention whilst holding on to individualist explanations for social problems (see Davin, 1978; Lewis, 1982, 1984; for an interesting counterview see Dwork, 1987, pp. 226–30). Among the reforms of this period were those aimed at improving the health of infants, particularly through education of their mothers – notification of births (1907), school meals for the needy (1906), medical inspection in schools (1907), the Children's Act, and importantly the 1918 Maternity and Child Welfare Act which formally established clinics with health visitors. A vast number of voluntary societies aimed at promoting child welfare and domestic hygiene also came into existence. State intervention to supervise women's care for their children not only marked a shift in the relationship between state and family but it represented an attempt to increase the birth rate, to lower infant mortality and to provide the population who would maintain the Empire. Maintaining the 'Imperial Race' was seen as an utmost priority: quality of the 'race' for national efficiency, quantity for the imperial army. A propaganda film entitled 'Motherhood' made in 1917 to celebrate National Baby Week expressed the view that 'the Race marches forward on the feet of the children'. Anna Davin expresses the essence of these policies thus:

A powerful ideology of motherhood emerged in relation to these problems of the early 20th Century, though it was firmly rooted in the nineteenth-century assumptions about women, domesticity and individualism. Motherhood was to be given new dignity, it was the duty and destiny of women to be 'mothers of the race', but also their reward. But just as it was the individual mother's duty and reward to rear healthy members of an imperial race, so it was her individual ignorance and neglect which must account for infant deaths or sick children. Thus, moral blackmail, exploiting the real difficulties and insecurities of many mothers, underpined their lofty status. Nor did their elevation mean an end to subordination. To be good mothers they now needed instruction, organized through the various agencies of voluntary societies and local government, in the skills of what came to be known as mothercraft, as they were being defined by the medical profession. Doctors, district nurses, health visitors were all asserting their superior knowledge and authority, establishing moral sanctions on grounds of health and national interest ... *The authority of state over individual, of professional over amateur, of science over tradition, of male over female, of ruling class over working class, were all involved in the redefining of motherhood in this period.* (Davin, 1978, p. 13, my emphasis)

And it was sustained by a powerful ideology of the supremacy of British culture and the British race over others.

A second example of the interconnections of these issues can be seen in the unemployment policies of the 1920s. In different ways these policies, along with the earlier 1908 Old Age Pensions Act and health insurance in the 1911 National Insurance Act, discriminated against women and 'aliens', aspects which were not contested by the labour movement. In the case of 'aliens' what we see in these policies is, first, the beginnings of a popularly accepted idea that entitlement to forms of welfare provision should be restricted by *nationality*, which in practice meant white, Christian and English-speaking, and secondly, the interconnection of welfare provision with immigration control which worked in two ways: either by using denial of access to welfare as a form of control, or by using the welfare agencies themselves to police foreigners' access to benefits. The 1905 Aliens Act was passed to impose restrictions on Jewish immigrants who arrived, many as refugees from Eastern Europe and Russia, from the 1880s onwards. The campaigns for immigration control often concluded in abusive anti-semitism, and found support from all the major political parties as well as from trade unionists like Ben Tillett, the dockers leader. Bruce Glasier of the ILP wrote in the *Labour Leader* in 1904: 'Neither the principle of the brotherhood of man nor the principle of social equality implies that brother nations or brother men may crowd upon us in such numbers as to abuse our hospitality, overturn our institutions or violate our customs' (quoted in Cohen, 1985, p. 76). The Aliens Act demanded that no person who could not support herself or himself, or who might need welfare provision, should be allowed in, and that any who within 12 months was homeless or living in overcrowded conditions or living off poor relief be deported. The 1908 Pensions Act denied a pension to anyone who had not been both resident *and* a British subject for 20 years. In the health insurance scheme of the 1911 National Insurance Act, non-British citizens who had not been resident for five years received lower rates of benefit (seven-ninths) even though they had paid contributions (Cohen, 1985). Women too were only eligible for three-quarters of the rate. Furthermore women were penalized by not being able to claim for time off for childbirth.

In 1918 increases in mass unemployment following the ending of the First World War led to some of the discriminations being removed because the administrative costs of operating the complex procedures were too high (see Cohen, 1985, pp. 83–4). At the same time, however, the administration of the 'out-of-work donation' – a non-contributory, non-means-tested, relatively generous benefit for ex-soldiers *was* clearly racist. The Ministry of Labour refused to grant the donation to aliens and in 1919 sent secret instructions to labour exchange managers that unemployed Black seamen should be kept ignorant of their rights to 'out-of-work-donation' (Fryer, 1984, p. 299). Rising unemployment and post-war jingoism combined to make the lives of Jewish and Black people severely restricted. After the war racist attacks took place on Black workers and families in South Tyneside, Liverpool and Cardiff. The Aliens Act was further tightened in 1919 and 'all Jewish aliens were obliged to carry identity cards, to notify the authorities if they were absent from home for two weeks, to

The Historical Cast of Welfare Reforms   159

keep out of designated "protected areas", and to fill in a special register if
they stayed overnight at a hotel. At the same time the police were given
power to close clubs and restaurants "frequented by aliens"' (Cohen, 1985,
p. 87).

Interestingly, following the 1920 Aliens Order, which gave the police
greater powers to investigate illegal immigration, it was the Special Irish
Branch, whose role previously had been to hunt out Irish nationalists, who
were given the job. Although 'aliens' referred at this time mainly to Jewish
people, there were attempts, justified in terms of the high unemployment
rates amongst seamen, to repatriate Black seamen. In the event these
failed, but immigration controls on Black seamen increased. As Gordon
comments, these controls have modern parallels, since they

were initially imposed to reduce the perceived costs of immigration and, later, to
protect the labour market for the indigenous white working class. Although
supposed to be applicable only to people who were not British subjects, in practice
all black people were at risk. Finally, the controls suggested the ultimate solution of
repatriation, and, as was made clear in the highest official circles at the time, such
repatriation need not be compulsory, but could also be induced and encouraged.
(1985, p. 8)

By 1921 the Ministry of Labour was forced to re-introduce non-contributory benefits for those who had run out of entitlement to national
insurance benefit. The Ministry was, however, obsessed with the possibility
of scroungers and thus introduced a 'genuinely-seeking-work test' (GSWT)
whereby a claimant had to prove she or he was genuinely seeking work
(Deacon, 1976, 1977). This was aimed largely at restricting the eligibility of
married women workers to benefit since the view was that their work in the
munitions factories during the First World War had been a temporary role
and that now they should not expect either to work or receive benefit. The
other restrictive legislation was the introduction in 1922 of a means test – a
test of household means – and the forerunner of the much-despised means
test of the 1930s – to deem whether or not a claimant needed benefit. At the
same time certain groups were automatically denied benefit, including
married persons with a partner in work and, the other object of government paranoia, aliens. Interestingly, while the operation of the means test
was vigorously campaigned against by the trade unions and the National
Unemployed Workers Movement (NUWM) there was little concern
initially about the GSWT (Deacon, 1977). This was probably because
married women were the main target of the GSWT whilst the means test
affected married men whose interests were given priority by the labour
movement. Indeed when the first Labour government came to power in
1924 it abolished the means test but actually tightened up the GSWT. After
the defeat of the General Strike the Conservative government reintroduced
the means test and severely tightened up the GSWT. Although women and

aliens again were the main groups to suffer from this, the general effect of
the tightening up was to deny benefit to able-bodied men too. At this point
the NUWM and the TUC campaigned for the withdrawal of the GSWT,
though the TUC was happy simply to demand a reversal to the original
interpretation. The Anomolies Act of 1931 replaced the GSWT and
deemed that any woman who had left the workforce had retired. This was
followed by a cut in health insurance benefits to married women in 1932
after an inquiry showed that more women than was considered
appropriate were claiming health insurance.

These policies represent part of the longer-term marginalization of
women from paid work and a reinforcement and redefinition of their
domestic role. For the Jewish and Black workers they represent the ways in
which nationalism and racism, immigration and internal controls were
intrinsic to the welfare state *before* the main arrival of Black immigrants in
the late 1940s. What it also shows is that the labour movement (which also
involved active Jewish, Black and women workers) was unable to sustain
any principled stand on racist immigration control and welfare practice,
nor to expand its focus of interests to include financial independence of
women. The divisions within its own ranks between respectable and unre-
spectable, between employed and unemployed, of gender and of 'race' were
reconstituted by the state in the welfare reforms the movement demanded
and won. This is not to say that there were no forms of support for
women's struggles. The famous rent strikes in Glasgow and Leeds from
1912 to 1914 were initiated by women and supported by the labour
movement and led to state-imposed rent control in 1915. But this was an
exception rather than the rule (Lewis, 1984, p. 27). Other battles were
fought and lost over this period, most notably the struggle to retain local
democratic control over the distribution of poor relief symbolized by
Poplarism (see Ginsburg, 1979, p. 59). By 1934 all benefit-setting and
administration was under central control. The more centralized provision
became the more the demands for reforms were limited to *access to* bureau-
cratically run and professionally administered welfare rather than *control
over* welfare. It was not until the women's movement of the 1960s and
1970s that fundamental questions about bureaucratic control and
professional authority were raised in any major way. The period discussed
here, from the 1880s to 1930, and the resolutions and antagonisms of class,
'race' and gender within it, have been described as the 'crucible years' (Hall
and Schwarz, 1985), in other words, the analysis of the period from 1880 is
crucial to an understanding of the developments over the following
century.

As a postscript to this period of welfare history it is suggested that the
framework of analysis which identifies Work, Family and 'Race'/Nation as
the key underlying principles of welfare development is useful in throwing
light on the welfare policies which were developed for another oppressed

group – the 'mentally deficient' (as the 'mentally handicapped' or people with learning difficulties were then labelled). The 1913 Mental Deficiency Act led to the grading of the 'mentally deficient' and their institutionalization in 'colonies' where they were segregated, not only from their families and communities in the outside world, but from the opposite sex. The aims of such a policy were in keeping with the predominant ideologies of class, 'race' and gender of the period. 'Mental defectives' and their supposed characteristics served almost as a metaphor for all that could undermine or destroy the progress of British capitalism, the British Family and the British Imperial Race. These characteristics included indolence, disorderliness, disobedience, immorality and promiscuity. The policy of institutionalization and segregation was not simply occasioned by a concern for these people's exclusion from waged labour and their consequent dependency but in order to prevent them from having children and further deteriorating the Race (see Ryan and Thomas, 1987). The Report of the 1929 Wood Committee on Mental Deficiency underlined this point:

Let us assume that we could segregate as a separate community all the families in this country containing mental defectives of the primary amentia type. We should find that we had colleced among them a most interesting social group. It would include as everyone who has extensive practical experience of social service would readily admit, a much larger proportion of insane persons, epileptics, paupers, criminals (especially recidivists), unemployables, habitual slum dwellers, prostitutes, inebriates and other social ineffecients than would a group of families not containing mental defectives. The overwhelming majority of the families thus collected will belong to a section of the community which we propose to term the 'social problem' or 'subnormal group' ... If we are to prevent the racial disaster of mental deficiency we must deal not only with the mentally defective persons but with the whole subnormal group from which the majority of them come ... The relative fertility of this (subnormal) group is greater than that of normal persons ... (Quoted in Ryan and Thomas, 1987, p. 108)

Scientific, moral, social and political ideas combined to frame a policy which encountered little opposition, apart from those for whom it was designed, and which effectively deprived a small oppressed section of the population of its human rights in the name of 'welfare'.

The 1945 Post-war Reforms

The next crucial phase in the development of the welfare state was the period of post-war reforms from 1945 to 1948: this saw Beveridge's National Insurance system and Family Allowances, the creation of the National Health Service in 1948, the implementation of the 1944 Education Act and a massive council house building programme. There is no doubt that these were significant developments for the welfare of the working class and that they went some way in meeting their aspirations and demands. At the same time, national and male chauvinism were built into the structure of these provisions. Woman's dependent status and her role as mother were reinforced by the developments, and the nationalist and imperialist sentiment of many of the policies created a ready framework for the unchallenged development of institutionalized racism. When Beveridge announced his attack on the five giants – Want, Squalor, Idleness, Ignorance and Disease – he hid the giants Racism and Sexism, and the fights against them, behind statues to the Nation and the White Family. In some ways the national unity which had previously appealed to a sense of Empire was now replaced by an appeal to a sense of British justice and fairness represented by the welfare state. These developments did not go unchallenged nor did they meet fully the demands for welfare policies made by women like Eleanor Rathbone, for family allowances, a recognition of women's domestic work and rights to equal pay. In the event the family allowances were set at much lower than the rates that had been recommended. A more radical opposition to Beveridge's policies came from Mrs Abbott and Mrs Bompass of the Women's Freedom League (Abbott and Bompass, 1943) based on the failure to give women independent status in the income maintenance schemes.

At the points where compromises were made by the post-war Labour government (and many were) it was often at the expense of women, the poor and the newly arrived Black workers. For example, the compromises Aneurin Bevan made in introducing and getting support for the National Health Service are well documented – he allowed consultants to continue their private practice while employed by the health service and assured general practitioners of their professional independence and autonomy, rather than becoming, like teachers and social workers, salaried local authority employees. Less well known is that he also decided against making provision for birth control under the health service on the grounds that it would arouse too much opposition (though women's organizations had long demanded it), and that he gave assurances that steps would be taken to prevent 'abuse' by foreigners (see Cohen 1985, p. 89).

Chapters 1–5 of this book have already pinpointed significant aspects of this familism and nationalism and the consequent failure of social policy in the post-war period, either conceptually or practically, to deal with the welfare needs of Black people or women. The following account therefore briefly points to the major effects of policy in the immediate post-war period for women and for the Black immigrants who arrived in the early 1950s.

One important aspect of this period was the increase in the proportion of married women working in response to the labour shortage in developing manufacturing industries and the services of the public sector. The other source of labour was, of course, Black immigration. But the majority in both groups remained, throughout the period, concentrated in low paid, unskilled work. As far as women were concerned, the welfare state of the immediate post-war years had idealized motherhood – 'the white woman's burden' (Dale, 1986) – and housework but failed to give women financial or practical support. Family allowances were set lower than recommended and the plans for communal laundries, nurseries and restaurants never materialized. In the following years the welfare state also failed to provide a structure of support for women workers, particularly those with children. The reforms in the 1960s and 1970s in divorce, abortion, equal pay and sex discrimination helped accommodate rising dissatisfactions but fundamentally the emphasis of social policies was to maintain the 'stability' of the family. In the 1950s this took the form of an elaboration of warnings of the 'emotional deprivation' (contrasted with the concern of physical deprivation of earlier years) which the children of working mothers could suffer. The solution to this heightened sense of responsibility became, for many white women, part-time work. In this way, their Black sisters who had had to leave their children behind until they were settled, or who had to work at jobs with long hours and low pay, were seen already to have failed as mothers. White family supremacy abroad became white family supremacy at home.

Since areas like housing and social security policies treated women as dependents of their wage-earning, tenancy-holding husbands, these failed to be able to respond to the changing situation of increasing numbers of female earners, single parents and elderly women. Secondly, much policy and provision, particularly housing and childcare, was based on the assumed predominance of the nuclear family form. This served to marginalize or stigmatize those not living in such a household, like single people, single parents, partners of the same sex and the elderly. It also led to the view that the steady departure from this norm constituted a problem in itself rather than a new set of needs to be met. In 1961 nuclear families (two parents with dependent children) represented 38 per cent of all households, by 1982 they represented 29 per cent (Watson, 1987, p. 131), yet single parents and the elderly continued to be amongst the main groups in poverty. Thirdly, progress for women was uneven and contradictory. The opening up of higher education in the 1960s generally benefited white middle-class girls. However, whilst these girls entered the labour market at a professional level, they found the gender inequalities here almost as prevalent as for their semi-skilled and unskilled sisters. Similarly, whilst the National Health system improved the general health of women, this was much less marked for working class and Black women. Fourthly, state provision to meet the specific needs of women – for contraception or abortion for example – was also accompanied by state regulation of women's lives through determining who had access to such provision.

In relation to the experience of Black people, one important aspect of this period is the extent to which the ground was already laid for the subsequent racism that occurred. For example, personal accounts of Caribbean workers' lives in Britain as forestry workers and service workers (see Ford, 1985; Sherwood, 1985) show that these people met with vicious racism. Somerset County Council automatically took into care any illegitimate baby born to a British woman but fathered by a *Black* American GI (BBC TV, 1986). Residency qualifications meant that council housing was not open to the new arrivals. In many cases Black people had to organize welfare provision for themselves; for example, in Liverpool in 1948 the Colonial People's Defence Committee organized for the welfare of Black seamen who were denied benefits when unemployed even though many of them were war veterans (Channel 4 TV, 1987). In an examination of the discussions by the post-war Labour government of the problem of shortage of labour and how it should be met, Heather Joshi and Bob Carter (1984) show that the spirit of these discussions reveal unreconstructed imperialist and racist attitudes. The immigration of Black workers was construed as a 'problem' where the racism of the white population and the labour movement was to be appeased rather than challenged. No consideration was given to the welfare needs of the new arrivals; indeed the concern was more about the possibilities of 'scrounging' and assuring the white population that no special privileges were being granted.

When black workers began to arrive here in some numbers in the 1950s, there was no progressive anti-racist political/ideological framework which would have enabled the working class to 'make sense' of a Black presence in Britain. Before the working class could fashion a response from within its collective traditions and experiences of poverty and hardships, its reformist leadership had structured such a response around 'colour' as a 'problem'. (Joshi and Carter, 1984, p. 55)

To begin with, then, Black immigrants entered a racist society where they were seen primarily by policy-makers as units of disposable labour. This framed subsequent immigration policy which aimed to limit the numbers of Black immigrants as well as to reduce rights of settlement. Whilst the 1962 Immigration Act sought to restrict entry to skilled or qualified workers or those who had jobs to go to, in fact the question of jobs was not the central issue in the propaganda for controls. The issues were the numbers of Black people and their 'drain' on the welfare services, and the restrictions were in terms of those who were thought to become a burden on the welfare state. The idea that Black people were actual or potential scroungers became institutionalized in law and practice even though no empirical evidence existed for such abuse. Nevertheless, in 1963 the Ministry of Health issued a memorandum to hospital authorities offering 'guidance' in treating 'visitors from overseas' (Cohen, 1985, p. 91). The 1971 Immigration Act tightened up the rights of Black people to enter and stay in Britain in an explicitly racist manner by use of the concept 'patrial' – citizens of the UK and colonies who had a parent or grandparent born in the UK or who had been 'ordinarily resident' in the UK for five years by 1973. These persons were not to be subject to immigration controls. This in effect created a distinction between white and Black potential immigrants from the Commonwealth. After this Act implementation of immigration controls through the welfare services became much more widespread. Instructions were sent to health officials, for example, in 1974 and 1979 on the non-eligibility of suspected short-stay residents. The crucial effect was to legitimize the racist practice of withholding welfare benefits from any Black person until proof of eligibility was established. The Act also widened scope for deportation and gave wider powers to the police for arrest without warrant in the case of suspected breach of immigration controls, with the effect of heightening police intervention in the Black communities. The 1982 Nationality Act brought nationality into line with the racist definitions in the 1971 Act. Varied elements of the controls combined sexism with racism: in 1979 a ban on the immigration of male fiances and husbands created the situation where men but not women could bring in their fiances or spouses.

Four further aspects characterize this period in relation to Black people's relations to the welfare state (see also chapters 4 and 7). First, the universal interests which the welfare reforms hoped to meet and sustain were heavily male, English-speaking and white. Universal provision meant treating all alike irrespective of specific needs. Similarly, social problems were generically conceived as 'deprivation' and 'poverty' which failed to acknowledge the specific needs of Black people or women. Secondly, in so far as racism was recognized, particularly when it threatened social stability, it was recognized and treated as a separate issue of attitude or culture, as particularly represented in the Race Relations Acts of 1965 and 1968, and the integrationist, assimilationist and multiculturalist policies of the 1960s and 1970s. Thirdly, Black immigrants in general entered the declining working class areas marked by poor and insufficient housing, health care and educational provision. In relation to schools they entered a process which was already operating to control and select children for a hierarchically structured labour market according to class and gender. These processes took on a racialized and racist dimension. The inadequacies of working-class culture which had explained working-class failure at school became reformulated as the inadequacy of Asian, African or Caribbean culture, to explain Black children's underachievement. Fourthly, and finally, in so far as the specific needs of Black people came to be acknowledged they were underpinned by a 'deficit model', that is to say, by a view of the problems faced by Black people as being caused by their own inappropriate family lives, cultures, languages or aspirations. (These aspects are covered in more detail in chapter 7.)

In general, the organized white working-class movements over the post-war period, whilst winning some significant victories for themselves, failed to face up to the challenges posed by the resistance of Black communities and groups, and by the growth of the women's movement. Not until the mid-1970s were there signs that this might change, in, for example, the mobilization of the labour movement to defend the attempt to limit access to abortion, and the support given to the anti-fascist and anti-racist campaigns of the same period (though organization for both was initiated outside the labour movement and support for the latter fell away as fascist groups declined, even though racism increased). The development of the labour movement as representing white male interests has already been described. A further aspect of trade unionism in the 1950s – its concentration upon workplace wages and conditions – also precluded the incorporation of women's and Black people's interests. This point is argued by Joshi and Carter:

> Black workers thus offered the labour movement the opportunity to break the reformist distinction between the 'political' and the 'economic' precisely because as a 'racialised' fraction of the working class, they could not improve their access to better jobs and housing through purely economistic action at the level of the shop floor. (1984, p. 69)

Economic Recession and the New Right

Policies affecting women and Black people appear to have gone in two contradictory directions since the mid-1970s. On the one hand there have been reforms such as the Equal Pay Act (1970) and Sex Discrimination Act (1975), and a significant tightening up of the Race Relations Act (1976); there has been the development of equal opportunities policies for women and, particularly since the 1981 riots, for Black people, and the pursuit of anti-racist and anti-sexist strategies in some local authorities and some areas of private industry; and there has been the continued development, and sometimes local authority support of, a whole range of local, grass-roots organizations aimed at meeting the needs of Black people and women in the community – education, training, freedom from violence, homelessness, health care. On the other hand, the welfare cutbacks and the failure to stem unemployment by both Labour and Conservative governments since 1975, along with the development of policies and ideologies from the New Right-influenced Conservative governments of 1979 onwards have served to weaken much of the progress made. These policies can be identified as having four different effects:

1 A *worsening* of some of the general material conditions which exacerbate gender and racial inequalities – for example, poverty, unemployment and low pay.

2   An *intensification* of those aspects in welfare policy which reproduce women's and Black oppression – for example, community care policies, immigration controls, law and order policies.

3   A *weakening* of the attempts to counter or challenge these – for example, through the disempowerment of the unions and the local authorities, as well as by the marginalization of women's struggles and Black resistance.

4   A *reworking* of the themes of the Family, Nation and Culture, into a justification for the minimizing of state-provided welfare, for inequalities and for the strong law and order state.

The impact of these processes upon women and Black people exemplifies the way in which the policies involved are a combination of a *general* attack upon the interests of the working class as well as a *specific* attack upon the interests of women and Black people. These processes are now examined in turn.

The first cutbacks in public expenditure were made by the Labour government in 1975. As a result of the economic crisis of that year the government applied to the International Monetary Fund for a loan; the IMF granted this on condition public spending was cut back. Over the following two years social service expenditure was cut by 6.5 per cent (Gough, 1980). Since 1979 the Conservative government has attempted to cut back expenditure but in fact it has never succeeded in cutting as much as planned. Overall between 1978/9 and 1986/7 public expenditure (including defence, up 28 per cent to £18.6 billion, and overseas aid, down 15 per cent to £1.2 billion) has increased by 14 per cent to £145.9 billion (Hills, 1987, quoting from Government Expenditure Plans, Cmnd 8789 and 56) and has remained, as such, at a fairly constant proportion of the national income. However, what this increase hides is the escalation of social needs. These needs include rising unemployment, an increase in the proportion of elderly people and single parents, as well as the social costs, like ill-health, of poverty. Within this overall picture there are particular variations: the housing budget has been more than halved in real terms (down 55 per cent). The result of this has been, along with the sales of council housing, a dramatic reduction of council housing stock as well as increases in council rents. However the impact of such cuts is to re-emerge as increased social costs in other budgets, for example, social security for the unemployed and board and lodging costs for the homeless. The increase in social security spending disguises not only the increased need, but also the cuts and their effects that have taken place within the social security budget. Pensions for example – the largest component – now are no longer linked to earnings, only to prices. Though there have been improvements in the state earnings related pension scheme, this move affects those whose main source of pension is the basic state pension. Child benefits have failed to keep up with inflation, and there have been cuts in housing benefit, as well as the means testing in April 1987 of the maternity grant and the death grant and the replacement of needs payments for claimants with a discretionary loan through the new social fund. The overall effect has been an intensification of poverty and a failure to meet the needs of those in poverty.

Unemployment and the social costs of the Conservative government's welfare policies have been borne disproportionately by the poor, particularly women and Black people. Between 1979 and 1986 male unemployment rose by 143 per cent and female unemployment by 189 per cent (EOC, Annual Report 1986), though the unemployment of many married and cohabiting women and mothers remains invisible in the unemployment statistics. However, the unemployment rate for Black women was almost twice that for white women even before 1979 – 10.8 per cent compared with 5.7 per cent (Arnott, 1987). The unemployment rate for workers of Caribbean origin is twice that for white workers; for those of Pakistani/Bangladeshi origin it is three times. This is more pronounced for Black youths aged 16–24; their white counterparts have an unemployment rate of 16 per cent, for youths of Caribbean origin it is 34 per cent, and for those of Pakistani/Bangladeshi origin it is 48 per cent. For older workers over 45 years of age the respective percentages are 7 per cent (white), 15 per cent (Caribbean), 34 per cent (Pakistani/Bangladeshi) (Taylor, 1987, p. 73). These figures hide particular concentrations in inner-city areas: a local survey in Liverpool in 1986 found *80 per cent* Black unemployment (Arnott, 1987).

Different racist and sexist processes have produced a situation where historically women and Black people have worked in the low paid industries, including the public sector (see chapter 7). This feature and the low levels of pay and the consequent lack of eligibility to certain forms of state protection and benefits have been intensified by recent policies. Public sector wages have fallen behind levels in other industries, and additionally the number of jobs cut back or given over to private contract and/or to part-time status has involved a worsening of conditions and pay (see Beechey and Perkins, 1987). The 1986 Wages Act removed wages council minimum wage protection from workers under 21 and weakened the protection for adults. This has particularly affected women workers, many of whom work in part-time low paid work, and industries like hotel and catering where Black men are highly represented (Arnott, 1987).

For white working-class women and Black women their marginalization into casualized part-time work and home-based piece-work reflects a restructuring of employment taking place on an international scale. This restructuring strategy aims, as Swasti Mitter describes, to 'nullify the rights and privileges that organized labour had won, especially in the West, through many years of struggle'. And she continues,

These workers are precisely the ones who have so far been marginalized in the mainstream labour movement. Their very vulnerability has made them a preferred labour force in an evolving pattern of business organisation that tends to rely on flexible and disposable workers. The transnational corporations, with their immense resources, engineer access to such workers by restructuring labour nationally as well as globally on the basis of race and gender. Colour and sex have thus become the main principles behind the most recent international division of labour. (1986, p. 6)

In this situation, access to employment rights and social security benefits has decreased. For example, someone working less than 16 hours a week, and with less than 5 years' continuous service has no rights with regard to sickness pay, unfair dismissal, redundancy pay or reinstatement after maternity leave. The recent reinforcement of the role of occupational pension and sick pay schemes takes non-manual, full-time, unbroken employment as the norm and thereby renders those who do not fit these patterns – like many Black and women workers and young workers – considerably worse off (see Land and Ward, 1986; Arnott, 1987; Glendinning and Millar, 1987).

As well as unemployment and low pay, the declining value of state benefits, of pensions, supplementary benefits (SB) (5 per cent increase compared with 14 per cent increase in incomes), income support, child benefits, widow's benefits and the losses of entitlement in housing benefit, free school meals, maternity grant, disablement allowance, young people's allowances, all contribute to the creation of more and more people living on the poverty line. In 1984 nearly 8 million people were dependent on SB, an increase of 77 per cent since 1978 (Piachaud, 1987). Women are particularly represented here, not just because of unemployment and low pay but because they constitute the majority of the elderly who are dependent upon SB, as well as the majority of the increasing numbers of lone parents who also suffer a high risk of poverty: in 1983 60 per cent of lone parents lived on supplementary benefits or had incomes on or just above the SB level (Glendinning and Millar, 1987).

In spite of some limited moves towards equality for women in accordance with the European Economic Community requirements (for example, the right for either a man or a woman to be the claimant of social security – though still not both), many aspects of social security and unemployment policy still continue to reinforce the idea of the woman's role as dependent wife and mother. Since 1982 a woman must satisfy the DHSS that her children will be cared for to be eligible for unemployment benefit. In 1984 married women's access to employment on the MSC's Community Programme was limited. These moves are also reflected in the direct and indirect ways in which women's unpaid work in the home is being increased. For example, the policy of community care for elderly, infirm, disabled people and people with learning difficulties has much to commend it, but without adequate domiciliary, housing and social provision, it is women within families who will shoulder much of the caring responsibilities. Cutbacks in provisions such as school meals also increase the work in the home normally assigned to women.

For Black men and women who are disproportionately represented in these groups in poverty, this has also been accompanied by moves which reinforce a racial division of labour which identify Black people as scroungers and/or aliens. The MSC programmes have not challenged but accommodated the racism of employers so that Black youths have a far smaller chance of eventually gaining employment (see De Sousa, 1987). Access to benefits has been linked up more tightly to immigration controls in social security, education and health so that access to provision is dependent upon proof of settlement status (see 'Internal Controls' in chapter 7). In 1987, consequent upon the immigration authorities' refusal of entry to people in need of housing, some local authorities refused to accept responsibility for housing homeless families without any length of residency in their borough. In Tower Hamlets this included recently arrived families of longstanding Bangladeshi male workers (Bopari, 1987). In addition, the introduction of the Community Charge or 'Poll Tax' will be financially detrimental to those on low incomes, part of larger households living in inner-city areas. It will also deter recently arrived immigrants from signing the electoral register or using local services in case this precipitates harassment on the grounds of suspected illegal status (Oppenheim, 1987). Indeed any test of residence status runs the risk of being racially discriminatory.

Whilst trends in social security legislation represent attempts to reassert the role of social security in disciplining the labour force and encouraging the acceptance of low paid work, they also reinforce with new vigour the age-old but continuing element in poor relief, national assistance and supplementary benefit – the deserving and undeserving poor. The 1986 Social Security Act revives this particularly through the social fund, whereby special needs, such as urgent needs payments, clothing, heating payments, and so on, will be by discretionary loans, without any recourse to appeal, as well as through encouraging claimants to apply to charities. Discretion paves the way for the reinforcement of sexist, moralistic and racist views of who constitutes the 'undeserving'.

Cuts in public expenditure, increasing unemployment and the failure to mitigate poverty have particularly affected women and Black people. These factors have aided, not caused, the processes of racism and sexism under capitalism which give rise to this situation, and have aggravated the *consistent* failure of the welfare state to acknowledge them.

We turn now to the second aspect, the ways in which present welfare trends serve to intensify some of the processes that contribute to the oppressions of women and Black people. These include the reprivatization of welfare services and the introduction of private market principles into state welfare; the shift in emphasis from care to control; the shift of domestic and caring responsibilities to women and financial responsibilities to the family; and the emphasis on voluntarism and self-help. All of these have 'race' and gender implications.

Perhaps the most apparently new shift in government welfare policy is its privatization schemes. These have taken two major forms: the encouragement of the development of a private sector alongside the state sector, and the introduction of private sector and of market principles within state welfare. For example, in the first category there have been incentives to develop private hospitals and private nursing homes, for employers to take out private medical insurance for their workers and for consultants to do private work in pay beds in the NHS hospitals. In addition the right-to-buy one's council house and tax relief on mortgages have encouraged owner occupation and the balance of subsidies has shifted now towards owner-occupiers (Murie, 1983).

The other side of the coin has been the introduction of the private sector – in the name of efficiency and savings – into state welfare by contracting out cleaning, catering, building and maintenance services in local authority housing and education provision and in hospitals. This marks, in addition, the increasing priority given to cost-benefit analysis in the assessment of social service provision, rather than need. An example is school dinners: following the 1980 Education Act it was left to local authorities' discretion whether to provide school milk, transport and dinners. This meant that national standards governing nutritional standards were dropped as were nationally determined meal prices. For some local authorities school dinners have been seen, through the introduction of fast (and often 'junk') foods as a potential source of saving: prices have risen as standards have declined and the yardstick is no longer the nutritional needs of children but the lowering of costs.

Increases in charges for services make the state service resemble more the cash nexus of the private market, and at the same time pave the way for the acceptability of welfare provision through payment. Prescription charges rose by 60 per cent between 1979 and 1983 (Rees, 1983); dental and optical charges have gone up; some local authorities have introduced charging for homehelps and attendance at training centres for the mentally and physically handicapped. Many schools now charge parents for books, outings, music lessons and the cost of school dinners went up, on average, by 150 per cent between 1977 and 1987 (personal calculation). Between 1979 and 1982 council house rents more than doubled (Murie, 1983). The language of the private market extends to the users of welfare who are now encouraged to see themselves as 'consumers' shopping wisely in the welfare market of choice for their health care, their children's education and the home of their dreams.

Further rationalization of changes in welfare policies is given in terms of the prioritization given to the *needs of industry*. Thus it is argued that the growth of the social security budget should be stemmed because it is responsible for a major share of the current heavy tax burden on individuals and companies and 'could severely damage prospects for economic growth' (HMSO, 1985). Education and training too have to be streamlined and graded to meet the needs of industry.

The combined effect of these trends is to residualize certain areas of state pension or council housing and turn them into poor people's provision. Twice as many council tenants are supplementary benefit claimants compared with other forms of tenure, and single-parent families tend to be allocated poorer council properties on the worst council estates (Watson, 1987, p. 135).

These processes particularly effect women and Black people as consumers of and workers in, welfare. The privatization of many of the ancillary services, where those two groups are highly represented, has reduced the pay and conditions of work of the employees in these services. Secondly, the residualization of, for example, council housing, has a particular 'race' dimension. Although few local authorities monitor their right-to-buy applicants, studies suggest that very few Black tenants are exercising this 'right' (Lawrence, 1987, p. 4). This is in part because they do not have the means but also because racist allocation procedures have led to many Black tenants (along with single parents) occupying the worst council housing which neither they nor anyone else would want to buy. Thirdly, in spite of anti-discriminatory legislation, building societies still discriminate against single women and women with higher earnings than their husbands (Watson, 1986, p. 74) as well as against Black applicants. For example, in one study, the granting of loans to Afro-Caribbeans and Asians compared with whites in down-market inner-city property was rated at 51 per cent, 43 per cent and 73 per cent respectively (Glazer and Young, 1983). In general the principles of the private market reinforce existing inequalities even more rigidly than the state. To prevent racism and sexism against workers and patients in private residential homes is even more difficult than in local authority homes where – in some places at least – recourse to publicly stated equal opportunities policies is possible. Private medical insurance is not viable for those whose 'race', class or gender render them more susceptible to illness, accident, stress or violence. Further, the 'needs' of industry are, as we showed earlier, for a flexible, exploitable and unskilled workforce at one extreme – Black and white youth and Black and poor working-class women – and highly paid technocrats at the other – usually white middle-class men. In this context moves towards anti-racism or anti-sexism are too often marginalized as irrelevant (property of the 'loony left').

A second major shift in welfare policies is from 'care' to 'control'. This is reflected in increased spending on law and order and also by policies for the control of the 'depraved' rather than care of the 'deprived'. Between 1978/9 and 1983/4 law and order and defence spending increased more rapidly than social expenditure (Loney, 1986, p. 181). The New Right's theme of 'law and order' is heavily entwined with nationalism and racism and the associated vilification of certain groups – 'the enemy within' – working against the national interests. These include Black youth and Black immigrants as well as 'scroungers' and strikers, feminists, gays and lesbians, who between them are identified as posing a threat to morality and social stability. This has led to an intensification of policing in Black communities (see for example the 'Swamp '81' operation conducted by the police before the Brixton riots described in the Scarman Report, 1981), of policing Asian immigrants, as well as more militaristic policing in Northern Ireland (the permitted use of the plastic bullet) and during the miners strike in 1984/5. In fact, Hall et al. (1978) and the authors of *The Empire Strikes Back* identify the growth of authoritarianism emerging with the responses to economic recession from the early 1970s.

During this period, transformations in the *form* of state power were secured through a political discourse which emphasized the drift of British society into 'violence' and 'disorder' as a way of securing and re-ordering the relative balance between the ideological and repressive roles of the state. This is particularly true of the ways in which the policing role came to be defined but it was also a clear tendency in the fields of industrial relations, social welfare and race relations. (CCCS, 1982, p. 25)

These shifts to the exercising of greater state control are mirrored within welfare. Policy for the treatment of juvenile offenders in the 14–17 years age group has substantially shifted away from the 'caring' philosophy of the 1969 Children and Young Person Act by introducing 'short sharp shock' detention centres for young offenders. Social security legislation has aimed to contain expenditure on benefits and reduce numbers of civil servants. But at the same time it has increased certain areas of expenditure. One area of increase has been in staff in the fraud inspectorate: the number of special investigators doubled between 1978 and 1980 to 1,000 (McGregor, 1981). The ideological nature of such an attack on scroungerism can be seen when the £3.2 million fraudulently claimed from the DHSS is set against the £27 million evaded by non-payment of taxes. At the same time in 1985 £2 billion social security payments went unclaimed (Bradshaw, 1985). Within education there have been increases in the numbers of disruptive units, as well as the disproportionate numbers of Black children sent to them (Carby, 1982a). In this way these trends represent a general shift from 'care' to 'control' but one with specific consequences for minority groups. The policy responses to the development of the disease AIDS also exemplify how what is essentially a health care issue has been treated as if it were an issue of crime and disorder whose perpetrators are homosexual men and female prostitutes in the Third World (Small, 1988). Policy prescriptions have concentrated on individual morality on the one hand (one partner, safe sex) and the possibility of social controls on the other – immigration controls, compulsory testing, segregation and further discrimination and hostility against gay men and lesbian women, such as the prohibition against local authorities' promoting homosexuality and lesbianism instituted by the government in 1988.

The moves towards 'community care' policies – that is the deinstitutionalization of older people, disabled people and people with learning difficulties – rest on the assumption of women's availability to care, for these policies have not been matched by financial commitments in the community. Home helps, meals-on-wheels, respite care aids and adaptations have not been expanded to meet the needs of those who need constant or even occasional help (Finch and Groves, 1983). This is not so much a shift as a reinforcement of what has continually been the case: women taking unpaid responsibility for the young, sick and elderly. The idea that families take greater responsibility for their ill and elderly relatives, or for their children's discipline and sexuality, has been rein-forced by, first, particular developments which increase families' financial responsibilities (borne often by women who have the job of making ends meet), for example, cuts in schools' provisions of meals, or books, or outings, or the reduction of benefits for the under-25s which lengthens their dependence on their families. Secondly, the Conservative policy rhetoric has linked this to its economic philosophy of individualism and freedom of choice: 'Freedom and responsibility go together. The Conservative Party believes in encouraging people to take responsibility for their own decisions. We shall continue to return more choice to individuals and their families' (Conservative Party Manifesto, 1983, p. 24). This philosophy has also been articulated through the emergence of 'family' issues in political debate, for example, the 1980 Education Act gave supremacy to parental authority in the take-up of sex education in schools (David, 1983).

Alongside this the values of voluntary work, thrift and self-help have also been stressed. In 1984 the DHSS set up a 'Helping the Community to Care' programme which allocated £10.5 million through voluntary bodies to self-help groups, such as home-from-hospital projects for the elderly. Clearly the unpaid labour on which many of these projects depend is that of women in their families. In schools, failure by the local education authorities to maintain 'non-essential' school services – school meals, books, transport, swimming-pools – means that parents are obliged to make, pay for or raise funds for such items (Bull and Wilding, 1983). Although nursery and day-care places have declined, pre-school playgroups and voluntarily run bodies have been encouraged (David, 1983). Increasingly abortion services are being taken up by charities, with a fall in the numbers of abortions performed by health authorities (Illiffe, 1985). The intervention of the 'Task Forces' in the inner cities – an attempt to put limited extra resources into areas of high unemployment – stress the idea of the communities helping themselves with the aid and supervision of private business. The other side of the coin of self-help is 'blaming the victim' – that those who are poor, ill, unemployed have only themselves to blame because they have not helped themselves or exercised responsibility for themselves. This has been a persistent feature in explanations of social problems concerning working-class mothers and Black families. Since the 1960s working-class mothers' child-rearing habits have been blamed for the lack of educational achievement of their children and the social problems faced by Black families on their 'cultures'. Since the 1980s, however, this kind of explanation has been used more systematically: anti-smoking and anti-drugs campaigns have emphasized individual restraint over and above the structural aspects which give rise to these behaviours – stress, unemployment, insecurity. In 1986 the Junior Minister of Health, Edwina Currie, explained that the greater morbidity in the North of England was due to irresponsible eating habits and mothers giving their children the wrong food.

Thirdly, one development which has a particular effect on weakening the areas where anti-racist and anti-sexist struggles were beginning to have some impact is the curtailing of powers of the local authorities, and the consequent centralization of control over spending and decision-making. Spending by local authorities has not only been reduced but measures have been taken to ensure central government has control over this spending, for example, in 1984 'rate capping' was introduced which imposed limits and penalties on the higher-spending left Labour councils. Similar tightening of the channels of control resulted from the reorganization of the health service in 1982. In both cases local bodies have found themselves responsible for cutting local expenditure or facing confrontation with central government (Lambeth Area Health Authority, Liverpool City Council). Along with the dissolution in 1986 of the GLC and the metropolitan county councils these processes have led to the cutting back of grants which fund autonomous women's organizations or Black community groups, although in some cases those councils themselves use cutting back as an argument for marginalizing what are seen as 'minority' issues.

Whilst what has been described reflects some of the major trends in welfare policy it is worth briefly pointing out that these developments are not without their internal contradictions. For example, there are limitations to the profitability of private welfare. The falling off of private health insurance subscriptions in the early 1980s, the reduced profits of organizations like BUPA and the fact that in 1984 up to one-third of all beds in private acute hospitals were empty suggest that private medical care has reached saturation point (Mohan, 1986). Secondly, the social costs and social unrest resulting from increased poverty and unemployment and more authoritarian and racist policing in the inner cities have led to increases in public spending in those areas. The government has had recourse to greater state intervention, not less, to ensure that the family exercises parental authority over the discipline and sexual behaviour of its children, and that it assumes greater financial responsibility for them. Furthermore the increases in women's paid employment, smaller and more mobile families and increases in divorce mean that women's availability to care cannot be presumed. It would not be accurate, either to see the effects of these developments as entirely unprecedented. Private welfare, selectivity, social control, less eligibility, failure to redistribute or to meet the needs of women and Black people, or to reduce significantly their inequalities, have all been part of post-war welfare provision. In addition, some aspects of current developments – public expenditure cutbacks and increased policing of the Black communities – began under the mid-1970s Labour government. What does mark a difference, however, is my fourth and final point: the *reworking* of the ideologies of Family, Nation and culture to particular effect.

In the historical development of welfare policies the appeal to notions of the family, to national unity and to British culture has been consistent, but how these three ideals are constituted has differed. Although they have differed, however, they have also had shared assumptions, sometimes intentional and sometimes not so, of women and ethnic minorities, particularly Black people, as subordinate. Up until the Second World War national unity and British cultural supremacy tied the development of welfare policy to imperialism abroad. The welfare state became central to the reconstruction of post-war Britain and it represented Britain's civilizing mission brought home again, built with the bricks of the family and the mortar of national unity, by the labour of low paid women and newly arrived Black workers. What was crucially different was that, then, the ideology of the traditional family, of national unity and of British culture was used to *justify* state intervention and a limited form of white male egalitarianism. The use of these ideologies in the 1980s by the New Right has been to justify *less* state intervention, the supremacy of the market, and the existence of inequalities. It has attempted this by elevating the family to a high position of responsibility for the welfare of its members, for exercising freedom of choice in the selection of private and/or state welfare provision – schools, health care, housing and so on – and for responsibility for morality, discipline and the transmission of British cultural values. The family in its traditional form thus provides a vital link between moral principles and cultural life on the one side, and market principles and economic life on the other. But the cultural values the family is asked to defend are derived from its days of high imperialism and, as such, are essentially British, white and Christian. As right-wing writer Alfred Sherman explains:

The imposition of mass immigration from backward alien cultures is just one symptom of this self-destructive urge reflected in the assault on patriotism, the family – both as a conjugal and economic unit – the Christian religion in public life and schools, traditional morality, in matters of sex, honesty, public display and respect for the law – in short all that is English and wholesome. (Sherman, 1979, quoted in Solomos et al., 1982)

The assertion of British culture affirms the national interest, and the national interest is the reassertion of the freedom of the market and the associated revival of Britain as a major competitor in the world economy. This assertion of British culture requires the minimizing, in the name of national interest, of the influence of other cultures. The process is clearly visible in educational debate and recent education policy. In a collection of essays *Anti-Racism: an Assault on Education and Value* (Palmer, 1986), New Right educationalists argue that anti-racist initiatives in schooling have contributed to a lowering of standards and constitute an assault on the traditional British values in education. The 1987 proposals for educational reform also link three elements: the need for a core curriculum and the reintroduction of testing and selection procedures, the reassertion of traditional moral and cultural values, and the rights of parents to choose schools appropriate to their cultural aspirations. These three elements are all seen as contributing to education by being able to meet industry's needs and thus restore Britain once more to greatness. Appeals to family responsibility and British cultural tradition, secure the maintenance of inequalities of class, 'race' and gender, and justify the continued oppression of women and Black people, in the name of moral and economic regeneration.

7 The Welfare State as Part of a Racially Structured and Patriarchal Capitalism

Introduction

In this chapter I shall present an analysis of the role that Black men and women and white women play in the welfare state as workers, unpaid and paid, as consumers and as people involved in struggles over welfare. Returning briefly to Gough's model of the welfare state, we noted that the welfare state, in fulfilling the function of social reproduction, serves also to maintain conditions favourable to capital accumulation as well as the maintenance of social harmony. However, none of this process is straightforward or cut and dried. Since it is difficult clearly to separate these functions (for example, the containment and control of disaffected groups – legitimation/repression – may be partially carried out by the education system which also fulfils the function of social reproduction), this chapter highlights particular and significant elements of these areas in relation to 'race' and gender. We examine these in three sections: first, the role that Black workers and Black and white women have played in maintaining lower social expenditure; second, social reproduction in terms of the reproduction of sexual and racial divisions of labour and in terms of the maintenance (and non-maintenance) of the non-working population; third, forms of social control in relation to 'race' and gender – Black pathology, containment and incorporation, internal controls and maintenance of female dependency and subordination. Finally we look at the issues raised by the struggles of women and Black people against oppression and their implications for welfare strategy. As will be clear from the following accounts, the dimensions of 'race', class and gender can each have a specific as well as a combined effect on the provision and experience of welfare

The Role of Black Men and Women Workers and White Women Workers in Maintaining Lower Social Expenditure

The post-war expansion of the welfare state drew its workforce, skilled and unskilled, from the 'reserve army of cheap labour' – Black and white women and Black men. As well as constituting the low paid workers in the welfare services, women, Black and white, have been the unpaid welfare workers in the home and the unpaid voluntary workers in the community. In addition to this, the British state has shown at best an ambivalence about bearing the social costs of Black immigrant workers. These five factors in different ways and at different times over the post-war period have played an important role in keeping down the 'relatively rising costs' of welfare provision. By attempting to keep down the costs of welfare, the state hopes to stave off possible conflict between capital and labour whom it would otherwise have to approach to foot the bill.

Welfare services are labour-intensive and provide far less possibility than manufacturing industry to use automation as a way of offsetting rising costs. Black and immigrant workers are one section who play an important role, particularly in the health service, of limiting these rising costs. The study of Doyal, Hunt and Mellor (1981) shows clearly how, since the 1950s, the NHS has been dependent on overseas workers, both as contract labour and settlers, from the Caribbean, India, Ireland and Malaysia, at all levels of skills, though they tend to be concentrated on the lower grades and many of them are women. One third of the doctors and 20 per cent of student nurses working in Britain in 1981 were born overseas. In the London hospital in the Doyal study, 84 per cent of domestics and 82 per cent of catering workers were from abroad. Further, in spite of immigration controls, the NHS has continued to recruit skilled overseas workers and until recently, by a number of anomalies, unskilled labour. Since there are limits to the scope of rationalization of labour in such a heavily labour-intensive sector as the health service compared with private industry, the availability of cheap labour has been particularly crucial in keeping costs down. On the other hand, where rationalization and deskilling *have* taken place, this has been possible by the use of overseas nurses, concentrated in SEN training and less prestigious areas like the psychiatric and geriatric services. A further point related to the question of social costs being borne by the immigrant's country of origin is that many of the doctors and nurses have had their training paid for by their own – far poorer – countries, and the children of many of those women on contract labour are being cared for and educated in their own countries. In other words 'the need to reproduce labour power effectively while at the same time keeping down the costs of reproduction to capital as a whole ... helps to explain the need for migrant labour both historically and today' (Doyal et al., 1981, p. 68).

The issue of social costs of immigrant workers was an important debate in the late 1940s as the government looked for new sources of labour. The failure of the post-war government to acknowledge the social costs of the new immigrants, to make necessary adjustments in the provision of welfare, can be understood in terms of the priorities given to other issues in the debate about how to meet labour shortages. One of these issues was how to dispose of labour once it was no longer needed and the other was the effect upon the host population if the immigrants were to stay longer. The 1949 Royal Commission on Population emphasized that immigrants should be 'of good human stock and were not prevented by their religion or race from intermarrying with the host population and becoming merged in it' (quoted by Booth in Dummett, 1986, p. 117). In both these terms Europeans from Holland, Greece, Italy and Eire were not seen as posing great problems – they could enter the country on temporary work permits and thus return when no longer required, or if they stayed they would 'merge in'. Black immigrants, however, as Commonwealth subjects had rights of settlement and also were seen to be bearers of radically different – and inferior – cultures. In other words, they were seen even before their arrival as a 'problem'. However, at the same time, as Joshi and Carter (1984) point out, Commonwealth workers were cheaper than aliens because they were British citizens, and as such were deemed to have come 'individually and on their own initiative' and thus there was no need to make welfare provision for them. There was thus *no intention* to provide for them, and when Black immigrants *did* use welfare services they were seen as scroungers. The juxtaposition of these two features is pinpointed by Jacobs when he says: 'black workers were acceptable as cleaners, porters, kitchen staff, even nurses and doctors, but never wholeheartedly, as patients. They could build council houses but were not expected to live in them' (Jacobs, 1985, p. 13).

As it was, immigrants came from Europe, particularly Eire, and the Commonwealth, pushed by economic necessity as well as pulled by Britain's demands for labour. Yet the notion of an immigrant 'problem' was applied much more to the presence of Black immigrants, especially after manifestations of white racism like the Notting Hill riots of 1958 (although this is not to deny that forms of racism were and are still experienced by the Irish, the Italians, the Greeks, Jewish refugees and existing Chinese and Polish communities). The response of post-war governments was to bring the rights of Black Commonwealth immigrants more in line with the lesser rights of aliens, but in a way that would not break up the Commonwealth.

The introduction of the first set of immigration controls, the 1962 Commonwealth Immigrants Act, which marked the beginnings of the selective admission of immigrants in terms of their skills, as well as the gradual erosion of their settlement rights, led to concern in academic and political circles about the *numbers* of immigrants and the costs to the country, and one of the main arguments *in defence* of the presence of immigrants was their cheap labour and their minimal social costs. The Conservative Home Secretary R. A. Butler, in 1961, argued 'our hospitals ... would be in difficulties were it not for the services of immigrant workers' and *The Times* wrote 'Britain's essential services could not carry on without immigrant labour' (both quoted in Cohen, 1985, p. 90). The appeasement of white racism and the need for cheap labour in the welfare and public services were therefore not without their contradictions. Nor were they without their challenges. Needless to say, Black workers had no time for this patronizing attitude: in the health service strikes against the pay freeze in 1972 and later against low wages and cutbacks in 1982/3, Black women ancillary workers were a major force (see Bryan et al., 1985, pp. 45–50).

A further dimension in this issue is the role that *women's work in general* plays in the welfare state. The state is the largest employer of women workers and most of these women work in the welfare services of health, education and the social services. Women constitute 75 per cent of the manual labour force in local authority employment (Coyle, 1985). At the professional level this has a long history, a history of class and gender divisions. At the beginning of this century this work was an important route for economic independence for middle-class unmarried women. At the same time, gender inequalities, male domination and the sexual division of labour were often reproduced in this work. Women could be nurses but not doctors; teachers, but not wives and mothers as well (the marriage bar was not removed until 1950, David, 1980). However, these women found themselves, as teachers, health visitors or social workers, directing their working-class sisters into marriage and motherhood, and once there, supervising them. The post-war expansion of the welfare state reveals this first process more markedly. Whilst women have provided the socialized forms of care they have done so consistently in the lower paid grades of the welfare state. What highlights the particularly exploitive nature of women's work is not simply that in many cases employers use the cleaning, cooking and caring skills that women have developed in their homes and label it as low paid *unskilled* work, but also that so much of this work is *part-time* and therefore low paid (Beechey and Perkins, 1987). This is particularly true of cleaning and catering, home helping, clerical and secretarial work, but is it also the case that professionally qualified staff – teachers and nurses especially – are employed as part-timers which has no comparison in the manufacturing sector. Part of the reason for this lies in management's need for flexibility – for example, where residential care has to be maintained day and night, or where peak times have to be covered – like crossing patrol wardens outside schools. However, to a large extent it is because much of this work is seen as *women's* work engaging *women's* skills and, in the absence of social provisions for women workers, it has been constructed as part-time and therefore low paid to fit in with domestic commitments. Men's work in equivalent areas, such as ambulance men and hospital porters, also requires full-time cover but is organized as full-time shift work. In the 1980s the trend has been to make more women's work in the welfare services part-time or temporary, for example school catering workers now receive no money during school holidays. Furthermore the part-time nature of much of this work has meant that its privatization has been that much easier to manage – for example, the contracting out of hospital cleaning (Coyle, 1985). In other words, women's vulnerable position in relation to the labour market, combined with the skills they offer by virtue of the sexual division of labour in the home, have provided the welfare state with the opportunity to limit its costs. Again it would be wrong to assume that women have been passive victims in this process. The major growth in post-war trade unionism has been in the public sector – NUPE, for example, where women are about 70 per cent of the membership (but only 10 per cent of the full-time officials), and significant struggles have been waged over many of these issues (see *Waged Work: A Reader, Feminist Review*, 1986b). However, at the same time some of these issues are marked by their failure to attract support from the bulk of the male trade union movement (see Coyle, 1985).

In addition to this, women provide much of society's welfare as unpaid workers in the home, caring for their children, disabled, or older relatives, as well as their entirely able-bodied husbands. That this is reinforced by social security legislation and the ideology of the social work, education and health services has already been discussed in Chapter 3. The fact that present trends by the Conservative government are to reduce the costs of welfare by transferring institutionalized care back into the 'community', testifies to the savings women continuously provide. 'Community care', as has relentlessly been explained by social policy writers, means care by the family, and that means women (Finch and Groves, 1980; Walker, 1982). In addition, when reports and reviews of 'community care' identify the informal or voluntary networks in the community (for example, the Barclay Report, 1982) these too refer to the unpaid work of women. Women's voluntary work has a long history dating back to Victorian philanthropy exercised by middle-class women. Changes over the last hundred years, however, suggest that women's ability to take on more unpaid labour is severely limited. Many more women combine paid work with their domestic commitments. Women comprised 41 per cent of the workforce in 1982 and in 1979 52 per cent of women with dependent children did paid work (Study Commission on the Family, 1983). The importance of a woman's wage to the family can be understood by the fact that the number of families living near the poverty line would increase three to four times if her wage were withdrawn (Study Commission on the Family, 1980).

Nevertheless, families, usually women, do still provide the main care for older and disabled relatives (see Ungerson, 1987). As discussed earlier, cutbacks in welfare and the disproportionate burden these place on the poor, on women and on Black people, represent the other side of the coin of the exploitation some members of these groups suffer as workers within the welfare state.

Social Reproduction

In general, the concept of social reproduction when used of the welfare state refers to its role in ensuring that labour power is produced, cared for, skilled and disciplined appropriate to the needs of capitalism. What we are concerned with here is what that means for women and Black people, as well as the extent to which this process also involves the reproduction of the social relations of patriarchal and racial domination. We look first at the involvement of the welfare state in reproducing racial and sexual divisions, and secondly at the maintenance of the non-working population.

Sexual and Racial Divisions of Labour in Welfare Provision

It is clear that women play a central role in producing, caring for and nurturing members of their family or household. They also play a crucial role in mediating between their family and the services provided. It is *they* who take their children to the doctor, who are expected by schools to help teach their children to read, and it is *women* who often provide the services themselves. The state then plays a major role in assuming a sexual division of labour in which women do these activities, and in defining and supervising the way they are carried out. The education system provides a good example of all these different operations. In the past, education policy-makers made clear divisions between the curriculum for boys and that for girls according to their assumed destinies. Some of this is now contested within and outside education, but a labour market structured on class, 'race' and gender lines still persists and influences the destinies of young women. Girls still tend to 'choose' arts and social science subjects, teachers allow boys to dominate in the classroom and playground, women or Black people are not represented in the teaching presentation of history, for example, and girls emerge with fewer qualifications, a situation compounded by 'race' and class. Girls not only learn that there are limited opportunities for them in paid employment, and that they will have domestic duties but that they should be subordinate to men (Stanworth, 1981). Some of these lessons are apparent to them in the organization of school-life where women work as teachers mainly on the lower grades and in certain subjects, or with pastoral roles, or as cooks and cleaners and caretakers' wives, often as part-timers, whereas men run schools, are full-time science and maths teachers or caretakers. Furthermore, it is mothers, as parents, who are deemed to bear the responsibility for their child's achievement or otherwise at school, for, it is presumed *by* schools that mothers are the ones who prepare their children for school by helping them to read and write, be dressing them and generally negotiating the passage of their child's education career. All these different operations described above are also shot through with class differences, so that it is working-class girls whose destinies are most limited and their mothers who receive most blame.

Of course these differences are shot through with 'race' too. The idea of the Black child and her/his family or culture as an educational 'problem' is a theme that runs through much educational thinking and official policy even though it has moved from assimilation, integration, dispersal and multiculturalism. Brah comments that the 'deficit model' of the aspirations, abilities and cultures of Asian and Afro-Caribbean children persists in educational thinking in spite of official policy having traversed the assimilation, integration and multicultural models (Brah and Deem, 1986). Young Blacks who dream of a better future are deemed as having 'unrealistic aspirations', and Asian girls are denied career opportunities because of assumptions about Asian culture and the 'passive' role of women therein. None of this is helped by the fact that only 2 per cent of teachers are Black, and that a study by the Commission for Racial Equality in 1986 found that the main reason for Black teachers leaving the profession was the racism of their pupils and colleagues.

The MSC's youth training programmes, juggling between the conflicting ideologies of equal access, 'special needs' and social control and containment, also reinforce existing racial (and gender) inequalities and structures as young Black people are filtered into the lower status Mode B schemes (Solomos, 1985; De Sousa, 1987).

Rex has also pointed out how the 1977 White Paper on Inner City Policy made racist assumptions about the occupational destinations of those living in the inner cities. It argued in effect that as the inner cities were revived and new industries developed, the present residents (mainly Black) would be unsuitable because of their lack of skills. The assumption is that Black people and their children can only work at unskilled levels (Rex, 1984a).

The welfare services themselves also reproduce racial divisions with

Black women in particular occupying the lowest grade positions. Hazel Carby makes the observation here that the employment of Black women as carers and cleaners in the health service is not so much an extension of their caring role but of their *servant* role in imperialist social relations (1982b).

A final example of racial divisions in welfare is council housing (see Jacobs, 1985). Jacobs describes the post-war relationship between council housing and 'race' as 'The British road to apartheid'. Qualifications of residency, the blaming of Black people for inner-city problems, racist allocations procedures, fears of a white backlash, dispersal (the spreading of Black tenants to white areas to avoid ghettoization), punishment and deterrence of Black homeless families have all contributed to a segregated system which furthers racial divisions:

> By locking the black working class in council ghettos, the state aims to perpetuate, through the generations, the immigrant status of the black community. The purpose is to ensure, without need of further immigration, that black Britain continually replenishes capital's reserve army of labour. Largely unopposed by the Labour movement it has been effortlessly achieved under the cloak of a caring welfare state in the name of socialist housing. (Jacobs, 1985, p. 25)

At a local level the policies for equal opportunities in local authorities and anti-sexist and anti-racist strategies in schools, colleges and social services represent an important initiative in attempting to raise these as issues to be fought (see later).

Maintenance of the Non-working White Population, but Limitation and Control of the Black

Part of the welfare state's role in social reproduction as identified by Gough (1979) is the maintenance of the non-working population – the elderly, the young, the unemployed. Once again the shifting relationship between the state, the family and women is crucial here in defining the *need* and *the source* of maintenance, and in particular in defining women as dependants of their husbands. Women cohabiting with their husband or male partner are deemed to be dependent upon him in social security legislation. Moves to equality in this area have merely given the woman the right to claim and make him her dependant. Similarly, a long-term unemployed spouse is deemed his/her partner's dependant. Basically the system works on the basis of a single family wage rather than the reality where both partners work but where, because of domestic commitments and low wages, the woman's wage is usually less, though still of vital importance in maintaining the family above the poverty line. The married man's tax allowance, an additional allowance granted to working men in recognition of their wife's dependent housekeeping status, further reinforces the notion of the dependent wife, and also discriminates against women earners. It is quite difficult for a woman unless she is above 21, never married and childless, to be regarded as an independent person in social security provisions. For example, if a woman with children makes claims for social security, efforts will be made to establish her 'liable relative' – the man responsible for maintaining her and her children (see Land, 1983). (Women are not the only people affected in this way. With the growth of youth unemployment, recent trends in social security eligibility have shifted the financial and housing responsibility for young people away from the state and back to the family.) The issue of divorce also raises starkly the question of women's limited opportunity for economic independence through the wage system and the reluctance of either husband or the state to accept responsibility. Where and when the state does accept financial responsibility for maintaining a woman (and her children), then she will be thrown on to the poverty line of social security subsistence level. For some women this poverty is often preferable to an oppressive marriage in which she had little control over her access to money: what Hilary Graham calls 'the two dimensions of lone mother-hood: their absolute poverty and their relative power' (Graham, 1987). For other women, like older women living alone whose major source of income is social security benefits, the poverty they endure in old age is merely a cruel intensification of their financial dependence and/or low pay during their lives (Peace, 1986). Though changes in pensions were made in 1978 which improve women's access to occupational schemes and acknowledge their 'non-working' years at home, ultimately women's access to a decent living in old age 'reflects the changes of the labour-market and the marriage-market' (Groves, 1983, p. 60). The main final point to be made here is that when women are not in receipt of a living wage then maintenance by a man is a risky and uncertain business and maintenance by the state almost inevitably means poverty. Women are a major group in poverty by virtue of either low state subsistence or inequality and financial dependency in marriage.

When we turn to the question of the maintenance of the *Black* non-working population then the 'race' dimension shifts the issue into different perspective. We have noted up to now the way the state reinforces women's mothering role but for Black women the emphasis has not been so much on the 'endowment' of motherhood and the maintenance of dependants, but on the *restriction* of motherhood and *limitation* and *control* of dependants. This is illustrated in two ways: immigration control and repro-ductive policies. Paul Gordon (1985) cites many examples of instances where normal rights afforded dependants through social security are denied to Black people, or where their having made claims renders them guilty of 'scrounging'. The Home Office ordered Nasreen Akhtar to be deported following the break-up of her marriage. Her having claimed supplementary benefit was cited as evidence of her intention to remain dependent on social security for as long as she could. The order was eventually overturned by the Immigration Appeal Tribunal (see Gordon, 1984). More generally, the concern about 'numbers' surrounding the 1962 and 1971 Commonwealth Immigration Acts, was about *'dependants'*, wives, children, and grandparents, and the shift that the immigration laws mark from citizen to migrant worker is precisely about the denial of benefits to those dependants and therefore about their limitation. Refusal of admission to many immigrants is on the basis of dependants having to prove they have no recourse to public funds and can be maintained by a relative or friend already resident. (This does not apply to Commonwealth citizens with right to abode or pre-1973 settlers.) Gordon also points out that although the 1977 Child Benefit Act was hailed as progressive for the way it transferred money for children from fathers to mothers, it also had the efffect of withdrawing financial support for children living abroad but with a parent working here, as child tax allowances could be claimed in this instance but child benefits cannot. The 'Sole Responsibility' rule of the 1971 Act also makes it difficult for single parents to bring their children into the country unless they have themselves solely maintained and *visited* them (Bryan et al., 1985, p. 157). The non-maintenance of Black dependants is reinforced further by the assumption that Asian cultures, in particular, are self-supporting and have no need for public provision. This underlies the lack of provision for older Black people. Yet, in one study 26 per cent of the Black older people interviewed had *no* family in Britain (Bhalla and Blakemore, 1981).

This concern with 'numbers' has also centred around the fertility of Black families. A crop of studies in the 1960s was directed at future estimates of the numbers of Black children given the rate of fertility of Black families. Such concerns are heavily influenced by eugenicist ideas, and racist ideas about Black sexuality. It is not surprising therefore that the rights of Black mothers to fertility are not always taken for granted as Black women's campaigns over the use of the long-lasting contraceptive injection Depo-Provera, abortion and sterilization have shown (Bryan et al., 1985, p. 103–4). In general then, as mothers, Black women's experience is not the same as that of white mothers.

Black women, as mothers, encounter other state agencies such as the DHSS, schools and so on in a very particular way; they may be asked to produce their passports before being considered eligible for benefit, or before their children are allowed to be enrolled in schools. (Bhavnani and Coulson, 1986, p. 84)

Social Control

The modification of behaviour, attitudes and practices towards work and family is a well acknowledged historical role of all aspects of the welfare state. It has particular resonance with the poor, the residuum, the undeserving (Piven and Cloward, 1972). But it intersects with 'race' and gender in a number of very particular ways. We look first at three ways in which social control is implemented and the racist justifications of that implementation: Black cultural pathology; Black people as a 'danger'; and internal controls – the use of welfare agencies to police immigration controls.

Black Cultural Pathology

The characterization of individuals, families or communities being to blame for their deprivation because of their way of life, their culture, has long been part of commonsense ideas in social work, education and health care. But deeply embedded notions of cultural and racial superiority, absorbed and reworked through different modes of racial domination, gave rise in the post-war period to specific and often contradictory ideas of the deficiencies of Afro-Caribbean and Asian families and cultures. They are particularly persistent in education, social work and health care. Hazel Carby points out that Black children are seen to fail at school either because their Asian mothers are too passive and withdrawn and stay in the home, or because their Afro-Caribbean mothers are too assertive and go out to work (Carby, 1982a). Illnesses, such as rickets, are seen as resulting from unsuitable diets rather than the need for a policy for vitamin D to be put into chapati flour or ghee. The problems of adolescents are translated in terms of their parents' maladaptive childcare practices. The Black Health Workers and Patients Group point out that 40 per cent of all Black people in NHS beds are psychiatric patients, and that 'multiculturalism' has affected psychiatric diagnosis in such a way as to reinforce racism: '"the hysteric" young Asian women in dread of arranged marriage ... the vicious and violent Afro-Caribbean male youth, perhaps already implicated in the social psychosis of Rasta' (1983, p. 32). This last example points to another variation in social control: potential danger and the need for containment.

Danger, Containment and Incorporation

The presentation of the presence of Black people as a cultural threat, a danger to the 'British way of life' has been a recurrent political and popular obsession since the 1920s. When riots happen these are given as evidence of the failure of Black people to adjust to British democracy. The theme has a long history and has been played on anti-Irish and anti-Semitic variations. The theme also has a variety of key signatures: not just the threat to 'culture' and 'democracy' but also to 'morality' and to 'health'. These latter two were also part of the moral panic of Black immigration in the 1950s and early 1960s. A Birmingham newspaper in 1956 carried the story of two white girls aged 15 and 16 found at night in the house of 'coloured men' who were recommended to be put into care for being in 'moral danger' (Joshi and Carter, 1984). In Bradford in 1961 a smallpox scare in the Pakistani community gave scope to scaremongering of the health risks that Black immigrants carried (see Gordon, 1983). At the same time little was done to resolve the overcrowding that Black families suffered. Lambeth Council for example decided it could not enforce the Public Health Act because they would have been forced to place Black families in council housing (Jacobs, 1985, p. 20). During the 1960s the moral and cultural threat shifted to a 'material threat' that Black people posed in terms of jobs and housing. In the 1970s and 1980s the two themes became forcibly intertwined.

Hall et al. (1978), Gilroy (1982), Solomos (1985), have all shown how policies on law and order, youth and unemployment have been constructed upon the image of Black youth in the 'urban ghetto' as a potential danger, in terms of increased crime and political instability. This has emerged particularly since the 1970s and the economic crisis and the identification of Black unemployed youth as part of the 'enemy within'. It is not only through law and order that containment policies are practised. In 1980 the ILEA provided £1.6 million for disruptive units in schools. Increasingly, evidence and suspicion mounted that there were disproportionate numbers of Black children being sent to them (as with the earlier incidence of ESN classes and schools), such that Black parents in Haringey demanded that the provision be stopped (Carby, 1982a, p. 205). According to the Black Health Workers and Patients Group (1983), Section 136 of the 1959 Mental Health Act which empowers the police to remove to a place of safety someone thought to be dangerous to themselves or others, is three or four times more likely to be used on Black people than white. Further, Black people are more likely to be offered drug or ECT treatment than therapy (Mama, 1984). Bryan et al. (1985) also claim that attitudes of cultural pathology and lack of access to housing and child care facilities lead to the likelihood of Black children being taken into care in the event of homelessness, or domestic violence. Indeed, as Jacobs points out, in the event of allocation, Black tenants are more likely to find themselves on more heavily controlled and policed estates (1985). The 1981 riots crystallized the rationalization of such policies for the right. But it should also be noted that the threat of political instability had also led to the voicing of a different approach – mostly notably by Lord Scarman. His line is away from the tough law and order approach to one of consensus through community consultation as well as the injection of money into deprived areas. This has been criticized as soft social control and incorporation by many:

Increasingly the effect of state funds on our community has been to neutralize its militancy; political mobilization has come to be seen as a salaried activity ... accountable not to the Black community but to the State which pays them. Their brief, however unwitting, is to keep the lid on the cauldron, and their existence is seen as proof of the government's 'concern' to soften the effects of its own institutionalized racism. (Bryan et al., 1985, p. 179)

Others argue that such policies at least expose the contradictions, and create openings and opportunities for anti-racist struggle and debate (Hall, 1982). More recently a new twist in the idea of Black people as a 'threat' has emerged. This is the New Right emphasis on the danger to British cultural values, discussed in the previous chapter.

Internal Controls

A third form of control adopted by the welfare state is that of policing the immigration control laws, which has already been described as having an important historical dimension. Gordon (1985) has documented the way medical techniques have been used as an administrative form of immigration control. Until a public outcry in 1979 doctors were used by immigration authorities to make 'virginity checks' on women from the Asian subcontinent entering Britain to marry their fiancés. In addition, until 1982 children entering Britain were turned away if they were not the age claimed, and the age was determined by the potentially harmful use of X-rays. Mental ill-health can also be grounds for refusal to entry, and the Home Secretary has the power to repatriate an alien receiving treatment for mental illness. In addition to these uses of medical techniques, medical care has been used as a method of immigration control. In 1979 a DHSS circular 'Gatecrashers' asked area health authorities in London to ensure that people 'not ordinarily resident' in Britain did not get free NHS treatment. In Leicester in 1976 nearly 200 women attending an ante-natal clinic were asked to show their passports. In 1982 the Government introduced 'charging' for overseas visitors. The effect of this is to encourage the questioning of right to free access of anyone who 'appears' to be foreign (Gordon, 1983).

The other aspect is the increased liaison between the welfare services and the administration of immigration control. Housing departments have liaised with the Home Office over the eligibility of people applying to be housed. Checking a passport is not uncommon nor is the evasion of responsibility to house homeless persons. An investigation by the Commission of Racial Equality, for example, found that the London Boroughs of Barnet and Kensington and Chelsea were refusing to house permanently work permit holders even though these workers were within their rights to be housed (Gordon, 1985, p. 88). In social security and further education too administrators have been required to act on behalf of the immigration authorities by checking up immigration status or by refusing access to services on the assumption that the client was not eligible. Such liaison has been made easier with the introduction of computerized information systems. However, the combined effects of these control processes is, first, to flout principles of confidentiality, secondly, to deny provision to bona fide immigrants like fiancees, work permit holders, students and others awaiting permission to stay on, or even subject them to deportation if they do 'have recourse to public funds', thirdly, to deter *all* Black people from claiming their rightful benefits, and legitimize and institutionalize racist practices in the provision of welfare, as well as, finally, criminalizing an area of activity – misuse of welfare provision by immigrants – the extent of which is neither particularly significant nor proved. What is most disturbing is the rootedness of these controls in the welfare state; as Cohen comments, 'welfarism is intimately linked to immigration control and cannot be understood other than as a construct of the basest nationalism' (1985, p. 92).

Social Control, Women and Welfare

It is clear that the welfare state operates in ways as to maintain the financial dependence of women in the home, their subordination to male authority in the home and at work, and to define, limit and constrain women's sexuality, their mothering, their reproductive powers and their access to an independent income. At the same time two qualifications have to be made. The first is that this process operates differently according to class and 'race', and the second is that this process is neither monotonous nor monolithic but both contradictory and contested. There are times when the welfare state has, for example, sought to make provisions for women with children to enter paid work, during the war for example, although this provision was ill-coordinated (see Riley, 1983). If we take health care as an example, we can see evidence of many of these different points: 'Health policy reflects and helps to maintain gender divisions that characterise society as a whole. In this sense medicine is a form of social control: a way of putting women in their place – wherever that place ought to be' (Oakley, 1983).

Women constitute 75 per cent of the health service workforce yet very few of them occupy positions of power and status. Approximately 10 per cent of hospital medical staff are women, and 10 per cent of consultants are women (DHSS, 1977, quoted in Oakley, 1983, p. 120). Women also use the health service more often than men. This is, amongst other things, because of their caring role and the fact they have children. Yet doctors' prescriptions for and treatments of women are significantly different from those for men. According to one survey, doctors classified their most troublesome patients as 'female', 'inadequate', not employed and working class with vague symptoms of psychiatric illness that were difficult to diagnose and treat' (study by Stimpson, 1976, quoted in Oakley, 1983, p. 105). Doctors are also more likely to diagnose women's health problems as neurotic or psychiatric requiring drug therapy or psychiatric treatment. Often the acknowledged aim of such treatment is to help the patient adapt to her housewifely, motherly duties. As an extreme example, Diane Hudson (1987) shows that a leucotomy (surgical removal of part of the brain) is twice as likely to be performed on a woman than a man presenting with depressive illness. Health policy and practice also identifies mothers as protectors of their family's health: exercising responsibility, self-sacrifice and good example. Such an analysis detracts from the social causes of ill-health as well as from the differential access women have to doctors and hospitals where transport, time and geographical area play an important part. In terms of women's own health, class differentials have widened over the years. Women who are married to semi-skilled and unskilled workers are 70 per cent more likely than women married to professionals and managers to die prematurely (1986 Office of Population Census and Statistics, quoted in Doyal, 1987). Women from the lowest social class group are also three times more likely than those in the highest group to suffer chronic illness (Doyal, 1987, p. 176).

The particular area where doctors increasingly exercise control over women's lives is in reproductive technology. Access to most forms of contraception, sterilization, abortion and infertility services is via the medical profession. Thus doctors' perceptions of acceptable female behaviour are extremely important in determining women's ability to have their needs met. Women wanting abortions may have to suffer the indignity of being considered inadequate or promiscuous or both. At the same time doctors may make their own decisions about patients who require sterilizations or more secure but dangerous forms of contraception which are based on pathological and racist views of Black and working-class families (Rakusen, 1981). The development of services for infertility exemplifies further these points. The provision of infertility services is patchy and, in common with other forms of provision, services are better in the more affluent parts of the country. However, 40 per cent of district health authorities have no special provision. This means time and money are necessary if patients wish to have consultations out of their area. On top of that, treatment is rarely entirely free; for example, for artificial insemination patients have to pay a £10–15 insemination fee (Mathieson, 1986, quoted in Doyal, 1987, p. 179). Most *in vitro* fertilization is carried out privately with total costs ranging from £2,000 to £2,500 with no guarantee of success (Doyal, 1987, p. 81). The availability therefore of such services to poorer women is limited. There is also sufficient evidence to suggest that some of the causes of infertility are, in common with much ill-health, more common amongst the poorer sections of society.

What further characterizes the operation of infertility services, however, is the ideology of appropriate motherhood. As Lesley Doyal points out a major contradiction exists between the idea that *all* women's ultimate ambition is to become a mother, and the practice of accepting only *some* women as suitable for infertility treatment: 'the allegedly biological maternal instinct is assumed to affect only those heterosexual women who are married or enjoying a "stable and happy relationship with a man"' (p. 182). Indeed the Warnock Report on human fertilization and embryology in 1985 stated: 'We believe that as a general rule, it is better for children to be born into a two-parent family, with both father and mother, although we recognise that it is impossible to predict with any certainty how lasting such a relationship will be' (pp. 11–12, quoted in Stanworth, 1987, p. 24). This attitude discriminates against lesbian and single heterosexual women, but a case in October 1987 of a woman turned down for *in vitro* fertilization (IVF) treatment on the grounds that she had once been a prostitute, even though she now fulfilled the criteria of heterosexual coupledom, shows that the administration of such a service can be both discriminatory and punishing.

The lessons women have learned from this apply to other areas of welfare: women need to be able to have the technology and the freedom to have children as well as the technology and the freedom not to have children. To be able to have these, women, as practitioners and clients, should play a major part in the decision-making of such services, with a recognition of the differential nature of women's experiences, whether fertile or infertile, Black or white, middle class or working class, heterosexual or lesbian, old or young. Those services themselves should be set in the context of a health service which provides a preventive approach to the social, environmental as well as physical causes of ill-health. Such a challenge does exist and the implications of this and other struggles are detailed in the next section.

The Implications for Welfare Analysis and Strategy of Struggles against Black Oppression and Women's Oppression

For [women] going into politics is a gesture of defiance, however timid, against their domestication, although they usually bring with them their experience of domestic responsbility. This is true whether we are talking of the Labour Party women's sections, the contemporary women's liberation movement or campaigns on issues which have been traditionally politicised by women – health, housing and children. (Campbell, 1984, pp. 191–2)

In the light of our experiences of racism in the field of health it is little wonder that Black women regard the State's surveillance of our lives through the combined Health and Social Services with growing distrust. Increasingly alienated from potentially beneficial provisions, we have been among the first to question the overall power of the Welfare State to record, control and intervene in our lives. (Bryan et al., 1985, p. 110)

The struggles by Black women and white women and the struggles by Black men and women, singly and together, are of extreme importance to welfare strategy. First they point to the importance of struggles in the *community*, often left out of account in mainstream and political economy writings, where the issues are precisely those about welfare provisions – housing, health, children, older people, poverty. Secondly, because of this they represent a major challenge to the narrow reformist, economist and nationalist concerns of the labour movement, organized in the workplace. Thirdly, these struggles highlight in its most stark way a major contradiction, a need for the provisions of welfare – decent housing, health and childcare facilities – violated by the reality of welfare services that have controlled and divided and rendered its users subordinate and dependent. Out of this contradiction has come a critique of bureaucracy, of professionalism, of hierarchy and most importantly the demand for *control* of welfare provision. The objectives of women's struggles have been to link the demands about home life to the demands about worklife, indeed the very process of such struggles requires the continual negotiation between the demands of private family life and the need to enter public political life. At the same time, the roots of much Black political consciousness lie in struggles against slavery and colonialism and international forms of exploitation, and potentially challenge the nationalist confines of welfare capitalism. These issues are now examined in greater detail.

Women's struggles for family allowances, for the right to determine their fertility, for legal and financial independence, for a financial recognition of their caring skills, for the right to define their own sexuality, for freedom from violent and oppressive relationships, all challenge the form, the nature and the objectives of welfare policy. They do this, first, by challenging the taken-for-granted areas of family life – the financial, emotional, physical relationships in the family. In particular they are able to challenge the notion of *dependency* and of *caring* by unlocking them from their assumed biological master – the fact that women bear children. Women's biology, as developments in reproductive technologies show, is a constantly changing phenomenon yet it is not this which determines women's oppression, but rather the social conditions and social relations under which that biology exists. In more general terms, they demand that that area known as reproduction becomes central to political demands for change, that questions of who cares, how and when, are central to any economic reorganization of society; secondly, they demand that the bureaucratic and professionally controlled relations of welfare have to be replaced by non-hierarchial, non-sexist and non-racist egalitarian relationships.

Finally, women's struggles have also highlighted the need to link the often conflicting needs for women in the here and now (an adequate benefit for carers, for example) with the long-term needs for women (to break free of the assumption that women are the carers, for example).

Campaigns directed at social security legislation or the low rates of child benefit highlight the dependent status of women in the family and the insecurity and inequality of this. By challenging this assumption of dependency it can be argued that women have paved the way to question other conditions of dependency which are often taken as fixed. That is to say, women have questioned their own dependency and in so doing have challenged, not simply the assumption of financial dependency, but of physical and physic dependency which are assumed to give rise to financial dependency. Old age, disability, mental handicap and not least childhood create forms of dependency which have been challenged recently. All have pointed to an important issue for future welfare strategy: the need to disentangle dependency that is socially constructed by being denied access to an independent income through work and/or benefit, from emotional and physical needs. At present, state provision often serves not to remove dependency but simply to restructure and reinforce the boundaries of dependency. Present changes in unemployment benefit for young people lengthen the time for which they are financially dependent on their parents; compulsory retirement policies structure old age; the present push for 'community care' will, without the massive necessary funding for community-based provision, increase the dependency of older people, disabled people, mentally ill people and people with learning difficulties upon female relatives who are expected to care for them, and further render these women more dependent upon the wage of a male partner. This issue of dependency is doubly significant for women for it is in caring for the elderly or frail or sick or young that they themselves are rendered financially dependent. It is this perspective of a shared problem between the dependency of women and those for whom they care which is important to emphasize, otherwise, there is a danger of a polarization taking place between the needs of 'carers' and the 'cared for' (see Croft, 1986).

The issue of 'caring' – who does it and why – is central to welfare strategy and women's lives. The emphasis of its being unpaid and exploitive work carried out within the isolation of the home has been countered by some feminists keen to assert women's pride in their skills. This view celebrates women's special nature which emerges from their caring role as bearers of a nurturing and supportive, collective culture. The difficulty with this is that it can serve to lock women back into their 'special nature' away from the public world of production and power (see chapter 3). It is possible to understand women's caring role in materialist terms, that is, as the way patriarchal capitalism reproduces its labour power and maintains its non-working population, *and* at the same time recognize the importance of this caring experience for women's sense of the need to change the world. Ann Ferguson and Nancy Folbre explain it like this:

The social relations of our nurturance work account on the one hand for our oppression (sacrificing our own interests for those of men and children), and on the other hand for our potential strength as bearers of a radical culture: we support an ethic of sharing, co-operation and collective involvement that stands in clear opposition to an ethic based on individualism, competition and private profit. (1981, p. 329)

In this way, it is possible to acknowledge caring as part of 'women-centred values' without returning to a biological essentialism, and further, to see within these values important aspects which form the basis of an alternative model to the present bureaucratic, professionalized, authoritarian relations of welfare today.

What is interesting about many women's struggles is that the process of struggling has been as significant as the aims of those struggles. Fighting for rights at the political level in trade unions, or political parties, involves fighting for them at the personal level too. '"The first hurdle you have to get over is your husband", said a Midlands hospital worker in her forties with a family and a husband, who, like all of these women, had to negotiate her right to become a shop steward during the hospital workers' dispute' (Campbell, 1984, pp. 193–4). This necessity to combine personal struggle with political struggle has given rise to two significant general features. The first is the attempt to organize in ways which are themselves anti-sexist, anti-hierarchial, anti-racist and anti-bureaucratic. The Women's Health Movement, for example, has struggled for forms of health care where women are not treated as passive, and where their domestic role, maternal intentions, marital status, their 'race', sexual orientation, are neither abused nor assumed. This has also entailed the attempt to demystify and share with others medical knowledge, or the setting up of self-help groups, as well as challenging hierarchical forms of organization between the workers in welfare services, and most particularly in the relationship between the users and providers of the service. Another example is the establishment of women's refuges for women subjected to domestic violence. Many of these refuges, though certainly not all, have aspired to organize themselves in a collective and non-hierarchical way where decision-making is shared between residents, paid staff and volunteers where residents themselves play a major part in counselling and supporting other women who have been victims of male violence in the home. The attempt in both these cases is to struggle against unjust features of this society in ways which prefigure a new and better society (Rose, 1985). This attempt at 'prefigurative politics' is not just a feature of feminist women's organizations but reflects an aspect of many working-class community groups run by women, like tenants associations or action groups, who would not necessarily call themselves feminists: an attempt to inject politics with the essence of shared and collective living rather than with formality, bureaucracy and hierarchy.

The second general important point which emerges from the nature of women's struggles is that, in so far as these struggles are often situated in the community rather than the workplace and are battling over questions of reproduction and not just production, they begin to break down the distinction set by state and the labour movement alike. This is the distinction between work and home, where work is what men do, where they get paid and where they struggle against capitalism, and where home is where women's unpaid caring work is rewarded by men's pay, and improved by virtue of men's struggles. The idea that reproduction and production are seen as interdependent forms of equal importance and not separate forms in which the organization of reproduction follows in the wake of production has important implications for welfare analysis and welfare strategy. It means that the future of employment cannot be considered separate from the future of welfare. But more than that it means that the central questions of both are: who is dependent on whom and who cares for whom? Any integrated social and economic policy has to provide an answer to these questions in ways that recognize the diversity of needs and of household forms and in ways that do not oppress, exploit or assume the rights of others to do so.

Many struggles in the Black communities over, for example, high suspension rates amongst Black children in schools, over SUS – the disproportionate numbers of Black youths arrested for being a suspected person – over the need for the NHS to recognize sickle-cell anaemia, over transracial childcare, over homelessness, and over deportation, have often involved mainly, though not exclusively Black *women*. Such campaigns point to an experience where the welfare state, in setting women up, puts them down as well. They point to the differences in the ways the state oppresses different women. Where that process has involved racism it has been particularly controlling, subordinating, blaming and punishing. These struggles range from workplace to community, they address questions of culture, and of human need. Where women's struggles have demanded a reassessment of the relationship between production and reproduction, Black struggles raise a further dimension: the relationship between welfare policies, the state and the *international division of labour*. It is this internationalism – of connecting to the oppression and exploitation in the Third World, to the global division between North and South – which perhaps raises the greatest challenge to socialism in general, to welfare strategy in particular.

How are these issues of community struggle, human need, culture, the state and internationalism raised by Black and anti-racist welfare struggles?

Struggles at Grunwick, Imperial Typewriters and Chix linked workplace to community, for it was from the Black communities that financial and organizational support was forthcoming when the trade unions and welfare agencies failed. The organizations of Black parents against suspensions, harassment and even, in the case of Manchester Burnage High School, murder, are important welfare struggles which, while they focus on *specific* racial aspects, also challenge central issues concerning form and control in state provision. A different example of the link between community and workplace is provided by Paul Gilroy's suggestion that there was a 'continuity of protest which links the 1981 riots with the Health Service strike that followed them' (1987a, p. 37). Gilroy also suggests that in the political activity of Black Britain class antagonisms are felt as community antagonisms. It is in and through the community that struggles over state services, over cultural identity and for political autonomy or self-management take place.

Each of these features can be found in the recent history of Britain's black communities: struggle over the services provided by the state, particularly the quality of educational opportunities for black children have been intense; ... and the demands of community organisations have repeatedly focused on the need to gain a degree of control over the processes which shape day to day experience. Local campaigns for police accountability, prompted by concern about the organisation and role of the force in inner-city areas, perfectly illustrate the ... last category. (Gilroy, 1987a, p. 230).

In some cases experience of racism in the statutory services has led to the setting up of self-managed supplementary provision outside the state, like Saturday schools. These have operated in some Black communities as a reaction to schools' classifying Black children as 'educationally sub-normal' but also to teach about Black history and cultures. In challenging not simply the question of access to welfare, but the entire basis of welfare and the form of its provision, such struggles are about the politics of need – challenging the state's, the administrators' and agencies' definition of need: if your access to health care is determined by the need for a doctor or nurse who speaks your own language, then this becomes not a 'special' but a basic need. At the same time this issue of the assertion of cultural identity is a difficult one to negotiate, particularly in view of the emergence of a right-wing redefinition of cultural difference, which masks a racial superiority as well as the recent development of religious fundamentalism. What is necessary is to understand culture in materialist terms, that is to say, as the means by which oppressed groups struggle to retain solidarity against the material and ideological forces which oppress them. For example, Avtar Brah's discussion of the need for anti-racist schooling discussed in chapter 4 presents a nine-point strategy that involves reclaiming *culture* as 'an oppositional force which stands in a complex relationship with the material conditions of society' (Brah and Deem, 1986, p. 76). This extends far beyond multiculturalism and is important, for just as within the women's movement claims to 'women's special nature' run the risk of biological essentialism, so too do claims to cultural identity have to be able to counter the sort of cultural essentialist thinking which acknowledges the importance of culture but also claims a hierarchy of cultures and justifies racial domination. The materialist view of culture is exemplified nicely by Paul Gilroy in the following way: 'In our multicultural schools the sound of steel pan may evoke Caribbean ethnicity, tradition and authenticity yet they originate in the oil drums of the Standard Oil Company rather than the mysterious knowledge of ancient African griots' (1987b, p. 12).

After the riots of 1981 several local authorities began to introduce equal opportunities policies not only for Black people but for women and, in some areas, for disabled people and homosexuals and lesbians. Such policies include positive action in employment and training (for example, provision of training schemes for Black or women workers in areas where they are underrepresented); monitoring of, for example, housing allocations, or employment; reviewing appointment procedures; creating anti-racist and anti-sexist strategies in teaching or social work practice; creating forms of consultation with women's groups or Black groups in the community. In many ways these policies have been an important source of legitimation of Black people's and women's struggles. They have created a framework and sets of tangible objectives around which women and Black people can organize, and they have created the opportunity for an acknowledgement and unveiling of different processes of racism and sexism operating within institutional settings, rather than simply by individuals. As mentioned earlier, in some cases, particularly within the GLC, these policies have created the opportunity to influence the local state into less bureaucratic and formalized procedures, to 'prefigure' good practice to get local author-ities and trade unions to centralize 'social' issues, and provide blueprints for other organizations to follow. The fact that the Conservative govern-ment dissolved the GLC and the metropolitan counties in 1986 and has since begun to put into action its own inner-city initiative shows in a negative way some of the success such local authorities had in effecting, with community support and involvement, equal opportunities policies. At the same time, there are some aspects which inhibit the full effectiveness of such policies: first, they operate within the constraints of national economic policy – high unemployment and a restructuring of employment which render Black people and women badly off. Secondly, such policies have been seen as an attempt by the local state to incorporate the leader-ship of the Black communities and to create a layer of 'femocrats' to disarm grass-roots activities by women and Blacks. Thirdly, in relation to Black professionals, social services management, for example, may consider Black social workers more effective at social control of the Black population than white social workers and use equal opportunities policies to achieve such effectiveness. Fourthly, the operation of employer-led anti-racist training is sometimes counterproductive amongst white employees who see it as management telling them what to do. In fact, the successful implementation of anti-racist and anti-sexist strategies requires the involve-ment of white and Black people, female and male, and in schools, for example, parents and children, in the articulation and operation of policies. What these observations point to is the need for a significant transfer of power and decision-making to women and Black people in the community, and accountability to them, as well as the need for organizat-ions of the white working class to pursue equal opportunities policies and anti-racist and anti-sexist strategies. As far as trade unions are concerned, some local authority trade unions do operate their own equal opportunities policies on behalf of their members at work as well as within their organ-izations. Clearly the second strategy, particularly in creating policies to get women and Black people into positions of responsibility at all levels of union activity, is vital to ensure the effectiveness of equal opportunities by employers. A final aspect of these strategies is the danger of limiting the problems faced by women and Black people to national if not local policies, especially given the fact that many of Black women's and men's struggles have been informed by an internationalist consciousness.

We look finally at the challenge these struggles present to imperialist and nationalist ideology and practice. Many of those who came from Asia and Africa in the inter-war and early post-war years and became involved in trade unions or in community campaigns had long experiences of anti-colonial struggle. For example, Udham Singh was a skilled electrician, an active trade unionist and delegate on his local trades council, and founder in 1938 of the first Indian Worker's Association. In 1940 he was hanged for shooting Sir Michael O'Dwyer who had been Lieutenant Governor of the Punjab and in 1919 had been in charge of the forces responsible for massa-cring unarmed peasants and workers at Amritsar (Sivanandan, 1982, p. 3). This internationalist consciousness has been explained by Gilroy in the following way: 'The need to develop international dialogues and means of organisation which can connect locality and immediacy across the internat-ional division of labour is perhaps more readily apparent to black populations who have recent experience of migration as well as acute memories of slavery and international indenture' (1987a, p. 68).

The appeals to national strength, national unity and national identity have long underpinned the argument for welfare provision. The New Right's racism has colonized with particular strength the appeal to cultural nationalism, and used this to argue for a restructuring of welfare and an acceptance of inequalities. Demands which are able to counter the ideolog-ical and material effects of this nationalism are therefore very important. Struggles against immigration controls, for instance, are also struggles against the international exploitation of labour. In the late 1970s, for example, the exposure of the use of Depo-Provera, unwarranted termination and sterilization on Black women in this country made links to the use of Third World Black women as guinea-pigs in contraceptive drug trials. From Black feminists in this country has also emerged the important attempt to make links of solidarity between the female workers in the sweated industries of the West (many of them Black workers) with the female workers who work often in the same multinationals in the Third World. Swasti Mitter (1986) sees in this the possibility of a 'novel labour movement'. What further marks this novelty, is that the demands of these women workers incorporate demands against imperialism and against racism as well as a restructuring of domestic work and paid work. Mitter concludes,

the division between core male workers and peripheralized women workers in the international political economy is based precisely on the generally accepted role of women in the domestic sphere. Hence it would be futile to counteract the challenges of the global corporations until and unless there are extended social provisions for the care of the young and the elderly, and men are willing to share domestic work. (p. 162)

It is clear from this that these internationalist perspectives have implications for welfare strategy. In addition to these priorities suggested by Mitter, the connections between access to welfare and immigration status must be cut. Welfare provision should be available to all who live in this country. Links between welfare agencies and immigration authorities should be removed. Indeed the aims, principles, systems of categorization and assessment of immigration controls should be questioned. In the immediate situation, policies which make immigrants prove they will have 'no recourse to public funds', or which create entitlement to welfare benefits according to immigrant status, or tests of residence in relation to receipt of benefits and services, or requirements to check passports before granting access to benefits or provision, should be challenged. Gordon (1985) proposes that the decriminalization of immigration – the removal of police as enforcement agents – would be an important step towards the ending of the passport checking by immigration officials that exists in the welfare services. Storey (1986), suggests there should be strict guidelines on confidentiality with disciplinary sanctions taken against welfare officials who abuse or pass on information or use it for anything other than the purpose for which it was given. Local education authorities, for example, could operate a policy whereby they had no obligation to educate a child who would be staying in the country less than six months, which would then require no further investigation. Health authorities could treat all, including visitors, without charge on a 'Good Samaritan' policy. All these challenges rest on changing immigration policy. The restoration of 'no immigration controls' is feasible only as an ultimate goal achieved in cooperation with other countries of the world. This clearly would save money and bureaucracy and would allow families to be united and refugees to enter countries freely. However, in the meantime a move to a just and non-discriminatory immigration policy for Britain is probably more feasible. As a move in this direction Ann Dummett (1986), on behalf of the Action Group on Immigration and Nationality, suggests that international standards and conventions could be brought to bear on British immigration and nationality laws – for example, the rights to have family life respected and the elimination of racial discrimination are both tenets of international law on immigration and nationality. A different issue but nevertheless one which indicates the connections between welfare and international policies is the exploitation of Third World countries through the export of inappropriate forms of welfare aid, for example, drugs and medical technology which are unable to deal with and often reinforce the problems of ill-health in these countries (Doyal, 1979). The representation of this issue closer to home is the exploitation by polytechnics and universities of 'overseas students', often from the Third World, who are taught and trained – whether in science or social policy – on courses whose content bears no relation to the needs of the countries from which they have come and to which they will return. Part of an anti-racist strategy within higher education might involve addressing sensitively the needs of such students. At a broader level an internationalist perspective also demands a critical view of exhortations by policy-makers and politicians, of the left and right, to welfare strategies which appeal to the 'British Nation' or 'British interests' for the racism they, consciously or otherwise, generate.

Finally, this internationalist perspective forces us to reconsider on what basis welfare capitalism can progress. In the past the welfare state has represented – at some expense to women and considerable neglect of Black and other immigrants – an accommodation of capital's and labour's interests to guarantee social reproduction. But as Hilary Rose points out, 'even this view of the welfare state being about the gains of the male working class and the sacrifice of women – a history of partial progress at best – is precluded by the new forms of industrialisation' (Rose, 1986, p. 87).

These new forms of industrialization are the ones described by Mitter above, and Sivanandan earlier – the movement of capital and production to some Third World economies, high unemployment in Britain, with a labour market increasingly divided between a highly skilled, high waged, mainly white male sector and a low-waged/part-time/unemployed sector of women, unskilled men, young people and Black people, men and women, young and unskilled. In other words some acknowledgement is required, as Rose puts it, of 'the international dimensions of the crisis, in which production work is being moved out of the old societies, throwing into question the extent of the state's commitment to guarantee social reproduction' and secondly of 'the centrality of women within the crisis both within the deindustralising and the industrialising societies' (1986, p. 92).

This chapter has examined some of the main aspects in the relationship of 'race' and gender to welfare provision today in terms of the roles women and Black people play as providers of welfare, paid and unpaid, as claimants, patients, clients, tenants, parents and school children, and as people struggling, in any of these roles, over welfare issues. Such an examination has revealed a whole range of important issues: of caring – who cares for whom, why, and how – of dependency, of the relationship between home and work, of immigration controls on Black people, of the way the economic, political and cultural relations between the global North and South worlds are played out within the British welfare system, of the struggles to create forms of non-sexist and non-racist welfare practice which enhance ordinary people's control over the form and nature of welfare provision, of the importance of recognizing the specific needs that arise from sex differences or diversities in culture, but without returning to a biological or cultural essentialism. I hope too I have begun to show that these are important areas for the study of welfare, but also areas give rise to issues, demands and strategies which all those who are part of the institutions of welfare can (or will continue to) press for. In the following, concluding section I will look at these questions in a more general context.

8 Conclusion

This book set out to understand and explain the paradox whereby issues of 'race' and gender are marginalized in the discipline of social policy, whilst at the same time the concepts of Family and Nation have been salient features in the development of welfare policies. Secondly, it has examined and evaluated existing welfare theory and the challenges posed to it by a range of feminist critiques and work on 'race' and racism. Thirdly, it has created a framework for the analysis of welfare policy which can encompass 'race', gender and class as separate and convergent issues. From an evaluation of the different strands of thinking in feminism and work on 'race' and racism, I proposed that the feminist critique of welfare, taking into account Black feminism's criticisms of it, and the 'relative autonomy' approach to 'race' and class as well as the political economy of migrant labour could combine and create a more widely focused political economy of welfare. In other words, as it stands, the political economy of welfare approach provides a necessary but insufficient basis for a full understanding of the welfare experiences of women and Black people. What is required is a historical and materialist understanding of the welfare state as part of an imperialist, racially structured and patriarchal capitalism, where the relationship of the state to the family and women's position within that is seen as central, but not reduced in understanding to either the needs of capital on the one hand or the determinants of biology on the other. Furthermore, this analysis should be able to offer a materialist account of the relationship of the welfare state to 'race' and racism which is set in terms of the specific and changing relationship of capitalism to imperialism. However, this should not reduce racism to the needs of capital or the determinants of culture, but neither should it detach it so much from capitalism as to see it only as a set of undesirable prejudices.

In the previous two chapters I have attempted to elaborate such an approach in terms of both a historical account of the development of the welfare state and an analysis of contemporary welfare provision. I have argued that the themes of Family and Nation which were central to this development, both in the reforms from 'above' and the demands of the organized working class from 'below', had important implications for the provision of welfare for women, for immigrants and, after the Second World War, for Black immigrants. From the nineteenth century capitalism had absorbed and reconstituted the social relations of both imperialism and patriarchy (even if these three were not necessarily mutually accommodating: in times of war or labour shortage, the pulling of women into paid labour put the interests of nation and capital above those of the patriarchal family). This complexity was reflected in the ideas and practices of the ruling class and intelligentsia who found ways of rationalizing and justifying the superiority of man over woman, of white over Black, of ruling class over working class, of the respectable and deserving of the working class over the residuum and the undeserving. These found expression in a number of ways: in the interpretation of the scientific theories of Darwin as the right to destroy Black 'races' and promote the dominance of white 'races'; in medical ideas of women as frail and hysterical, or, if they came from the lowest social orders, as polluting and proliferative; in religious ideas of Christianity's civilizing mission to bring obedience, the work ethic and a dubious morality to the far-flung corners of the cities of Britain and the Empire; in sociological ideas of the nature, cause and relief of social problems. This is not to say that these ideas went unchallenged – they were challenged by internationalists, anti-imperialists, socialists and feminists; nor is it to say that they did not undergo changes – the shift from 'laissez-faire' to social collectivism at the beginning of the century was an important force for welfare reforms and for shifting the boundaries between the private and the public. What it does mean is that whilst at one level the developments of welfare reforms represented an important challenge by the working class to the social relations of capitalism – to get the state to safeguard the working class against the deleterious effects of capitalism – they represented, too, important accommodations to ruling class ideas, not only in an increasing faith in the capacity of the state to act wholeheartedly on behalf of the interests of the working class, but importantly, in accepting its conceptions of the Family and the Nation. Within the trade unions, strategies for reforms were based, for example, on the acceptance of the principle of the family wage, or on the rights of British white workers to benefits and provisions over and above 'aliens' or Black workers. Those who challenged these conceptions and practices were largely marginalized from the political processes which led to the winning or granting of welfare reforms. It would be wrong to infer from this that welfare reforms have been wholly detrimental to women or Black people or other immigrants, after all, they have not been exempt from the general improvements which welfare reforms bring to the living standards of the working class. At the same time such reforms contain specific internal contradictions for both women and Black people. Policies aimed at women as mothers, for example, have provided real material improvements for many women, whilst at the same time locking many women more securely into the sexual division of labour and financial dependency. Similarly, Black people's educational or social security needs may be met but in a way that reinforces their position as second-class citizens.

Chapters 1 and 5 showed how intellectual developments, of which the discipline of social policy was no exception, followed this pattern of accommodation. Part of the reason for this can be explained by the particular influence upon the discipline of early Fabian thinkers. For them the concepts of Family and Nation were essential components in their intellectual baggage. However, what is equally important is the extent to which the development since the 1970s of a more theoretically grounded and critical approach to social policy has also been slow to acknowledge the empirical and theoretical contributions of feminism and work on 'race' and racism. This is reflected in the reluctance to admit feminism into the male club of theoretical perspectives on welfare, in the failure to address questions raised by feminist approaches, and in the indifference to making any assessment of how the range of different perspectives on welfare – from the right through to the left – view the family and the relationship between women, the family and welfare provision, or how they view the relationship between 'race', racism and welfare.

By contrast, as chapters 3, 4 and 7 showed, these are areas to which feminist critiques and emerging anti-racist critiques of welfare have addressed themselves. In doing so they have added greatly to our under-standing of some central issues in social policy: feminist studies have explored the emotional, ideological, physical and political aspects of caring from the point of view of those most involved in those processes – women; they have challenged the assumptions of female dependency and its implications for women's eligibility to benefits, they have asserted the importance of tieing economic policy to social policy, particularly in the demand that paid work should be structured according to the needs of everyday life and not the other way round. Both sets of critiques have challenged the mystification of knowledge by welfare professionals and the bureaucratic, hierarchical, as well the sexist and racist forms of welfare provision and, through this, have pointed to the need for democratic involvement and, ultimately, control by users and workers over welfare provision. In doing this they have also widened the concept of welfare needs from a demand for more state provision to an insistence that such provision is responsive and flexible to the specific expressed needs of oppressed groups. At the same time they have challenged the notion of citizenship by demanding full political and civil rights to all, regardless of sex, ethic origin or immigrant status. They have legitimized the community as a site of defence and struggle and have shown the important role Black and women's organization can have in articulating their own unmet needs. In addition, Black and Third World feminists and those writing on 'race' have indicated relatively unexamined areas for social policy – the nationalist and ethnocentric underpinnings of welfare reforms, the relationship between welfare and imperialism, the political economy of migrant labour, immigration controls, international movements of capital and labour, and new forms of international solidarity – and they have stressed the need for an internationalist understanding of these issues.

Opening up the Discipline

The framework of analysis presented in chapter 7 of the relationships between 'race' and gender and welfare suggested that these relationships go beyond simple prejudice or discrimination but arise from the nature of the welfare state within patriarchal and racially structured capitalism. This drew our attention to the extent to which the welfare state had been built from the exploited labour of Black and other immigrant workers and women, to the ways in which it reproduces, in various material and ideological ways, international, racial and sexual divisions of labour, as well as racial domination and female subordination, all of which are compounded by class differences. At the same time women and Black people have struggled not only to retain state provision but to change and challenge it. Clearly there is scope for much more work in examining these relationships, processes, contradictions, struggles and strategies. Nevertheless, for students, teachers, researchers and practitioners it means that their work needs to try to do three things: (i) to take account of the welfare experiences as expressed by women and Black people themselves; (ii) to make explicit the specific roles and struggles enacted by women and by Black people in welfare provison; (iii) to examine the impact of welfare policies and practices and welfare strategies on women and Black people. More specifically, those involved in the study or practice of social policy might find the following (by no means exhaustive) checklist useful in their work. In examining or operating welfare policies and practice we can ask:

- Do they (welfare policies and practices) move in the direction of transforming or reinforcing the sexual divisions of labour at home and sexual and racial divisions of labour at work, and women's and Black people's limited opportunities in paid employment?
- How do they acknowledge unpaid care in the home? Do strategies enhance the choices of carers and cared-for?
- How far are economic policies geared towards caring needs within households?
- Do welfare policies and practices counter the privileging of a particular

household form (the married couple, male nuclear, breadwinner family which is not only detrimental to the needs of women within that household but also marginalizes the needs of single parents, single people, elderly people, cohabitees, lesbians, gays, young people, Black and other ethnic minority households, childless women, large households with no biological ties, poor households, households with disabled people, with mentally ill, people with learning difficulties, dependent, frail or older people, households of people with learning difficulties, travelling households and groups.

- Do political processes exist for the democratic involvement in welfare provision of women and of Black people and other racialized groups? And do they acknowledge different interests and experience between people in these groups (working-class women, Black women, lesbians, Asians, Africans, Caribbeans, providers and users of services)?
- Do welfare policies acknowledge the existence of racism? Do they challenge the idea of Black people and their cultures as 'problems', as 'scroungers' as dangerous, unhealthy, as passive, as only victims?
- Do they (welfare policies and practices) resist a racist conception of nationality, particularly in terms of eligibility rights to benefits and residence status qualifications?
- Do they counter ideas of white/British cultural superiority?
- Do they allow for the positive recognition of cultural differences without using these to mask experiences of racism or justify real differences in power?
- Do welfare policies expose and challenge the exploitation of the 'Third World' or the economic dependency of the Third World upon the industrialized Western world?
- How far is it acknowledged that national welfare programmes depend upon (or are threatened by) international forms of exploitation?
- Last, but not least, where are the spaces, the openings, the sites, in which these questions can be transformed into collective struggles?

By asking these questions it does not mean that social policy abandons its traditional concerns with poverty or redistribution but that these become informed by the specific and general ways these issues affect women and Black people as well as by the way these issues in turn are central to the lives of many women and Black people. Poverty, for example, has to take into account the 'feminization' of poverty, questions about the causes of women's financial dependency, and their specific relationship to the labour market; it must take on board too the patterns of global poverty and the political economy of migrant labour, the impact of racist immigration and nationality laws, as well as the racism in education, employment, housing and income maintenance services. In other words those issues of why women are dependent, why women care which are presently confined to the feminist margins of the subject, become central to the explanations of social problems and policy-making as do the different roots, relations and directions of racism. If the discipline of social policy is to break free of its nationalist concerns, it must adopt an internationalist approach. One part of this is the important recent development of comparative social policy. Material that compares welfare provisions, mortality ratios, policies for women and so on is important in three ways. First, it shows us discernible trends common to countries of similar or differing political and economic systems of organization: for example, in Europe, including Eastern Europe, the entry of women into paid work has been a common development, so too has the maintenance of a sex-segregated and in most cases relatively lower paid labour market, and the movement of women from private unpaid caring in the home to paid caring in the public sector. However, we can also discover within this that there may be specific national and historical variations in policy, for example, the large numbers of women in part-time work and history of poor provision of socialized care for pre-school children is a characteristic particular to Britain. Looking to other countries' social policies we can also begin to see that, even within capitalism, the state can be shifted much further in meeting need than it has gone in Britain: by looking at provisions which allow women to enter the labour market that exist in Denmark and Sweden, for example, or even by examining international law on immigration and nationality we can be reminded that by these standards our own policies and laws are contemptible. However, we should, at the same time, be aware of the dangers of creating 'models of achievement' from countries with different economic and social histories. We have, also, to be open to critical accounts from those countries themselves. Taking again the example of Denmark and Sweden, Anette Borchorst and Birte Siim (Sassoon, 1987) argue that the development of the advanced welfare state in these countries has made significant improvements in the social and economic position of women since the 1960s: women are much more able to support themselves and their children independently either through the labour market or through the state and their large-scale entry into the labour market has generated comprehensive services of childcare, health care and care for the elderly so that they stand in a much stronger position as mothers, as workers and as consumers (rather than clients) of welfare compared with women in Britain or the United States. However, the other side of this development has been what Borchorst and Siim call 'a shift in the locus of oppression from the private to the public sphere' (Sassoon, 1987, p. 152): the weakening of family patriarchy and the strengthening of social patriarchy. 'Redistributive corporation', on which these countries' social democracy is based, is a system of legitimation and institutionalization of class conflict whereby representatives of government, trade union bodies, industry and professional experts are all involved in political and economic and social decision-making. This has given rise to a concentration of male domination in politics and work which has both helped and resulted from the maintenance of patriarchal power in terms of legitimizing women's double burden as both mother and worker. They argue that this is not intentional but results from, for example, working conditions which are negotiated according to male norms, and on the assumption of women's extra home responsibilities. Policies that benefit women have resulted from broader political and economic goals rather than a commitment to women's equality or breaking down the sexual division of labour in the home. Women as objects rather than subjects of social policies have therefore been particularly vulnerable to political and economic change: cuts in welfare services in Denmark have, as in Britain, hit women particularly hard. If we were to draw lessons it would be to recognize the importance of such advanced welfare states' policies for strengthening women's position but to insist also on the centrality of women's interests, together with a recognition of the class differences within them, in political and economic decisions and on the importance for opportunities for women to be centrally involved in that decision-making.

Such comparisons are, then, clearly enlightening, but there are further dimensions to an internationalist perspective. These look at the relationship between countries as well as inside them; they consider how far exploitation across continents affects welfare provision within those continents; they look at the power relations behind the nationalist boundaries of welfare obligation, and at how movements of capital as well as labour effect the potential for welfare provision, and what new international forms of solidarity, struggle and, ultimately, demands for welfare arise from these.

Strategies for Welfare

Welfare strategies that counter racism and those that counter sexism have to be both *specific* and *linked* both to each other as well as to those strategies that recognize the importance of class. They should recognize the need for Black and women welfare workers and consumers to organize separately and autonomously as teachers, social workers, tenants or patients, for example. At the same time the demands and issues raised by such groups should be supported by mixed organizations – trade unions, political parties, welfare pressure groups, community groups – and become incorporated into and linked to their own demands. Thus, for example, the specific vulnerability of single women and of Black people to homelessness requires a strategy which not only aims to increase the availability of low-cost housing but also unlocks that availability from the assumptions of family forms and dependency as well as from immigration controls, residency status and racist allocation of housing. Demands to reform social security could take on board the disaggregation of social security benefits – a system of benefits for all carers, for example – as well as seeking an ending to entitlement based on immigration status, to links between the Home Office and the DHSS, to discrimination against those with dependants abroad and to the imposition of British cultural norms, and additionally supporting calls for the provision of information in minority languages. In addition it should be recognized that whilst many of the issues raised by racism and sexism are specific to Black people's and women's needs, they are also general, in the sense that the ideologies and practices of welfare capitalism that they challenge are those which also oppress the working class in general. Thus anti-racist and anti-sexist strategies in schools have the potential of challenging with renewed vigour the hierarchical selection and grading processes on which capitalist schooling is based; similarly, challenges to the racist and sexist procedures in housing allocation and management challenge also the bureaucratic, authoritarian and individualizing nature of such provision. This exemplifies how many of the issues raised by struggles over 'race' and gender are not 'extras', luxuries we cannot afford in the crisis when the working class is struggling even to preserve its right to strike. On the contrary they raise, differently and with new perspective, issues which are central to the long-term interests of the working-class.

This view, that 'race' and gender raise welfare issues which are both specific from but at the same time central to class issues, differs from two currents of thought about strategy which are now popular. The first is that since the New Right has attacked the welfare state, has weakened the labour movement and has made unemployment a fact of life, the best strategy is one of economic growth, full employment, and a defence of the welfare state: 'This may not lead us any closer to socialism but at the very least we would have won back the political and ideological initiative from the right. If the choice is between Thatcherism and welfare capitalism, we should surely opt for the lesser evil' (Mishra, 1986b, p. 17).

The second position, rather than dismissing the untimeliness of the radical implications of the women's movement and Black resistance, elevates them to a position of a new vanguardism which has replaced the old class antagonisms of capital and labour. According to this argument the working class has been weakened by the collapse of a manufacturing base in Britain and by the ability of capital to move around the world, to pick its workforce, whilst other oppositional forces have strengthened: these forces are the 'new social movements', which include the women's movement, peace movement and Black resistance. All of these are

in part non-class based. They involve relatively decentralised forms of organisation and often stem from conflicts structured around the contradiction between 'the people' and the state – where the state *not* the capitalist class, is the major problem. They split the working class since the white-based labour movement is often part of the problem for women, for environmentalists, for advocates of new community-based policies, and for black and Asian people. (Lash and Urry, 1987, p. 16)

I would not hold with either current, though I recognize the partial truths of both. The first position underestimates the marginalization of women and Black people (as I hope I have shown) from the ideals of 'full' employment (which only ever meant full, white, male employment), from welfare capitalism and from the labour movement whose incorporation is required for such a strategy. In so far as proponents of such a strategy look to the Scandinavian corporatist advanced welfare state model for support for the idea that such a system can provide significant improvements in the lives of women, then they are right. However, as the brief discussion above on Denmark and Sweden implies, this in itself is not enough: women's interests need to be seen as central, not additional, to economic strategies and provision of welfare, and this involves an explicit, conscious and detailed programme for women's access to political power. In addition, the Scandinavian corporatist system can only provide a limited model for the elimination of racism. The historical relationship of these countries to imperialism is very different from Britain's. Furthermore, the corporatist solution not only replaces class conflict with a form of class collaboration, but represents an essentially *national* solution which could serve to intensify, not eliminate, the racist nationalism inherent in British welfare policies and practices, particularly as few guarantees currently exist within the British labour movement for the acknowledgement of the importance of separate Black organizations which would highlight such issues. It could also be argued that rather than waiting for a strategy from which women and Black people would benefit in a passive way, on the contrary, that since the subordination of women and Black people features so centrally in the restructuring of the economy and the welfare state, precisely *now* is the time to assert their interests.

The second position overestimates the unity of the new social movements – which after all have their own class positions: the history of liberal feminism, or the emergence of a new Black professionalism testify to this; it overestimates too the 'newness' of these movements – has not Black resistance long traditions in anti-colonial and anti-slavery struggle? And it underestimates the extent to which the radical issues raised by the women's movement or Black resistance are in themselves profoundly anti-capitalist, and share common interests with class struggles. The 1984 miners' strike represented not only a defence of jobs but of a community and in doing so was subject to substantial police intervention and heavy control, an experience common to many of the Black communities. Finally, in its alleged decomposition of the working class it exaggerates the demise of class politics and also fails to recognize the struggles of the new working class – in the sweated labour of women in the Third World and Europe who, through all of this, have begun to find new forms of class solidarity in which anti-racism and anti-sexism feature as an important part of their struggle for better wages and conditions.

In this book I have argued for the need for gender and 'race' to be taken to the heart of an analysis of the welfare state within capitalism. I hope I have shown how work on women and welfare and on 'race' and welfare raises new and important dimensions for welfare analysis and strategy, and, at the same time, throws new light on existing social policy issues. Finally, I have begun the construction of an analytical framework, drawn from the development of the British welfare state, which is able to generate an account of the ways in which the welfare experiences and welfare needs of women and Black people are both specific *and* central to welfare analysis and welfare strategy.

When the oppressed demand, as they do now, more than the right to accommodate themselves to the society around them, when they demand that it is society itself which must change and be accommodated to them and their needs, then we must listen, for in doing this they provide us with the signposts to a more human and humane world.

Bibliography

Abbot, E. and Bompas, K. (1943) *The Woman Citizen and Social Security*, London, Katharine Bompas.

Abel-Smith, B. and Titmuss, K. (eds) (1987) *The Philosophy of Welfare: Selected Writings of Richard Titmuss*. London, Allen and Unwin.

ABSWAP (Association of Black Social Workers and Allied Professionals) (1983) *Black Children in Care*. Evidence to the House of Commons Social Services Committee. London, Association of Black Social Workers and Allied Professionals.

Ahmed, S., Cheetham, J. and Small, J. (eds) (1986) *Social Work with Black Children and their Families*. London, Batsford.

Alexander, Z. and Dewjee, A. (eds) (1984) *The Wonderful Adventures of Mary Seacole in Many Lands*. London, Falling Wall Press.

ALTARF (All London Teachers Against Racism and Fascism) (1984) *Challenging Racism*. Nottingham, Russell Press.

Amos, V. and Parmar, P. (1984) 'Challenging Imperial Feminism', *Feminist Review*, no. 17.

Arnott, H. (1987) 'Second-class Citizens', in Walker and Walker (1987).

Arnott, M. (1985) *Race and Gender: Equal Opportunities Policies in Education*. London, Pergamon/Open University.

Ashton, F. and Whitting, G. (eds) (1987) *Feminist Theory and Practical Policies*. Bristol, School for Advanced Urban Studies.

Ballard, C. (1970) 'Conflict, Continuity and Change', in Khan (1979).

Ballard, R. (1979) 'Ethnic Minorities and the Social Services', in Khan (1979).

Banks, O. (1981) *Faces of Feminism*. Oxford, Martin Robertson.

Barclay, P. (1982) *Social Workers: Their Role and Tasks*. London, Bedford Square Press.

Barker, M. (1981) *The New Racism*. London, Junction Books.

Barrett, M. (1980) *Women's Oppression Today: Problems in Marxist – Feminist Analysis*. London, Verso.

Barrett, M. and McIntosh, M. (1982a) *The Anti-social Family*. London, Verso.

Barrett, M. and McIntosh, M. (1982b) 'The "Family Wage"', in Open University (1982a).

Barrett, M. and McIntosh, M. (1985) 'Ethnocentricism and Socialist Feminist Theory', *Feminist Review*, no. 20.

Bartels, E. (1982) 'Biological Sex Differences and Sex Stereotyping', in Open University (1982a).

BBC TV (1986) *She Married a Yank: the women who married American GIs* (documentary).

Bean, P. and MacPherson, S. (eds) (1983) *Approaches to Welfare*. London, Routledge and Kegan Paul.

Beechey, V. and Perkins, T. (1987) *A Matter of Hours: Women, Part-time Work and the Labour Market*. Cambridge, Polity Press.

Ben-Tovim, G. and Gabriel, J. (1981) 'Race, Left Strategies and the State', *Politics and Power*, 3.

Ben-Tovim, G., Gabriel, J., Law, I. and Stredder, K. (1986) *The Local Politics of Race*. London, Macmillan.

Beresford, P. and Croft, S. (1984) 'Welfare Pluralism: the New Face of Fabianism', *Critical Social Policy*, issue 9.

Beveridge, W. (1942) *Social Insurance and Allied Services* (the Beveridge Report). London, HMSO, Cmnd 6404.

Bhalla, A. and Blakemore, K. (1981) *Elders of the Ethnic Minority Groups*. London, All Faiths for One Race.

Bhavnani, K. and Coulson, M. (1986) 'Transforming Socialist-Feminism: the Challenge of Racism', *Feminist Review*, no. 23.

Bhavnani, R. (1986) 'The Struggle for an Anti-racist Policy in Education in Avon', *Critical Social Policy*, issue 16.

Black Health Workers and Patients Group (1983) 'Psychiatry and the Corporate State', *Race and Class*, XXI.

Bland, L. (1982) '"Guardians of the Race" or "Vampires upon the Nation's Health"? Female Sexuality in Early Twentieth Century Britain', in Open University (1982a)

Bland, L. (1985) '"Cleansing the Portals of Life": the Venereal Disease Campaign in the Early Twentieth Century', in Langan and Schwartz (1985).

Blatchford, R. (1902) *Britain for the British*. London, The Clarion Press.

Borchorst, A. and Siim, B. (1987) 'Women and the Advanced Welfare State – a New Kind of Patriarchal Power', in Sassoon (1987).

Bopari, N. (1987) '"Intentionally Homeless" Bangladeshis!', *Foundation, Race and Housing Journal*, no. 3.

Bosanquet, N. (1983) *After the New Right*. London, Heinemann.

Bourne, J. (1980) 'Cheerleaders and Ombudsmen: the Sociology of Race Relations in Britain', *Race and Class*, XXI (4).

Bourne, J. (1983) 'Towards an Anti-racist Feminism', *Race and Class*, XXV.

Bourne, J. (1987) 'The Shape of Things to Come: Don't Write Race out of Class Politics', *New Socialist*, March 1987.

Bowles, S. and Gintis, H. (1976) *Schooling in Capitalist America*. London, Routledge and Kegan Paul.

Boyson, R. (1971) *Down with the Poor*. London, Churchill Press.

Bradshaw, J. (1985) 'Tried and Found Wanting: the Take-up of Means-tested Benefits', in S. Ward (ed.), *DHSS in Crisis*, London, Child Poverty Action Group.

Brah, A. and Deem, R. (1986) 'Towards Anti-sexist and Anti-racist Schooling', *Critical Social Policy*, issue 16.

Brah, A. and Minhas, R. (1985) 'Structural Racism or Cultural Differences? Schooling for Asian Girls', in G. Weiner (ed.), *Just a Bunch of Girls*. Milton Keynes, Open University Press.

Brent Asian Women's Refuge and Resource Centre (1984) 'Brent Asian Women's Refuge and Resource Centre', *Feminist Review*, no. 17.

Brent Community Health Council (1981a) *It's My Life Doctor*: Annual Report. London, Brent Community Health Council.

Brent Community Health Council (1981b) *Black People and the Health Service*. London, Brent Community Health Council.

Bridges, L. (1975) 'The Ministry of Internal Security: British Urban Social Policy 1968–74', *Race and Class*, XVI (4).

Brittan, A. and Maynard, M. (1984) *Sexism, Racism and Oppression*. Oxford, Basil Blackwell.

Brixton Black Women's Group (1984) 'Black Women Organising', *Feminist Review*, no. 17.

Brownmiller, S. (1975) *Against Our Will: Men, Women and Rape*. New York, Simon and Schuster.

Bryan, B., Dadzie, S. and Scafe, S. (1985) *The Heart of the Race: Black Women's Lives in Britain*. London, Virago.

Bull, D. and Wilding, P. (1983) *Thatcherism and the Poor*. London, Child Poverty Action Group.

Campbell, B. (1984) *Wigan Pier Revisited*. London, Virago.

Campbell, B. (1986) *The Iron Ladies: Why do Women Vote Tory?* London, Virago.

Carby, H. (1982a) 'Schooling in Babylon', in CCCS (1982).

Carby, H. (1982b) 'White Woman Listen! Black Feminism and the Boundaries of Sisterhood', in CCCS (1982).

Castles, S. and Kosack, C. (1973) *Immigrant Workers and Class Structure in Western Europe*. Oxford, IRR/Oxford University Press.

CCCS (Centre for Contemporary Cultural Studies) (1982) *The Empire Strikes Back*. London, Hutchinson.

Channel 4 Television (1987) *Bert Hardy – Photographer* (documentary).

Chowdorow, N. (1978) *The Reproduction of Mothering*. Berkeley, Ca, University of California Press.

Clarke, J., Cochrane, A. and Smart, C. (1987) *Ideologies of Welfare*. London, Hutchinson.

Coard, B. (1971) *How the West Indian Child is Made Educationally Sub-normal in the British School System*. London, New Beacon Books.

Coates, K. and Silburn, R. (1970) *Poverty, the Forgotten Englishman*. Harmondsworth, Penguin.

Cockburn, C. (1983) *Brothers: Male Dominance and Technological Change*. London, Pluto Press.

Cohen, S. (1985) 'Anti-semitism, Immigration Controls and the Welfare State', *Critical Social Policy*, issue 13.

Commission for Racial Equality (1986) *Survey on Teaching*. London, Commission for Racial Equality.

Community Relations Commission (1970) *Between two Cultures: a Study of the*

Relationship between Generations in the Asian Community in Britain. London, CRC.

Connelly, N. (1988) *Care in the Multiracial Community.* London, Policy Studies Institute.

Conservative Party (1983) *Manifesto.* London, Conservative Party.

Coote, A. (1981) 'The AES: a New Starting Point', *New Socialist*, November/December.

Corea, G. (1985) *The Mother-machine: Reproductive Technologies from Artificial Insemination to Artificial Wombs.* New York, Harper and Row.

Corrigan, P. (1979) 'Popular Consciousness and Social Democracy', *Marxism Today*, December.

Coward, R. (1984) *Female Desire.* London, Paladin.

Coyle, A. (1985) 'Going Private: the Implications of Privatization for Women's Work', *Feminist Review*, no. 21.

Croft, S. (1986) 'Women, Caring and the Recasting of Need: a Feminist Reappraisal', *Critical Social Policy*, issue 16.

Crosland, A. (1956) *The Future of Socialism.* London, Jonathan Cape.

Cross, M. (1981) 'Racial Equality and Social Policy: Omission or Commission?', in *Yearbook of Social Policy in Britain, 1980–81.* London, Routledge and Kegan Paul.

Cross, M. (1982) 'The Manufacture of Marginality', in E. Cashmore and B. Troyna, *Black Youth in Crisis.* London, Allen and Unwin.

Crossman, R. (1958) 'London Diary', *New Statesman*, 29 November.

Dale, J. (1986) 'Feminists and the Development of the Welfare State – Some Lessons from our History', *Critical Social Policy*, issue 16.

Dale, J. and Foster, P. (1986) *Feminists and State Welfare.* London, Routledge and Kegan Paul.

Daly, M. (1978) *Gyn/Ecology: the Metaethics of Radical Feminism.* Boston, Mass., Beacon Press.

David, M. (1980) *The State, the Family and Education.* London, Routledge and Kegan Paul.

David, M. (1983) 'The New Right in the USA and Britain: a New Anti-feminist Moral Economy', *Critical Social Policy*, 2 (3).

David, M. (1985) 'Motherhood and Social Policy – a Matter of Education?', *Critical Social Policy*, issue 12.

David, M. (1986) 'Morality and Maternity: Towards a Better Union than the Moral Right's Family Policy', *Critical Social Policy*, issue 16.

David, M. and Land, H. (1983) 'Sex and Social Policy', in Glennerster (1983).

Davin, A. (1978) 'Imperialism and Motherhood', *History Workshop Journal*, no. 5.

Davis, A. (1981) *Women, Race and Class.* London, The Women's Press.

Davies, M. Llewellyn (ed.) (1915/1978) *Maternity Letters from Working Women.* London, Virago.

Deacon, A. (1976) *In Search of the Scrounger.* Occasional Papers in Social Administration, no. 60. London, G. Bell and Sons.

Deacon, A. (1977) 'Concession and Coercion: the Politics of Unemployment Insurance in the 1920s', in A. Briggs and J. Saville, *Essays in Labour History.* London, Croom Helm.

Deacon, B. (1983). *Social Policy and Socialism. The Struggle for Socialist Relations of Welfare*. London, Pluto Press.

Deakin, N. (1987) *The Politics of Welfare*. London, Methuen.

Delphy, C. (1984) *Close to Home: a Materialist Analysis of Women's Oppression*. London, Hutchinson.

Department of the Environment (1977) *Policy for the Inner Cities*. London, HMSO, Cmnd 6845.

De Sousa, E. (1987) 'Racism and the YTS', *Critical Social Policy*, issue 20.

Donnison, D. (1975) *Social Policy and Administration Revisited*. London, Allen and Unwin.

Donovan, J. (1986) 'Black People's Health: a Different Approach', in Rathwell and Phillips (1986).

Doyal, L. (1979) *The Political Economy of Health*. London, Pluto Press.

Doyal, L. (1987) 'Infertility – a Life Sentence? Women and the National Health Service', in Stanworth (1987).

Doyal, L. and Gough, I. (1984) 'A Theory of Human Needs', *Critical Social Policy*, issue 10.

Doyal, L., Hunt, G. and Mellor, J. (1981) 'Your Life in Their Hands: Migrant Workers in the National Health Service', *Critcal Social Policy*, 1 (2).

Dummett, A. (ed.) (1986) *Towards a Just Immigration Policy*. London, The Cobden Trust.

Dwork, D. (1987) *War is Good for Babies and Other Young Children: a history of the infant and child welfare movement in England, 1898–1918*. London, Tavistock.

Dworkin, A. (1981) *Pornography: Men Possessing Women*. New York, Perigee/G. P. Putnam's.

Edgar, D. (1986) 'The Free and the Good', in R. Levitas (ed.), *The Ideology of the New Right*. Cambridge, Polity Press.

Ehrenreich, B. and English, D. (1973a) *Complaints and Disorders: the Sexual Politics of Sickness*. London, Readers and Writers.

Ehrenreich, B. and English, D. (1973b) *Witches, Midwives and Nurses: a History of Women Healers*. London, Readers and Writers.

Ehrenreich, D. and English, B. (1979) *For Her Own Good: 150 Years of the Experts' Advice to Women*. London, Pluto Press.

Eisenstein, H. (1984) *Contemporary Feminist Thought*. London, Allen and Unwin.

Ely, P. and Denney, D. (1987) *Social Work in a Multi-racial Society*. Aldershot, Gower.

Engels, F. (1884, reprinted in 1976) *The Origin of the Family, Private Property and the State*. London, Lawrence and Wishart.

Equal Opportunities Commission (1986) *Annual Report*. Manchester, EOC.

Feminist Review (1984) 'Many Voices, One Chant, Black Feminist Perspectives', *Feminist Review*, no. 17.

Feminist Review (1986a) 'Feminism and Class Politics: a Round-table Discussion', *Feminist Review*, no. 23.

Feminist Review (ed.) (1986b) *Waged Work: a Reader*. London, Virago.

Ferguson, A. and Folbre, N. (1981) 'The Unhappy Marriage of Patriarchy and Capitalism', in Sargent (1981).

Finch, J. (1984) 'Community Care: Developing Non-sexist Alternatives', *Critical*

Social Policy, issue 9.

Finch, J. and Groves, D. (1980) 'Community Care and the Family: a Case for Equal Opportunities', *Journal of Social Policy*, 9 (4).

Finch, J. and Groves, D. (eds) (1983) *A Labour of Love: Women, Work and Caring*. London, Routledge and Kegan Paul.

Finkelstein, V. (1980) *Attitudes to Disabled People*. New York International Exchange of Information in Rehabilitation monograph, no. 5.

Firestone, S. (1970) *The Dialectic Sex: the case for Feminist Revolution*. New York, Bantam Books.

Fitzgerald, T. (1983) 'The New Right and the Family', in Loney et al. (1983).

Flett, H., Henderson, J. and Brown, B. (1979) 'The Practice of Racial Dispersal in Birmingham, 1969–1975', *Journal of Social Policy*, 8 (3).

Foot, P. (1965) *Immigration and Race in British Politics*. Harmondsworth, Penguin.

Ford, A. (1985) *Telling the Truth: the Life and Times of the British Honduran Forestry Unit in Scotland 1941–44*. London, Karia Press.

Friedman, M. (1962) *Capitalism and Freedom*. Chicago, Chicago University Press.

Fryer, P. (1984) *Staying Power: the History of Black People in Britain*. London, Pluto Press.

Gabriel, J. and Ben-Tovim, G. (1978) 'Marxism and the Concept of Racism', *Economy and Society*, 7 (2).

Gabriel, J. and Ben-Tovim, G. (1979) 'The Conceptualisation of Race Relations in Sociological Theory', *Ethnic and Racial Studies*, 2 (2).

George, V. and Wilding, P. (1976) *Ideology and State Welfare*. London, Routledge and Kegan Paul.

George, V. and Wilding, P. (1985) *Ideology and Social Welfare*. 2nd rev. edn. London, Routledge and Kegan Paul.

Geras, N. (1983) *Marx and Human Nature: Refutation of a Legend*. London, Verso.

Gilroy, P. (1980) 'Managing the "Underclass"', *Race and Class*, XXII (I).

Gilroy, P. (1982) 'Steppin' out of Babylon – Race, Class and Autonomy', in CCCS (1982).

Gilroy, P. (1987a) *There Aint't No Black in the Union Jack*. London, Hutchinson.

Gilroy, P. (1987b) *Problems in Anti-Racist Strategy*, London, Runnymede Trust.

Gittins, D. (1985) *The Family in Question: Challenging Households and Familiar Ideologies*. London, Macmillan.

Ginsburg, N. (1979) *Class, Capital and Social Policy*. London, Macmillan.

Glazer, N. and Young, K. (1983) *Ethnic Pluralism and Public Policy*. London, Heinemann.

Glendinning, J. and Millar, J. (eds) (1987) *Women and Poverty in Britain*. Brighton, Wheatsheaf.

Glennerster, H. (ed.) (1983) *The Future of the Welfare State*. London, Heinemann.

Glennerster, H. (1988) 'Requiem for the Social Administration Association', *Journal of Social Policy*, 17 (1).

Golding, P. (1983) 'Rethinking Commonsense about Social Policy', in Bull and Wilding (1983).

Gordon, P. (1983) 'Medicine, Racism and Immigration Control', *Critical Social Policy*, issue 7.

Gordon, P. (1984) *Deportations and Removals*. London, Runnymede Trust.

Gordon, P. (1985) *Policing Immigration, Britain's Internal Control*. London, Pluto Press.

Gordon, P. (1986) 'Racism and Social Security', *Critical Social Policy*, issue 17.

Gordon, P. and Klug, F. (1984) *Racism and Discrimination in Britain. A Select Bibliography 1970–83*. London, Runnymede Trust.

Gordon, P. and Klug, F. (1986) *New Right, New Racism*. London, Searchlight Publications.

Gordon, P. and Newnham, A. (1985) *Passport to Benefits? Racism in Social Security*. London, Child Poverty Action Group and Runnymede Trust.

Gough, I. (1978) 'Theories of the Welfare State', *International Journal of Health Services*, 8 (1).

Gough, I. (1979) *The Political Economy of the Welfare State*. London, Macmillan.

Gough, I. (1980) 'Thatcherism and the Welfare State', *Marxism Today*, July.

Gough, I. (1981) 'Poverty in the United Kingdom': Review Article, *International Journal of Health Services*, 11 (2).

Graham, H. (1987) 'Being Poor: Perceptions and Coping Strategies of Lone Mothers', in J. Brannen and G. Wilson (eds) (1987), *Give and Take in Families: Studies in Resource Distribution*. London, Allen and Unwin.

Griffin, S. (1980) *Woman and Nature: the Roaring Inside Her*. New York, Harper Colophon.

Groves, D. (1983) 'Members and Survivors: Women and Retirement – Pensions Legislation', in Lewis (1983).

Gupta, P. S. (1978) *Imperialism and the British Labour Movement*. London, Macmillan.

Gurnah, A. (1984–5) 'The Politics of Racism Awareness Training', *Critical Social Policy*, no. 11.

Hadley, R. and Hatch, S. (1981) *Social Welfare and the Failure of the State*. London, Allen and Unwin.

Hall, S. (1980a) 'Race, Articulation and Societies Structured in Dominance', in UNESCO, *Sociological Theories: Race and Colonisation*. Paris, UNESCO.

Hall, S. (1980b) 'Thatcherism – a New Stage?', *Marxism Today*, February.

Hall, S. (1982) 'The Lessons of Lord Scarman', *Critical Social Policy*, no. 2 (2).

Hall, S. (1984a) 'Labour's Love Still Lost', *New Socialist*, January/February.

Hall, S. (1984b) 'Face the Future', *New Socialist*, September.

Hall, S. (1984c) 'The State – Socialism's Old Caretaker', *Marxism Today*, November.

Hall, S. (1985) 'The Gulf between Labour and Blacks', *Guardian*, 15 July.

Hall, S., Critcher, C., Jefferson, T., Clarke, J. and Roberts, B. (1978) *Policing the Crisis: Mugging, the State, Law and Order*. London, Macmillan.

Hall, S. and Schwarz, B. (1985) 'State and Society, 1880–1930', in Langan and Schwarz.

Hartmann, H. (1979) 'The Unhappy Marriage of Marxism and Feminism: Towards a more Progressive Union', *Capital and Class*, no. 8; revised in L. Sargent (ed.) (1981), *Women and Revolution*, London. Pluto Press.

Hayek, F. (1949) *Individualism and Economic Order*. London, Routledge and Kegan Paul.

Hayek, F. (1972, 1976, 1979) *Law, Legislation and Liberty* (3 vols). London,

Routledge and Kegan Paul.

Health and Race (1986) *Newsletter*, no. 7 (Leeds).

Hill, M. and Bramley, G. (1986) *Analysing Social Policy*. Oxford, Basil Blackwell.

Hills, J. (1987) 'What Happened to Spending on the Welfare State?', in Walker and Walker (1987).

Himmelweit, S. (1983) 'Production Rules OK. Waged Work in the Family', in Segal (1983).

Hinton, J. (1983) *Labour and Socialism: a History of the British Labour Movement 1867–1974*. Brighton, Wheatsheaf.

HMSO (1985) *Reform of Social Security*, Green Paper, Cmnd 9517.

Hobsbawm, E. (1969) *Industry and Empire*. London, Weidenfeld and Nicolson.

Hooks, B. (1982) *Ain't I a Woman: Black Women and Feminism*. London, Pluto Press.

Hooks, B. (1986) 'Sisterhood: Political Solidarity Between Women', *Feminist Review*, no. 23.

Hudson, D. (1987) 'You Can't Commit Violence against an Object: Women, Psychiatry and Psycho-surgery', in J. Hamner and M. Maynard (eds), *Women, Violence and Social Control*, London. Macmillan.

Illiffe, S. (1985) 'The Politics of Health Care: the NHS under Thatcher', *Critical Social Policy*, issue 14.

Jacobs, S. (1985) 'Race, Empire and the Welfare State: Council Housing and Racism', *Critical Social Policy*, issue 13.

Jagger, A. (1983) *Feminist Politics and Human Nature*. Totowa, New Jersey, Rowman and Allanheld, Brighton, Harvester.

John, G. and Humphrey, D. (1971) *Because They're Black*. Harmondsworth, Penguin.

Johnson, N. (1987) *The Welfare State in Transition*. Brighton, Wheatsheaf.

Jones, K., Brown, J. and Bradshaw, J. (1978) *Issues in Social Policy*. London, Routledge and Kegan Paul.

Joseph, G. (1981) 'The Incompatible Menage a Trois: Marxism, Feminism and Racism', in Sargent (1981).

Joshi, H. and Carter, B. (1984) 'The Role of Labour in the Creation of a Racist Britain', *Race and Class*, XXV (3).

Kellmer-Pringle, M. et al. (1980) *A Fairer Future for Our Children*. London, Macmillan.

Kenny, M. (1986) *Abortion: the Whole Story*. London, Quartet.

Kessler, S. and McKenna, W. (1982) 'Developmental Aspects of Gender', in Open University (1982a).

Khan, V. (1979) 'Migration and Social Stress: Mirpuris in Bradford', in V. Khan (1979) *Minority Families in Britain: Support and Stress*. London, Macmillan.

Klein, R. and O'Higgins, M. (eds) (1985) *The Future of Welfare*. Oxford, Basil Blackwell.

Land, H. (1976) 'Women: Supporters or Supported?', in S. Allen and D. Barker (eds), *Sexual Divisions and Society*. London, Tavistock.

Land, H. (1978) 'Who Cares for the Family?', *Journal of Social Policy*, 7 (3).

Land, H. (1980) 'The Family Wage', *Feminist Review* no, 6.

Land, H. (1983) 'Who Still Cares for the Family? Recent Developments in Income Maintenance, Taxation and Family Law', in J. Lewis (ed.), *Women's Welfare,*

Women's Rights. London, Croom Helm.

Land, H. and Ward, S. (1986) *Women Won't Benefit*. London, National Council for Civil Liberties.

Langan, M. and Schwarz, B. (eds) (1985) *Crises in the British State 1880–1930*. London, Hutchinson.

Lash, S. and Urry, J. (1987) 'The Shape of Things to Come', *New Socialist*, January.

Lawrence, E. (1982) 'In the abundance of water the fool is thirsty: Sociology and black "pathology"', in CCCS (1982).

Lawrence, E. (1987) Editorial, *Foundation, Race and Housing Journal*, no. 3.

Lee, P. and Raban, C. (1983) 'Welfare and Ideology', in Loney et al. (1983).

Lee, P. and Raban, C. (1988) *Welfare Theory and Social Policy: Reform or Revolution?* London, Sage.

Leonard, P. (1979) 'Restructuring the Welfare State', *Marxism Today*, December.

Levitas, R. (1986) 'Competition and Compliance: the Utopias of the New Right'. in R. Levitas (ed.), *The Ideology of the New Right*, Cambridge, Polity Press.

Lewis, G. and Parmar, P. (1985) 'Review Essay of American Black Feminist Literature', *Race and Class*, XXV.

Lewis, J. (1982) *The Politics of Motherhood: Child and Maternal Welfare in England, 1900–1939*. Beckenham, Croom Helm.

Lewis, J. (ed.) (1983) *Women's Welfare – Women's Rights*. Beckenham, Croom Helm.

Lewis, J. (1984) *Women in England, 1870–1950*. Brighton, Wheatsheaf.

LEWRG (London – Edinburgh Weekend Return Group) (1979) *In and Against the State*. London, Pluto Press.

Loney, M. (1986) *The Politics of Greed: The New Right and the Welfare State*. London, Pluto Press.

Loney, M. with Bocock R., Clarke, J., Cochrane, A. (1987) *The State or the Market: Politics and Welfare in Contemporary Britain*. London, Sage.

Loney, M., Boswell, D. and Clarke, J. (1983) *Social Policy and Social Welfare*. Milton Keynes, Open University Press.

Lorde, A. (1984) *Sister Outsider: Essays and Speeches*. New York, Crossing Press.

McGregor, S. (1981) *The Politics of Poverty*. Harlow, Longman.

McIntosh, M. (1978) 'The State and the Oppression of Women', in A. Kuhn and A. Wolpe (eds), *Feminism and Materialism*. London, Routledge and Kegan Paul.

McIntosh, M. (1981) 'Feminism and Social Policy', *Critical Social Policy*, 1 (1).

Mama, A. (1984) 'Black Women, the Economic Crisis and the British State', *Feminist Review*, no. 17.

Marshall, T. H. (1949) 'Citizenship and Social Class', republished in *Sociology at the Crossroads* (1963). London, Heinemann.

Meiksens-Wood, E. (1986) *The Retreat from Class: a New 'True' Socialism*. London, Verso.

Miles, R. (1982) *Racism and Migrant Labour*. London, Routledge and Kegan Paul.

Miles, R. and Phizacklea, A. (eds) (1979) *Racism and Political Action in Britain*. London, Routledge and Kegan Paul.

Miles, R. and Phizacklea, A. (1984) *White Man's Country: Racism in British Politics*. London, Pluto Press.

Millar, J. (1987) 'Lone Mothers', in Glendinning and Millar (1987).

Millet, K. (1970) *'Sexual Politics'*. New York, Avon Books.

Milner, D. (1973) *Children and Race*. Harmondsworth, Penguin.

Mishra, R. (1977) *Society and Social Policy*. London, Macmillan.

Mishra, R. (1981) Society and Social Policy, 2nd rev. edn. London, Macmillan.

Mishra, R. (1984) *The Welfare State in Crisis*. London, Wheatsheaf.

Mishra, R. (1986a) 'Social Policy and the Discipline of Social Administration', *Social Policy and Administration*, 20 (1).

Mishra, R. (1986b) 'The Left and the Welfare State: a Critical Analysis', *Critical Social Policy*, issue 15.

Mitchell, J. (1974) *Women and Psycho-analysis*. Harmondsworth, Penguin.

Mitter, S. (1986) *Common Fate, Common Bond: Women in the Global Economy*. London, Pluto Press.

Mohan, J. (1986) 'Private Medical Care and the British Conservative Government', *Journal of Social Policy*, 15 (3).

Molyneux, M. (1981) 'Socialist Societies Old and New', *Feminist Review*, no. 8.

Molyneux, M. (1984) 'Mobilisation without Emancipation? Women's Interests and Revolution in Nicaragua', *Critical Social Policy*, issue 10.

Moraga, C. and Anzaldua, G. (eds) (1981) 'This Bridge called My Back'. *Writings by Radical Women of Colour*. Watertown, Massachusetts, Persephone Press.

Mort, F. (1985) 'Purity, Feminism and the State: Sexuality and Moral Politics, 1880–1914', in Langan and Schwarz (1985).

Mount, F. (1982) *The Subversive Family: an Alternative History of Love and Marriage*. London, Jonathan Cape.

Murie, A. (1983) 'Housing: a Thoroughly Residual Policy', in Bull and Wilding (1983).

Murie, A. (1983) *Housing Inequality and Deprivation*. London, Heinemann.

Oakley, A. (1983) 'Women and Health Policy', in Lewis (1983).

O'Connor, J. (1973) *The Fiscal Crisis of the State*. New York, St James's Press.

Offe, C. (1984) *Contradictions of the Welfare State*. London, Hutchinson.

Office of Health Economics (1987) *Women's Health Today*. London, Office of Health Economics.

Office of Population Censuses and Surveys (1982) *General Household Survey, 1982*. London, HMSO.

O'Higgins, M. and Patterson, A. (1985) 'The Prospects for Public Expenditure', in Klein and O'Higgins (1985).

Ohri, A., Manning, B. and Curno, P. (1982) *Community Work and Racism*. London, Routledge and Kegan Paul/Association of Community Workers.

Oliver, M. (1985) 'The Politics of Disability', *Critical Social Policy*, no. 11.

Open University (1982a) *The Changing Experience of Women: a Reader*. Oxford, Martin Robertson.

Open University (1982b) *U221 Course Units: the Changing Experience of Women*, nos 1–16. Milton Keynes, Open University Press.

Oppenheim, C. (1987) *A Tax on all the People*. London, CPAG.

Orbach, S. and Eichenbaum, L. (1983) *What Do Women Want?* Glasgow, Fontana.

Owen, D. (1981) *Face the Future*. Oxford, Oxford University Press.

Owen, E. (ed.) (1986) *Comparing Welfare States and their Futures*. Aldershot,

Gower.

Pahl, J. (1980) 'Patterns of Money Management within Marriage', *Journal of Social Policy*, 9 (3).

Palmer, F. (1986) (ed.) *Anti-Racism: an Assault on Education and Value.* Nottingham, Sherwood Press.

Parekh, B. (1986) 'The New Right and the Politics of Nationhood', in G. Cohen, et al., *The New Right: Image and Reality.* London, Runnymede Trust.

Parmar, P. (1982) 'Gender, Race and Class: Asian Women in Resistance', in CCCS (1982).

Parsons, T. (1951) *The Social System.* London, Routledge and Kegan Paul.

Pascall, G. (1986) *Social Policy: a Feminist Analysis.* London, Tavistock.

Peace, S. (1986) 'The Forgotten Female: Social Policy and Older Women', in Phillipson and Walker (1986).

Pearson, M. (1986) 'The Politics of Ethnic Minority Health Studies', in Rathwell and Phillips (1986).

Petchesky, R. (1980) 'Reproductive Freedom: Beyond "A Woman's Right to Choose"', *Signs*, Summer.

Phillips, A. (1983) *Hidden Hands: Women and Economic Policies.* London, Pluto Press.

Phillips, A. (1987) *Divided Loyalties: Dilemmas of Sex and Class.* London, Virago.

Phillipson, C. (1982) *Capitalism and the Construction of Old Age.* London, Macmillan.

Phillipson, C. and Walker, A. (eds) (1986) *Ageing and Social Policy: a Critical Assessment.* Aldershot, Gower.

Phizacklea, A. (ed.) (1984) *One Way Ticket: Migration and Female Labour.* London, Routledge and Kegan Paul.

Phizacklea, A. and Miles, R. (1980) *Labour and Racism.* London, Routledge and Kegan Paul.

Piachaud, D. (1987) 'The Growth of Poverty', in Walker and Walker (1987).

Piercy, M. (1979) *Woman on the Edge of Time.* London, The Women's Press.

Pinker, R. (1971) *Social Theory and Social Policy.* London, Heinemann.

Pinker, R. (1979) *The Idea of Welfare.* London, Heinemann.

Piven, F. and Cloward, R. (1972) *Regulating the Poor: the Function of Public Welfare.* London, Tavistock.

Rakusen, J. (1981) 'Depo-Provera: the Extent of the Problem. A Case Study in the Politics of Birth Control', in H. Roberts (ed.), *Women, Health and Reproduction,* London, Routledge and Kegan Paul.

Rathwell, T. and Phillips, D. (eds) (1986) *Health, Race and Ethnicity.* Beckenham, Croom Helm.

Rees, T. (1983) 'Health and Welfare: Running to Stand Still', in Bull and Wilding (1983).

Reisman, D. (1977) *Richard Titmuss: Welfare Society.* London, Heinemann.

Report of the Mental Deficiency Committee (Wood) (1929) Part III – the Adult Defective. London, HMSO.

Rex, J. (1973) *Race, Colonialism and the City.* London, Routledge and Kegan Paul.

Rex, J. (1983) *Race Relations in Sociological Theory.* London, Routledge and

Kegan Paul.

Rex, J. (1984a) 'Black Marks for a White Paper', *Guardian*, 15 February.

Rex, J. (1984b) 'Social Policy and Ethnic Inequality', paper given at the Social Administration Conference, July, 1984.

Rex, J. and Moore, R. (1967) *Race, Community and Conflict*. London, Institute for Race Relations/Oxford University Press.

Rex, J. and Tomlinson, S. (1979) *Colonial Immigrants in a British City*. London, Routledge and Kegan Paul.

Rich, P. (1987) 'The Archers Revisited: the Mythology of National Community in Thatcher's Britain', *Times Higher Education Supplement*, 4 December.

Riley, D. (1983) *War in the Nursery: Theories of the Child and Mother*. London, Virago.

Robinson, C. (1983) *Black Marxism, the Making of the Black Radical Tradition*. London, 2nd Press.

Room, G. (1979) *The Sociology of Welfare*. Oxford, Basil Blackwell.

Rose, H. (1981) 'Re-reading Titmuss: the Sexual Division of Welfare', *Journal of Social Policy*, 10 (4).

Rose, H. (1985) 'Women's Refuges: Creating New Forms of Welfare?', in Ungerson (1985).

Rose, H. (1986) 'Women and the Restructuring of the Welfare State', in Owen (1986).

Rose, M. E. (1971) *The English Poor Law*. Newton Abbot, David and Charles.

Rose, R. and Deakin, N. (1969) *Colour and Citizenship*. Oxford, Institute of Race Relations/Oxford University Press.

Rowbotham, S. (1974) *Hidden from History*. London, Pluto Press.

Rowbotham, S. (1981) 'The Trouble with "Patriarchy"', in Feminist Anthology Collective (eds), *No Turning Back: Writings from the Women's Liberation Movement, 1875–80*. London, The Women's Press.

Rowbotham, S. (1985) 'What do Women Want? Women-centred Values and the World as It Is', *Feminist Review*, no. 20.

Rowbotham, S., Segal, L. and Wainwright, H. (1979) *Beyond the Fragments: Feminism and the Making of Socialism*. London, Merlin Press.

Ryan, J. and Thomas, F. (1987) *The Politics of Mental Handicap*. London, Free Association Books.

Sargent, L. (ed.) (1981) *Women and Revolution*. London, Pluto Press.

Sarup, M. (1986) *The Politics of Multicultural Education*. London, Routledge and Kegan Paul.

Sassoon, A. S. (ed.) (1987) *Women and the State*. London, Hutchinson.

Saville, J. (1957) 'The Welfare State: an Historical Approach' reprinted in E. Butterworth and R. Holman (1975), *Social Welfare in Modern Britain*. London, Fontana.

Sayers, J. (1982) *Biological Politics*. London, Tavistock.

Scarman, Lord (1981) *The Scarman Report into the Brixton Disorders 10–12 April 1981*. London, HMSO, reissued Harmondsworth, Penguin.

Schwarz, Bill and Durham, M. (1985) '"A Safe and Sane Labourism": Socialism and the State, 1910–24', in Langan and Schwarz (1985).

Scott, H. (1984) *Working Your Way to the Bottom: the Feminisation of Poverty*. London, Pandora Press.

Scruton, R. (1980) *The Meaning of Conservatism*. Harmondsworth, Penguin.

Segal, L. (ed.) (1983) *What Is to be Done about the Family?* Harmondsworth, Penguin.

Segal, L. (1987) *Is the Future Female? Troubled Thoughts on Contemporary Feminism*. London, Virago.

Seidel, G. (1986) 'Culture, Nation and "Race" in the British and French New Right', in R. Levitas (ed.) *The Ideology of the New Right*. Cambridge, Polity Press.

Semmel, B. (1960) *Imperialism and Social Change*. London, Allen and Unwin.

Shaw, G. B. (ed.) (1980) *Fabian Essays In Socialism*. London, The Fabian Society.

Shaw, G. B. (ed.) (1900) *Fabianism and the Empire*. London, The Fabian Society.

Sherwood, M. (1985) *Many Struggles – West Indian Workers and Service Personnel in Britain, 1939–45*. London, Karia Press.

Sivanandan, A. (1976) 'Race, Class and the State: the Black Experience in Britain', *Race and Class*, XVII (4).

Sivanandan, A. (1978) 'From Immigration Control to Induced Repatriation', *Race and Class*, XX (1), reprinted in Sivanandan (1982).

Sivanandan, A. (1979) 'Imperialism and Disorganic Development in the Silicon Age', *Race and Class*, XXIV (2), reprinted in Sivanandan (1982).

Sivanandan, A. (1982) *A Different Hunger: Writings on Black Resistance*. London, Pluto Press.

Sivanandan, A. (1985) 'Race Awareness Training and the Degradation of Black Struggle', *Race and Class*, XXVI.

Small, J. (1984) 'The Crisis in Adoption', *International Journal of Social Psychiatry*, 30 (1/2).

Small, N. (1988) 'Aids and Social Policy', *Critical Social Policy*, issue 21.

Solomos, J. (1985) 'Problems, but whose Problems? The Social Construction of Black Youth Unemployment', *Journal of Social Policy*, 14 (4).

Solomos, J. (1986) 'Varieties of Marxist Conceptions of "Race", Class and the State: a Critical Analysis', in J. Rex and D. Mason (eds), *Theories of Race and Ethnic Relations*. Cambridge, Cambridge University Press.

Solomos, J., Findlay, B., Jones, S. and Gilroy, P. (1982) 'The Organic Crisis of British Capitalism and Race: the Experience of the Seventies', in CCCS (1982).

Spring Rice, M. (1939, reprinted 1981) *Working-class Wives: Their Health and Conditions*. London, Virago.

Stanworth, M. (1981) *Gender and Schooling, A Study of Sexual Divisions in the Classroom*. London, Hutchinson.

Stanworth, M. (ed.) (1987) *Reproductive Technologies: Gender, Motherhood and Medicine.* Cambridge, Polity Press.

Stone, M. (1981) *The Education of the Black Child in Britain: the Myth of Multiracial Education*. London, Fontana.

Storey, H. (1986) 'United Kingdom Immigration Controls and the Welfare State', in Dummett (1986).

Stubbs, P. (1985) 'The Employment of Black Social Workers: from Ethnic Sensitivity to Anti-Racism?', *Critical Social Policy*, issue 12.

Stubbs, P. (1987a) 'Racism and the Left: a New Opportunity', *Critical Social*

Policy, issue 20.

Stubbs, P. (1987b) 'Crime, Community and the Multi-agency Approach: a Critical Reading of the Broadwater Farm Inquiry Report', *Critical Social Policy*, issue 20.

Stubbs, P. (1987) 'Professionalism and the Adoption of Black Children', *British Journal of Social Work*, vol. 17 no. 5.

Study Commission on the Family (1980) *Happy Families? A Discussion Paper on Families in Britain*. London, Study Commission on the Family.

Study Commission on the Family (1983) *Families in the Future*. London, Study Commission on the Family.

Sullivan, M. (1987) *Sociology and Social Welfare*. London, Allen and Unwin.

Taylor, B. (1983) *Eve and the New Jerusalem: Socialism and Feminism in the Nineteenth Century*. London, Virago.

Taylor, D. (1987) 'Living with Unemployment', in Walker and Walker (1987).

Taylor-Gooby, P. (1981) 'The State, Class, Ideology and Social Policy', *Journal of Social Policy*, 10 (4).

Taylor-Gooby, P. (1985) *Public Opinion, Ideology and State Welfare*. London, Routledge and Kegan Paul.

Taylor-Gooby, P. and Dale, J. (1981) *Social Theory and Social Welfare*. London, Edward Arnold.

Therborn, G. (1984) 'The Prospects of Labour and the Transformation of Advanced Capitalism', *New Left Review*, May/June.

Titmuss, R. (1943) *Problems of Population*. London, Association for Education in Citizenship/English Universities Press.

Titmuss, R. (1958) *Essays on the Welfare State*. London, Allen and Unwin.

Titmuss, R. (1967) *Choice and 'The Welfare State'*. London, Fabian Society Tract 370.

Titmuss, R. (1970) *The Gift Relationship*. London, Allen and Unwin.

Titmuss, R. (1974) *Social Policy*. London, Allen and Unwin.

Townsend, P. (1979) *Poverty in the United Kingdom*. Harmondsworth, Penguin.

Townsend, P. (1983) 'A Theory of Poverty and the Role of Social Policy', in Loney et al. (1983).

Townsend, P. (1984) *Why Are the Many Poor?* London, Fabian Society Tract 500.

Trivedi, P. (1984) 'To Deny our Fullness: Asian Women in the Making of History', *Feminist Review*, no. 17.

Ungerson, C. (ed.) (1985) *Women and Social Policy. A Reader*. London, Macmillan.

Ungerson, C. (1987) *Policy is Personal: Sex, Gender and Informal Care*. London, Tavistock.

Vogel, U. (1986) 'Rationalism and Romanticism: Two Strategies for Women's Liberation', in J. Evans, *Feminism and Political Theory*, London, Sage.

Wainwright, H. (1987) *Labour: a Tale of Two Parties*. London, The Hogarth Press, Chatto and Windus.

Walby, S. (1986) *Patriarchy at Work*. Cambridge, Polity Press.

Walker, A. (1982) 'The Meaning and Social Division of Community Care', in A. Walker (ed.), *Community Care: the Family, the State and Social Policy*. Oxford, Basil Blackwell.

Walker, A. (1984) *Social Planning. A Strategy for Socialist Welfare*. Oxford, Basil

Blackwell.

Walker, A. and Walker, C. (eds) (1987) *A Growing Divide: a Social Audit, 1979–87*. London, Child Poverty Action Group.

Wallas, G. (1890) 'Property under Socialism', in Shaw (ed.) (1890).

Warnock, M. (1985) *A Question of Life: the Warnock Report on Human Fertilisation and Embryology*. Oxford, Basil Blackwell.

Watson, S. (1987) 'Ideas of the Family in the Development of Housing Forms', in Loney et al. (1987).

Watson, S. with Austerberry, H, (1986) *Housing and Homelessness: a Feminist Perspective*. London, Routledge and Kegan Paul.

Waylen, G. (1986) 'Women and Neo-Liberalism', in J. Evans et al., *Feminism and Political Theory*. London, Sage.

Webb, S. (1907) *The Decline of the Birth Rate*. London, Fabian Society Tract 131.

Wedderburn, D. (1965) 'Facts and Theories of the Welfare State', in R. Miliband and J. Saville (eds), *The Socialist Register*. London, Merlin Press.

Weir, A. and Wilson, E. (1984) 'The British Women's Movement', *New Left Review*, 148.

Westergaard, J. and Rester, H. (1975) *Class in a Capitalist Society*. London, Heinemann.

Wicks, M. (1987) *A Future for All*. Harmondsworth, Penguin.

Wilensky, H. L. (1975) *The Welfare State and Equality*. Berkeley, Ca, University of California Press.

Williams, F. (1986) 'Recent Developments for Policies for Women in Hungary', *Critical Social Policy,* issue 16.

Williams, F. (1987) 'Racism and the Discipline of Social Policy: a Critique of Welfare Theory', *Critical Social Policy*, issue 20.

Wilson, E. (1977) *Women and the Welfare State*. London, Tavistock.

Wilson, E. (1980a) *Only Halfway to Paradise: Women in Post-War Britain, 1945–1968*. London, Tavistock.

Wilson, E. (1980b) 'Marxism and the Welfare State': Review Article, *New Left Review*, 122.

Wilson, E. (1982) 'Women, the "Community" and the "Family"', in A. Walker (ed.), *Community Care: the Family, the State and Social Policy*, Oxford, Basil Blackwell.

Wilson, E. (1983) 'Feminism and Social Policy', in Loney et al. (1983).

Wilson, R. (1985) 'Imperialism in Crisis: the "Irish Dimension"', in Langan and Schwarz (1985).

Index